9.14 (Ret) Barnes & Noble 9-67 (Swearingen)

STUDIES IN MEDIAEVAL HISTORY

Edited by GEOFFREY BARRACLOUGH

MEDIAEVAL GERMANY
911 — 1250

MEDIAEVAL GERMANY

911 — 1250

Essays by German Historians

Translated with an Introduction
by GEOFFREY BARRACLOUGH

Volume II. ESSAYS

BASIL BLACKWELL
OXFORD
1961

First Edition 1938
Second Impression 1948
Third Impression 1961

PRINTED IN GREAT BRITAIN
BY THE COMPTON PRINTING WORKS (LONDON) LTD., LONDON, N.1
FOR BASIL BLACKWELL & MOTT LTD.
AND BOUND BY
THE KEMP HALL BINDERY, OXFORD·

PREFACE

In view of the fact that this volume of essays has been preceded by an introductory study of certain phases and problems of German history, in the preface to which I have tried briefly to explain the objects of this work, few preliminary words are necessary in this place.

Nine essays by representative German historians are here presented to an English public in an English translation. The essays have been carefully selected, and together form a consecutive account of the history of Germany from the beginnings of a separate German kingdom in the tenth century to the end of the Hohenstaufen period. The volume starts with a general essay (I) which provides, in my view, the best short introduction to the history of mediaeval Germany, which is in existence. Here the determinative factors in the formation of mediaeval Germany are considered one by one, each element is assigned its place in the development of the German people as a whole, and the distinctive features of German development are emphasized by an illuminating comparison with France. The subsequent essays are arranged in an appropriate chronological order, divided into two groups by the great social and political upheaval which we call the Investiture Contest. We see (II) the legal foundations on which the relationship of church and state was built, not only in Germany but throughout Western Europe, before the revolutionary changes introduced in the eleventh century by the Cluniac movement and the Hildebrandine papacy; and we are thus able to understand the close co-operation of church and state, which was one of the main pillars of the old German monarchy. We see (III) the second influential factor in the early history of Germany: the vital forces embodied in the races comprised within the German state, and the strength of provincial life. We see, finally, the monarchy of Ottonian and early Salian days, the administration which it built up, the principles on which it

v

governed, the elements which gave it strength and the forces which weakened it (IV). These disruptive forces gained the upper hand during the Investiture Contest, and the civil wars under Henry IV and Henry V marked the end of the first period of German history. The Investiture Contest not only undermined the old system of government, but also stimulated into activity the forces which led to the growth of the new Germany of the later middle ages. We see the general effects of the Investiture Contest on the old constitution (IV), and we see further the precise process by which the German princes, profiting by their alliance with the papacy at the end of the eleventh and the beginning of the twelfth century, used the changes in the constitution of the German church in order to build up their local predominance and their territorial power (V). Already in the twelfth century they were able to use this early success to lay the foundations of the territorial principalities of the later middle ages; and one particularly lucid example, the " state " built up by the dukes of Zähringen in the Black Forest (VI), illustrates the methods they used, the new principles of government they introduced, and the changes in the political balance of power which resulted from the reclamation and colonization of new land. The immense tracts of newly colonized land, both within old west Germany and on the eastern frontiers, created new problems of social and political organization. At the same time, the Investiture Contest, which had undermined the old constitution, had also thrown the whole social organization of earlier centuries into the melting pot (VII); and the dissolution of the old society led to a process of social and political reconstruction. The question in the twelfth century was whether the reconstruction would be controlled by the crown, and would provide a new foundation for royal power, or whether it would establish the princes firmly in the saddle. We see the attempts which the Hohenstaufen made at reform and reconstruction (VII); and in particular we see their efforts to use feudalism, which became a potent force in Germany after the Investiture Contest, as an instrument for creating a strong feudal

monarchy, and holding the land together by feudal bonds
(VIII). Princes and emperor alike, all were engaged on
the task of introducing a new type of state and new forms
of political life (IX). But the early victory under Henry IV
had given the princes the initiative; the constitutional
reforms of 1180 were less a new foundation for royal
government than a compromise between crown and
princes; the latter knew better than the former how to
turn the growth of feudalism to profit, and it was on a
feudal basis that the princes built up their territorial states
in the thirteenth century (VIII). The Interregnum
between 1250 and 1272 enabled them to consolidate what
they had won in the preceding fifty years; and with this
victory a new age begins. When Rudolf of Habsburg
succeeded to the pillaged inheritance of the Hohenstaufen,
the age of princes succeeded the age of emperors. With
this new era of German history, however, the present work
is not concerned; we break off with the failure of the
Hohenstaufen to reorganize a strong monarchy, and with
the principalities firmly established on solid foundations.
Thenceforward the principalities are the factors which
dominate German history, right down to the nineteenth
century. Why the Hohenstaufen failed to master the
age-old tendency to separatism and particularism, is a
question which receives an indirect answer in more than
one of the essays which follow. For those readers who may
wish a fuller answer to this question, however, I have tried
to provide more detailed information in the last two
chapters in the first volume of this work. The sketch of
certain phases and problems of German history, which is
there attempted, thus rounds off the picture which the
nine essays in this volume provide, besides linking them
together and relating them to other recent work by German
historians of the twentieth century.

Acknowledgement of help and encouragement in the
preparation of this history of " Mediaeval Germany " has
already been made in the preface to the first volume. It
is not necessary to renew the expressions of gratitude there

set forth; but it is fitting that I should repeat here my deep sense of obligation to the eight German historians whose willing co-operation alone has enabled me to put this work before English readers. Their work follows, and speaks for itself.

G. B.

CONTENTS

ABBREVIATIONS

D (DO. II, DH. III, etc.) = Monumenta Germaniae historica, Diplomata regum et imperatorum Germaniae (DH. III = Diplomata Heinrici III).

HG. = H. Hirsch, Die Hohe Gerichtsbarkeit im deutschen Mittelalter (Prag, 1922).

HZ. = Historische Zeitschrift.

JL. = Ph. Jaffé, Regesta Pontificum Romanorum (ed. alt., ed. S. Loewen-feld, F. Kaltenbrunner, P. Ewald, Lipsiae, 1885—1888).

Lr. u. Sg. = H. Mitteis, Lehnrecht und Staatsgewalt. Untersuchungen zur mittelalterlichen Verfassungsgeschichte (Weimar, 1933).

MG. = Monumenta Germaniae historica.
  Const. = Constitutiones et acta publica imperatorum et regum.
  Epp. = Epistolae.
  in us. schol. = Scriptores rerum Germanicarum in usum scholarum.
  Lib. de lite = Libelli de lite imperatorum et pontificum saec. XI. et XII. conscripti.
  Script. = Scriptores.

MIÖG. = Mitteilungen des Instituts für österreichische Geschichtsforschung.

St. = K. F. Stumpf, Die Reichskanzler, Vol. II: Die Kaiserurkunden des X., XI. und XII. Jahrhunderts chronologisch verzeichnet (Innsbruck, 1865—1883).

ZRG. = Zeitschrift der Savigny-Stiftung für Rechtsgeschichte (*Germ. Abt.* = Germanistische Abteilung; *Kanon. Abt.* = Kanonistische Abteilung).

I

THE HISTORICAL FOUNDATIONS OF THE GERMAN CONSTITUTION[1]

By THEODOR MAYER

THROUGHOUT the long history of constitutional development in Germany there is one distinctive feature, as evident in the constitutions of 1871 and 1919 as in the days of the Holy Roman Empire, which clearly differentiates the German state from the centralized state as seen in France. It is this essential factor in the German constitution with which we are concerned here. The vital point is the antithesis between the German empire and the German principalities or territories; and the essential factor in this antithesis is that the rights of particular territories are not derived from a central governmental authority, that the territories possess indigenous rights of their own, so that it is possible to speak of a double source of public rights in Germany—of " dualism," as contrasted, for example, with the " monism " of France.

The constitution of the German empire as established in 1871 or in 1919 was, of course, the result of a momentary political situation, and it is therefore possible to explain the apparent anomalies in these constitutions as imperfections due to the political circumstances in which they were created. But it is equally legitimate to ask whether the dualism, which is apparent in them, is really only representative of a transitional stage in political development, having no deep roots in national character and therefore to be superseded in the interests of the German people, or

[1] " Geschichtliche Grundlagen der deutschen Verfassung. Festrede gehalten bei der Reichsgründungsfeier am 18. Januar 1933," *Schriften der Hessischen Hochschulen, Universität Giessen*, Jg. 1933, Heft I (Giessen: Alfred Töpelmann, 1933).—Thanks are due not only to the publisher but also to the Editorial Board of the University of Giessen for permission to translate.

2 TH. MAYER

whether we have to see in it an expression of German national individuality. This is no new question: as long as the empire has existed, the question of the relations of empire and constituent states has played a part in political discussion. Comparisons with other lands have been made, and it has been thought possible to see a difference between Germanic and Romanist conceptions of the state. BIS-MARCK himself spoke of " the German urge to division into narrow groups ".[2] Seventy years ago JULIUS FICKER[3] expressed the same thought, when he spoke of a " Roman theory of the state " with " a gradation from top to bottom, a unified mechanism", "which culminates in the head of the state and reaches through the manifold ranks of the hierarchy to the lowest grades of the dependent civil service and to the subject classes ", but in which " no spontaneous participation in government from below and no special civil rights are conceded ". He says further: " a centralized state may well be the most suitable form of government for a decrepit people, which has passed the zenith of its development ", but " not for a race full of vitality and in the vigour of its youth." The Carolingians (according to this theory) attempted to erect a centralized state, whereas Henry I recognized the racial units and their lands as constituent elements and tried to combine adequate force in the whole with as much free action by the members as was possible. So was produced a form of state in which all individual rights were left to the constituent parts, provided that their exercise did not run contrary to the interests of the whole.

Does this contrast, so clearly portrayed by FICKER, correspond to reality, or is it false ? Has it been superseded to-day or was it already erroneous seventy years ago ? In an age determined to seek new foundations for state and

[2] *Gedanken u. Erinnerungen* (ed. 1922), 339.
[3] *Das deutsche Kaiserreich in seinen universalen u. nationalen Beziehungen* (1861), 39 sqq., 54, 55 sq. Ficker discussed this question also, not only in his work *Deutsches Königtum u. Kaisertum* (1862), but particularly in the introduction to vol. I of the *Forschungen z. Reichs-u. Rechtsgeschichte Italiens*. Among more recent literature cf. W. Merk, *Der germanische Staat* (1927), particularly p. 12 and p. 39, together with the works cited *ibid.*, p. 12 n. 2.

for society the discussion of such questions is not super-
fluous. Historians have cast doubt on the contrast between
a Romanist and a Germanic form of the state,[4] because
Roman centralization itself was also a product of historical
development, and the tendency has been to speak of a
difference in time rather than of a difference in kind.
Discussing the rise of the modern ministries of state,
HINTZE[5] has said that German political development is
some three centuries behind that of the Western Powers.
FRITZ KERN[6] believes that Germany about 1250 was behind
France in its constitutional and political development, but
that about 950 it held the lead; and he attributes this
falling behind to the pernicious Italian policy of the German
emperors. Both HINTZE and KERN have this in common,
that they regard the difference between France and Germany as a disparity in time within an otherwise similar
development, whereas according to FICKER the contrast
was fundamental.

If we wish to compare constitutional development in
Germany and in France, we must first emphasize the fact
that both are inheritors of the tradition of Charles the
Great,[7] that both belong to the Romano-Germanic group
of peoples inhabiting Western Europe in the middle ages,
and that for both the same factors, Roman traditions,
Christianity, and Germanic powers of construction and

[4] Cf. R. Holzmann, *Reichsverfassung u. Gegenwart*, 14, where the
literature on the question is cited. Particular reference should be made
to A. Helbok, " Deutschland u. Frankreich, Länderstaat u. Einheitsstaat,"
Deutsche Rundschau, Jg. LVII (1931).
[5] " Die Entstehung der modernen Staatsministerien," HZ. C (1908),
110.
[6] " Der deutsche Staat u. die Politik des Römerzuges," *Aus Politik
u. Geschichte (Gedächtnisschrift für G. von Below*, 1928), 41.
[7] Cf. in general E. Patzelt, *Die karolingische Renaissance* (1924),
148—158, and F. Lot, *Etude sur le règne de Hugues Capet et la fin du Xe
siècle* (1903), 238—239. I cannot attempt, in what follows, any exhaustive
comparison of France and Germany, but wish only to bring forward some
objections to the idea that circumstances in the two countries were identical.
The marked economic contrast I have already noted, HZ. CXLIII, 146 sqq.
The method used by E. Mayer in his *Deutsche u. französische Verfassungsgeschichte*—namely the indiscriminate and simultaneous use of authorities
from the south of France and the north of Germany in proof of a particular
hypothesis—is particularly open to criticism. This case, it is true, is
exceptional; but few narratives make a sufficiently clear distinction between East and West Frankish authorities and circumstances.

political organization were decisive.[8] A similarity of
elements does not, of course, mean a similarity of development. Just as two chemical compounds, which contain
the same elements, but contain them in different ratios,
appear as different products, so it is with the states of the
Christian West. What is true for Italy is not true in the
same way for Spain or France; what is correct in regard
to the Romanized lands does not necessarily apply to Germany. The fact that Carolingian legislation was the same
in the eastern and western parts of the Frankish kingdom
is itself no proof that the actual legal position was the same
in both regions. Single documents from the western parts
of the Frankish empire cannot be used indiscriminately as
evidence of East Frankish or German conditions. Political
development in Germany, in short, must not be regarded
as a direct continuation of the Merovingian and Carolingian
constitutional order.

In the first place it must be emphasized that the whole
of France had belonged to the Roman empire. A constitution had not grown independently from French soil, but
had been imposed on the land as a finished growth by the
Roman conquerors. After the Frankish invasions, Frankish
counts had been introduced into this pre-existing Roman
administration,[9] which had become naturalized during some
five centuries of Roman provincial life, in order to direct it
in accordance with the interests of the new Frankish
governing class. The West-Frankish count, who often
resided in the city, had subordinate officials at his side.[10]
But the Roman machinery of government, and above all
the fundamental principle of a state administration, were
not destroyed, but were taken over, developed and trans-

[8] Cf. in general A. Dopsch, *Wirtschaftliche u. soziale Grundlagen der europäischen Kultur von Cäsar bis Karl d. Gr.* (2nd ed., 1922), and also the numerous French and German narratives of general and constitutional history.
[9] Besides the general constitutional histories, see particularly F. Kiener, *Verfassungsgeschichte der Provence seit der Ostgotenherrschaft bis zur Errichtung der Konsulate* (1900), 50 sqq. Cf. Dopsch, *Grundlagen* II, 342 sqq.
[10] Regarding the representatives of the "patricius" in Provence, cf. Kiener, 58, 64 sq., 67; regarding the representatives and subordinates of the count, *ibid.*, 116, 136 sqq.

formed. We can see the same thing in the position of the numerous bishops within the state[11]—bishops who, like the church as a whole, were weighty supporters of ancient tradition. Roman law remained in force and was valid for the Gallo-Roman population.[12] The Roman system of state taxation was still demonstrably in existence, in its rudiments, as late as the Danegeld levied in the tenth century.[13] The continuity of settlements can be fully demonstrated, although many villages and manorial centres have disappeared. The towns suffered seriously during the storms of the period of tribal migration, but they were not utterly destroyed. Above all else, however, the Gallo-Roman population itself remained. Far from being reduced politically and socially to a subordinate position, it was strong enough, on account both of its numbers and of its cultural influence, first to prevent or very quickly to suppress any considerable racial differences, which as such might have been of political significance, and then to romanize the Germanic population and displace, in part very rapidly, both Germanic law and Germanic judicial institutions.[14] The monistic conception of the state after the Roman pattern was not destroyed in France; and Roman institutions therefore proved to be an invaluable foundation for the French state of the middle ages and of modern times.

With this picture let us now compare Germany. Only a part of Germany had belonged to the Roman Empire; in Germany the Roman state had never exercised the unifying influence which it had exercised in France; the German tribes were incorporated into the Frankish kingdom one by one at different times. It is true that here also the Roman cultural inheritance did not completely vanish, but

[11] In general cf. Dopsch, *Grundlagen* II, 253 sqq., who is, however, speaking of the episcopacy as a political power.
[12] It is only necessary to recall the various "Leges Romanae"; cf. Schröder-v. Künssberg, *Deutsche Rechtsgeschichte* (6th ed., 1919), 248 sqq.
[13] Cf. Dopsch, *Wirtschaftsentwicklung d. Karolingerzeit* (2nd ed.) I, 346 sqq.
[14] Cf. Brunner-v. Schwerin, *Deutsche Rechtsgesch.* (2nd ed.) I, 207, Kiener, *op. cit.*, 85 sqq.

6   TH. MAYER

east of the Rhine its survival was very fragmentary.[15]
The remnant of the Roman population lived for the most
part in reduced and subordinate circumstances and was
nowhere able to leave its mark on political or social life.[16]
With few exceptions the boundaries of the German dioceses
were not those of Roman administrative districts,[17] and
consequently the church here was not an agent of Roman
tradition to the same degree as in France.   For Württemberg, where invaluable researches have been carried out,[18]
the persistence of Roman institutions is proved to have
been very small, and, as in Bavaria also, the introduction
of Christianity was the work of missionaries from the
Frankish kingdom.   In the whole district occupied by the
Germanic invaders about the year 260 not one single
bishopric was to be found: instead it was divided up
ecclesiastically among the bordering dioceses of Augsburg,
Constance, Basel, Strassburg, Speier, Worms, Mainz and
Würzburg.   In the German lands on the right bank of the
Rhine Christianity was therefore not a direct inheritance
from the Romans.   Even on the left bank of the Rhine,
where the occupation by the Germanic invaders was later
and less violent, Roman institutions only survived in small
measure.   It is true that the Roman cities mostly continued
to be used as settlements, but the far-reaching changes in
their topography, the shrinkage and transplanting of the
urban centre, make it clear that the social function of these
settlements and consequently the whole social system had
become entirely different.[19]   The Bavarian *dux*, again, was

[15] Besides Dopsch, *Grundlagen*, see particularly H. Aubin, *Mass und
Bedeutung der römisch-germanischen Kulturzusammenhänge* (XIII. *Bericht
d. röm.-germ. Kommission*, 1922), and " Die wirtschaftliche Entwicklung
des römischen Deutschlands," HZ. CXLI (1929).
[16] Cf. O. Paret, *Die Römer in Württemberg*, III: " Die Siedlungen des
römischen Württemberg " (1932), 267 sq.; W. Veeck, *Die Alemannen in
Württemberg* (1931), 124 sqq.
[17] In the German territories on the left bank of the Rhine the Roman
administrative boundaries continued, e.g., in the diocesan boundary on
the Vinxtbach.
[18] P. Gössler, " Die Anfänge des Christentums in Württemberg,"
Blätter f. Württemberg. Kirchengesch. (1932), 149 sqq.; cf. also E. Mayer,
Zeitschr. f. bayr. Landeskunde (1932).
[19] Cf. Aubin, " Zum Übergang von der Römerzeit zum Mittelalter auf
deutschem Boden," *Hist. Aufsätze Aloys Schulte gewidmet* (1927); F.
Wagner, *Die Römer in Bayern* (4th ed., 1928), 58—61.

not the successor of a Roman administrator but of a Frankish official,[20] and it seems likely that the Bavarian ducal family of Agilolfinger was of Frankish origin.[21] Roman law did not remain alive in Germany. The Roman theory of the state was therefore not a foundation of government in Germany, as it was in France. But there remains the further question, whether or how far the German state was based on the Frankish state, how far the Roman inheritance may have been transmitted to Germany by the Franks. In this connexion it is important to realize that the Frankish counts, who are found in Germany, were not introduced (as in France) into a pre-existing administrative organization, but were the agents through whom the administrative organization of a centralized state was for the first time to be set up. The count had no state officials under him. The German judicial system, also, in origin was not simply an organ of central government: on the contrary, jurisdiction was exercised for the most part in the hundred courts as a popular jurisdiction, and the popular courts remained in existence side by side with the count's courts until late in the middle ages.[22]

[20] Cf. Dopsch, *Grundlagen* II, 27 sq.; W. Varges, " Das Herzogtum," *Aus Politik u. Geschichte* (1928), 17 sqq.; H. Zeiss, " Bemerkungen z. frühmittelalterl. Geschichte Bayerns," *Zeitschr. f. bayr. Landesgesch.* II (1929—1930), 353 sq. and " Herzogsname u. Herzogsamt," *Wiener Prähistor. Zeitschr.* XIX (1932).
[21] M. Doeberl, *Entwicklungsgeschichte Bayerns* (3rd ed.) I, 30.
[22] Cf. E. Mayer, *Deutsche u. franz. Verf.-gesch.* II, 111, where it is stated that the king had originally no jurisdiction at all; H. Hirsch, *Die hohe Gerichtsbarkeit im deutschen Mittelalter* (1922), 185 sqq.; E. Wohlhaupter, *Hoch- u. Niedergericht in der mittelalterlichen Gerichtsverfassung Bayerns* (1929), 24, 28—33, 41—45; and H. Aubin in the *Geschichte des Rheinlandes* (1922), 9.—The question of the introduction of the county organisation into Germany is one of the most important problems of legal history from the Frankish period onwards. It is naturally beyond doubt that the Frankish counts were introduced into Germany, and it is therefore to be supposed that the whole of Germany was covered by a network of counties, although they can hardly, on account of the numerous forests, have formed a closed system. On the other hand, it is not true that the basic object of the county organisation, the execution of criminal justice and of other administrative functions by the counts, was actually carried into effect. The dualism in the judicial organisation, which finds expression in the relations between count and hundredman, was not surmounted by the introduction of the Frankish counts. We have to take into account further the relationship, not always clear and far from immutable, between count and duke, and the fact that the latter's position also was subject to considerable fluctuations. It is this peculiarity of public law and county

In Germany, in short, the independent community, which took charge of certain functions of government and whose rights were not derived from the state, existed from the beginning and proved a durable element in public life.[23] The introduction of the Frankish *Schöffengericht* with its jury of sworn doomsmen controlled by the state—an institution which might have brought minor jurisdiction under the control of government—was far from being a complete success in Bavaria, Swabia and Saxony.[24] The institution of *missi* probably never penetrated into Germany at all,[25] or at any rate broke down very quickly, and the palatine counts had lost their significance as early as the ninth century.[26] No system of state taxation is in evidence in Germany before the later middle ages.[27] Capitulary legislation, uniform legislation for the whole realm, ceased in Germany immediately the Frankish empire was divided, whereas it continued for another fifty years in the west and, in spite of the decline of the central power, had outstanding achievements to its credit. In France, we have seen, the fusion of races was very rapid: in Germany, on the other hand, the separate tribes remained in existence as strong racial units, though it would be an exaggeration to regard them also as the possessors of direct political rights. The German provinces were therefore later able to draw support from the political aspirations of the races and to set themselves up as guardians of racial and cultural peculiarities, in spite of the fact that provincial and racial boundaries nowhere fully coincided, and although it was the central authority of the Frankish rulers which, by setting down the tribal laws in writing, provided the

administration in Germany which makes intelligible the developments regarding the forest to which we shall return later. The problem of county organisation in Germany is still in need of further investigation: the final answer is not likely to be the same for all districts and periods. Cf. Hirsch, *Hohe Gerichtsbarkeit* 191, 229 sq.

[23] Cf. F. Steinbach, *Geschichtliche Grundlagen der kommunalen Selbstverwaltung in Deutschland* (1932).

[24] Brunner-v. Schwerin, *Deutsche Rechtsgesch.* II, 301.

[25] *Ibid.*, II, 262.

[26] M. Lintzel, "Der Ursprung der deutschen Pfalzgrafschaften," ZRG. *Germ. Abt.* XLIX (1929), 262.

[27] Cf. G. v. Below, "Die älteste deutsche Steuer," *Probleme d. Wirtschaftsgeschichte,* 622 sqq.

essential contribution to the development of tribal unity.[28] Germany was a land conquered by the Franks, into which Frankish institutions were introduced; but that does not mean that Frankish institutions obtained mastery there and dominated German public life. For this reason it cannot be said that the elements on which the mediaeval state in France and Germany was built, were at a parallel stage of development in the early middle ages, and for this reason it is impossible to agree with KERN's opinion that France was behind Germany in its constitutional development about the year 950.

As a political power Germany about the year 950 was certainly superior to its neighbour. After the decline of the ninth century, Germany in the tenth century raised itself to the position of the leading power in the Christian west. But that in no way implied that its political institutions kept pace with this advance. In a state the institutions of which are still unfixed, personality necessarily counts for more than it can ever count in a state with a definitely established constitution and administration. At that period Germany had the fortune to be governed by a series of outstanding rulers who held the state together by will and personal ability. They understood how to bind men to themselves, and how to build up on the basis of the personal relationship of fealty a substantial political system. They had also, in the crown demesne, an extensive property at their disposal, which provided a real basis for royal power. But they did not succeed in erecting a state

---

[28] In addition to the older literature—above all F. Kauffmann, *Deutsche Altertumskunde,* and R. Much, *Deutsche Stammeskunde* (2nd ed., 1920)—I would refer particularly to the introduction to K. Beyerle's edition of the *Lex Baiuvaiorum,* where the strong influence exerted by the Frankish central authority is admirably demonstrated. The tribal laws contributed much to the formation of the tribal units, for these groups were not always in existence, but were themselves gradually formed, and their formation had not been completed before the formulation and writing down of the tribal laws; cf. Dopsch, *Grundlagen* II, 26, and Aubin, " Das deutsche Volk in seinen Stämmen," in *Volk u. Reich der Deutschen* (ed. B. Harms, 1929). The conception of the races as bearers of political rights expounded by Rosenstock, *Königshaus u. Stämme* (1914), is exaggerated and overlooks the fact that the races were neither politically nor ethnically sufficiently united to be able to exercise such rights in practice; cf. v. Dungern's criticism, MIÖG. XXXVII (1917), 494 sqq.

administration which really achieved their objects, for the church, which should have discharged this function, was lost to the crown with the suppression of the " proprietary church system " during the Investiture Contest.[29] After the Concordat of Worms the bishops' relationship with the crown was similar to that of the lay princes.[30] All stood in a personal relationship of fealty to the king, which was often close and strong, but which can be called neither official nor feudal, although it contained elements of both.

The change in the relationship of crown and episcopate after the Investiture Contest is very striking, both as an indication of a weakening of royal control and as a revelation of the growing influence of feudalism. Are we, then, to attribute to the growth of feudalism the failure of the German monarchy to achieve its objects ? Was feudalism the decisive factor in the constitutional situation ? Because the decline of state authority and the gradual penetration of the state by feudalism went hand in hand in the western parts of the Frankish empire, feudalism itself has usually been regarded as the main element of disintegration and the chief cause of decline.[31] It is essential to ask ourselves whether this view is correct.

There can be no doubt, in the first place, that the intrusion of feudalism into public law meant that public offices and functions came to be regarded as fiefs. Revenues, usually lands, were connected with offices and functions, and the conception soon took root that the office or the exercise of administrative duties and of governmental rights was bound up with the landed property which in intention was merely its endowment—that the endowment, in short, was the primary factor. Offices were frequently

[29] On the proprietary church régime or the *Eigenkirchenwesen*, and its destruction during the Investiture Contest, cf. Stutz, *infra*, 35–70.

[30] For the reign of Barbarossa, cf. Hampe, *Das Hochmittelalter* (1932), 186. Regarding the significance of fealty in the Germanic state, cf. W. Merck, *Vom Werden u. Wesen des deutschen Rechts* (1925), 73, 76 sq., and *Der germanische Staat* (1927), 43.

[31] Cf. for example Kiener, *op. cit.*, 136. On feudalism generally cf. O. Hintze's far-reaching but sociological rather than historical essay, " Wesen u. Verbreitung des Feudalismus," *Sitzungsberichte d. preussischen Akademie, phil.-hist. Kl.* 1929, and Dopsch's important observations, " Benefizialwesen u. Feudalität," MIÖG. XLVI (1932).

handed down from father to son and were gradually appropriated by the families of their holders. Thus there resulted both the disintegration of state administration and the dissolution of society into smaller groups similar to petty states. Because enfeoffment was the usual form for the concession of an office, offices themselves were regarded as equivalent to fiefs. The bond between feudal lord and vassal was accepted as the connexion between the growing local powers and the central authority of the state. But was the tendency for administrative offices to become hereditary due solely to the fact that they were now being conferred according to the rules of feudal law ? It is easy to think of feudalism as essentially anarchic in tendency; but it would be truer to say that, although it may determine the external structure of a state and mould the forms of its institutions, feudalism itself is never a force working in any particular political direction. Indeed, it must be emphasised that no feature is more characteristic of the feudal state than the fact that, however loosely it may be knit together, all fiefs and all rights connected with them are essentially and fundamentally derived from the central authority.[32] In this respect the feudal system is very similar to a bureaucratic form of government; for the dependence of the whole system on the crown shews that the feudal state, like the bureaucratic state, is essentially " monistic " and not " dualistic " in character. But it would be a mistake to exaggerate the significance of feudalism as a constitutional principle, for even if the dissolution of state authority has frequently enough resulted in the rise of a feudal system, feudalism itself can never exert a decisive influence over the actual political situation.[33] Above all else, it certainly does not necessitate a collapse of the power of the state. On the contrary, feudalism provides a strong central authority, wishing to organize a more rigid form of government, with an excellent legal basis for the extension of its power. On the other hand

[32] Cf. Ficker, *Forsch. z. Reichs- u. Rechtsgesch. Italiens* I (1868), xxviii, and Dopsch, MIÖG. XLVI, 24.

[33] Cf. Lot, *op. cit.*, 237.

in different circumstances, it may place the necessary means
in the hands of the disintegrating elements.

Powerful rulers have always arranged the administration
to suit themselves. Whether the concession of offices took
the form of enfeoffment or not, was of little significance,
for the official character of any office could always be maintained. As an example we may take the German duchies
which, at the time of Conrad I and Henry I, were considered
not as offices derived from the crown but as units of independent origin. The very term " stem duchy," which is
ordinarily used to describe them, itself indicates their
primary character. Yet it was the feudal bond that brought
them under the control of the central authority, and the
very act of enfeoffment explicitly demonstrated that the
duke's authority was derived from above. Throughout the
tenth, eleventh and twelfth centuries dukes were not infrequently dismissed, and this indicates the official character of their position no less than the fact that the kings
themselves surrendered their duchies at the beginning of
their reigns. Yet their position was not entirely official,
but was rather a compound of feudal and official elements;
and for this reason it would be well, in attempting to define
the legal position, to renounce the idea of an exact differentiation between office and fief. But the legal position
was only one side of the question, and, as far as political
measures were concerned, was definitely not the decisive
factor; while it was the political measures taken by the
royal government which ultimately determined the course
of the nation's political life.

The fact is that, in political life, legal forms and rules
can never be decisive.[34] Incomparably more important is
the way in which the law is handled and the question
against whom it is enforced. And this was particularly
true of feudal law and feudal society. It was of little
account whether the small knights' fees were handed down
from father to son, but of real importance whether the great
dukes were to be allowed to establish hereditary succession.
This question, however, was not determined by feudal law

[34] Cf. Hampe, *Hochmittelalter*, 184.

or constitutional principles, but was dependent on political circumstances. Much depended also on the question whether the main emphasis in feudalism was laid on the benefice conferred or on the close personal relationship established by the bond of vassalage. It is characteristic, for example, that Charles the Great conferred influential positions on his *vassi* because in this way the growing weakness in the structure of the state could be combated.[35] In the same way, no mediaeval states were so thoroughly centralized as the Norman feudal monarchies in England, Normandy and Sicily. The feudal state added to the ordinary bond between subject and ruler the particularly binding engagement between lord and vassal. All rights and tenures were derived from the feudal lord, and the supreme feudal lord was the king. Feudal law thus became a real public law and the basis for extreme centralization.

In the West Frankish kingdom feudalism was already penetrating into governmental organization during the Frankish period, and was prevalent in France by the ninth century.[36] When the central authority collapsed, the powers of government passed so completely into the hands of the greater feudal vassals, the feudal princes, who had originally been officials, that the principalities became real states, independent in practice and only theoretically dependent on the king as feudal lord.[37] But in spite of the collapse of the central power political and cultural life continued: the local administration as such was not destroyed, but merely changed its character and position in constitutional law. The cohesion of the state, the connexion between the feudal principalities and the crown, rested on the personal relationship of fealty, the strength of which depended on political conditions.[38] When, in the course of

[35] Cf. Dopsch, MIÖG. XLVI, 24.
[36] Brunner, *Forschungen z. Gesch. d. deutschen u. französischen Rechts* (1894), 65. For France in general, cf. R. Holtzmann, *Französische Verfassungsgeschichte* (1910).
[37] Lot, *op. cit.*, 191, 215; Flach, *Les origines de l'ancienne France* IV (1917), 12 sq.; Mühlbacher, " Die Treupflicht in den Urkunden Karls des Grossen," MIÖG. *Ergänzungsband* VI (1901).
[38] Flach, *op. cit.* III, 56. Flach strongly contests the supposition that feudalism prevailed in France from the tenth to the twelfth centuries, and that feudal law took the place of public law. He places its predominance

the eleventh century, such relationships were brought within the framework of a defined and logical system of feudal law, a favourable basis for the French state was formed, which Philip Augustus was immediately able to employ in order to bring about a vast extension of the authority of the crown.

What, on the other hand, was the position in Germany? When Tassilo, duke of Bavaria, was forced to submit to Pippin in 757, he had to swear an oath of allegiance, through which his duchy was once again to be firmly united with the Frankish empire. After Tassilo's fall, indeed, the duchy was suppressed and the administration of Bavaria, like that of Saxony, was placed in the hands of Frankish counts. More important that this, however, is the fact that, although the ducal office in Bavaria had probably originated as a Frankish official position, the situation in Tassilo's day was essentially different: whatever its origin, it was, at the time in question, definitely regarded as a " stem duchy " with roots of its own in the past,[39] in which neither powers nor functions were derived from the monarchy. The contrast with the West Frankish region is obvious.

in the period after the battle of Bouvines (*op. cit.* IV, 4, 13) and for earlier times will only admit a relationship of fealty. But he goes too far in his otherwise justified reaction against the tendency towards exaggerated systematisation and idealisation of feudalism. Feudalism had great significance in France from the ninth to the twelfth century, much greater for example than in Germany, as is clearly shown by the charters of the period, in which (e.g. in donations) the relationship to the *senior* plays a great part, or by the famous letter of Odo of Blois to king Robert in 1023; cf. L. Halphen, " La lettre d'Eude II de Blois au roi Robert," *Revue historique* XCVIII (1908), 287 sqq. The political significance of feudalism, however, and its power as a force of political organisation depended very directly on the extent of royal power, for only by means of the royal power was it possible to make the pretensions of the feudal overlord effective in practice. Feudal law was present before 1214, and was important, especially within the great feudal principalities like Normandy, but the relations of the crown with the feudal princes were determined by the question of political power. Flach's mistake is to underrate the importance of feudal law on account of its relatively small effect on public affairs during the ninth, tenth and eleventh centuries, while a vast influence over practical politics is usually attributed to it which it did not possess, at least so far as the relations of the crown with the great feudal principalities were concerned. Here political factors were decisive, and in this regard what mattered was the political balance of power.

[39] Cf. Doeberl, *Entwicklungsgesch. Bayerns* I, 36, 78.

Feudalism reached Germany from the west, but can hardly be considered to have penetrated into public law to the same degree as in France, and was very much later in making its influence felt.[40] Not until the time of Barbarossa was feudal law logically and systematically enforced, in such a way as to provide a " monistic " legal foundation for the state.[41] In the legal literature of the thirteenth century—the *Sachsenspiegel* and the other law books— feudal law is systematized, but previously administrative law and feudal law had faced each other in outspoken rivalry. Both feudal law and administrative law, however, had one factor in common: each recognized the central power of the crown as the origin of public rights. How far this recognition went in practice, depended on political circumstances. Because political circumstances in the early period were more favourable in Germany than in France, feudalism was never so important a factor in the constitution of the German state as it was in France, and was also slower in reaching real significance. Here again is an important difference from the west. But in Germany there were, furthermore, public rights which were in no way derived from the king,[42] and in regard to which the feudal system, which centred in the king, was therefore originally of no importance.

Here we come to what is without doubt the most striking difference of all between the two countries. A whole class of German society—the " dynasts " or high nobility—had far-reaching rights of government on their estates and properties, which were not derived from the crown. The high nobility exercised criminal justice in matters of life and limb without obtaining licence or authorisation from the ruler. In this way they were able to form districts which were exempt from the county administration of the state, and which are known as " jurisdictions " or " secular

---

[40] Brunner, *Forschungen*, 66; Ficker, *Forschungen* I, xliii; Dopsch, MIÖG. XLVI, 35.
[41] Brunner, *Forschungen*, 62; Hampe, *Hochmittelalter*, 217.
[42] F. Keutgen, *Der deutsche Staat des Mittelalters*, 8 sqq. There is no need in this connexion to discuss the well-known contrast between " folk law " and " royal law ", which makes itself evident, for example, in the hundred courts.

16TH. MAYER

immunities ". A group of families, estimated to be not more than three hundred in number and recognizable from the middle of the ninth century onwards, was for some three centuries in possession of all governmental rights in Germany, and all countships and dukedoms were the exclusive preserve of its members.[43] These families, with their exclusive prerogatives, are known as the older princely class, to distinguish them from the later princely class which was defined at the end of Barbarossa's reign and was characterized by its immediate feudal relationship with the crown. The later princes were the highest rank in the feudal hierarchy, the tenants-in-chief, and their position was therefore determined by feudal principles: the older princely class, on the other hand, the exclusive class of " dynasts ", was a nobility of birth, and its prerogatives were its inalienable birthright.

What was the origin of the special prerogatives of the older German princely class ? How, indeed, did the dynastic nobility itself arise ? To these questions there is, at present, no certain answer, and until quite recently even the existence of the secular immunity, which was the mark of the aristocracy's privileges, was regarded as very doubtful. To trace the origins of the whole class back to an ancient Germanic nobility is out of the question, ever though it is possible that particular families may reach back to ancient times. On the other hand, it is conceivable that the high aristocracy was descended from the Carolingian official nobility, from Carolingian dukes and counts who may, as in France, have appropriated the prerogatives accruing from their official positions. But this explanation also has not proved completely satisfactory, correct though it may be in a few particular cases. Holders of royal demesne have also been considered, since royal demesne by its very nature possessed immunity from the ordinary administration. We know more or less accurately where

[43] O. von Dungern, *Adelsherrschaft im Mittelalter* (1927), 4. His success in establishing the fact of dualism in public law is important, for otherwise the false idea of a usurpation of public rights by the nobility—which, though it may be true in certain specific cases, is untenable as a generalisation—might still continue to dominate.

the royal demesne lay—practically exclusively in early
colonized regions—and we know also that many families
acquired such property; but such families were already
almost without exception members of the princely class
at the time when they obtained royal estates, as also, for
example, were the advocates of royal churches. Thus,
once again, we get no satisfactory answer to our question;
and the answer is rendered still less satisfactory by the
fact that the crown lands lay within the zone of early
colonization, since it was not here that the principal estates
of the dynastic nobility were to be found. HIRSCH has
declared that our knowledge is not yet far enough advanced
to make an answer to these problems possible;[44] and for
my part, I should add that the theories hitherto put forward
indicate that the problems are beyond solution, if reliance
is placed solely on the written evidence.

But there is other evidence besides the written evidence;
and in view of the failure of the written authorities to provide a conclusive answer, it may be suggested that a consideration of the position in east colonial Germany may open
up new perspectives. There, as we know,[45] the bishop of
Breslau made use of the reclamation of forest and waste

[44] H. Hirsch, *Jahresberichte f. deutsche Geschichte* (1927), 310. Cf.
Dopsch, *Grundlagen* II, 91 sqq., 110, and *Verfassungs-u. Wirtschaftsgesch.
des Mittelalters*, 45–50; G. Seeliger, *Die soziale u. politische Bedeutung d.
Grundherrschaft im frühen Mittelalter* (1903), 123 sqq., and *Staat u. Grundherrschaft in der älteren deutschen Geschichte* (1909), 21–32; v. Dungern,
Der Herrenstand im Mittelalter (1908), and *Adelsherrschaft im Mittelalter*
(1927); H. Hirsch, *Die Klosterimmunität seit dem Investiturstreit* (1914),
11 sqq.; K. Beyerle, *Zeitschr. f. Gesch. d. Oberrheins, Neue Folge* XXII
(1907), 112—113 (where the existence of " secular immunities " is still
contested); H. Aubin, *Die Entstehung der Landeshoheit* (1920), 124 sqq.,
164 sqq., 170 sqq., 286 sqq., and his article in the *Gesch. d. Rheinlandes*
(1922), 10; S. Hofbauer, *Ausbildung d. grossen Grundherrschaften im Reich
der Merowinger* (1927), 94 sqq.; A. Schulte, *Fürstentum u. Einheitsstaat
in der deutschen Geschichte* (1921), 13.—The questions raised here were the
particular concern of G. v. Below, *Der deutsche Staat des Mittelalters*.
Von Below still maintained the point of view that all rights were either
derived from the crown or usurped; cf. for example, p. 259. A discussion
of his attitude is impossible in this place; cf. however Dopsch's critical
essay, " Der deutsche Staat des Mittelalters," *Verf.- u. Wirtschaftsgesch.
des Mittelalters* (1928).

[45] Cf. J. Pfitzner, " Die älteste Geschichte d. Stadt Zuchmantel in
Schlesien," *Zeitschr. d. Ver. f. Gesch. Schlesiens* LVIII (1924), and *Besied-
lungs-, Verfassungs- u. Verwaltungsgesch. d. Breslauer Bistumslandes* I
(1926), 59 sqq.

to form a great consolidated principality with Neisse as its centre. Reclamation determined the boundary between the episcopal lands of Breslau and the district of the dukes of Silesia. In Bohemia, also, development followed an exactly similar course.[46] Here again, reclamation brought with it such far-reaching rights of government that the leading figures in the colonization threatened to throw off the yoke of their sovereign prince, the king of Bohemia. The question arises, however, whether the position in the east German zone of colonization can supply us with a real analogy. To this question I would reply generally that conditions and events in the colonial east were not fundamentally different from those in Old West Germany, but rather that they provide an indication, usually in a particularly intelligible form, of the position in the older lands, which, considered independently, is often far from clear.[47] We can, moreover, point to a connecting district in which east and west meet. This is the demesne of the archbishops of Salzburg,[48] which lies near the boundaries of the old German lands, and which offers us an excellent example of the actual growth of a princely state. Without ever having received an explicit grant of count's rights or of jurisdiction, the archbishops, beginning with their reclaimed lands, succeeded in forming a magnificent territorial principality.[49] But once we start to consider re-

[46] Th. Mayer, " Aufgaben d. Siedlungsgesch. in den Sudetenländern," *Deutsche Hefte f. Volks- u. Kulturbodenforsch.* I (1930),133 sqq.

[47] Cf. Th. Mayer, " Haupttatsachen d. wirtschaftlichen Entwicklung," *Vierteljahrschr. f. Sozial- u. Wirtschaftsgesch.* XXI (1928), where I have referred to the fundamental differences between indigenous economic growth, with roots in the soil and its beginnings in small groups, and the derivative economic types, in which development begins with a mature system transferred from elsewhere. Such differences are of equal account in constitutional history, and no example illustrates this fact better than a comparison of France and Germany. This example also shows that it is not enough to prove the fact of borrowing and to compare single elements, but that a comparison of the situation as a whole is always necessary.

[48] Cf. E. Richter, " Untersuchungen z. historischen Geographie d. ehemaligen Hochstiftes Salzburg," MIÖG. *Erg.-Band* I, 617, and H. Widmann, *Geschichte v. Salzburg* I, 326.

[49] The archbishops of Salzburg profited greatly from the fact that a whole series of dynastic families died out, particularly the counts of Plain, who were the archbishop's *advocati*. In this connexion cf. F. Martin, *Die kirchliche Vogtei des Erzstiftes Salzburg* (1906), 17. As to the significance of the extinction of families of count's rank in Bavaria, cf. Doeberl, *Entwicklungsgesch.* I, 259.

clamation and colonization as a source or creator of public rights, we can point to more than one instance within the central German district of Hesse and the old duchy of Franconia. For the moment I will only mention the county of Wittgenstein, of which we possess a most valuable study.[50] There reclamation was beyond all doubt the driving force in the formation of the lordship. And from the same district it is possible to collect a whole series of further instances,[51] which show above all else that conditions in east and west Germany were in this respect by no means basically different. The rôle of colonization in the development of the east is obvious enough and has long been understood; but if conditions, as we have seen, were fundamentally similar in east and west, may we conclude that internal colonization had the same constitutional effects in west Germany as external colonization is known to have had in the east colonial lands ? What contribution, in short, did colonization make to the growth of the old princely families to political and constitutional predominance ?

Once we have obtained sufficient facts to formulate the questions at issue we can safely undertake a more detailed examination of the position in Hesse and more generally in the district round the middle Rhine and the Main, where conditions were very typical. Hesse, in all its three provinces, comprises land which was colonized at an early date, like Rheinhessen or the Wetterau. But these early settlements are joined by other districts which were only colonized and brought under cultivation after the Frankish period. As such I would mention the Pfälzerwald, the Hunsrück, the Taunus, the Vogelsberg, the Büdingerwald, the Spessart and the Odenwald. If we enumerate the dynastic families of this neighbourhood and their landed property, we obtain a very remarkable picture. The families in question are those of Leiningen, Sponheim,

[50] G. Wrede, *Territorialgesch. d. Grafschaft Wittgenstein* (1927).
[51] Cf. M. Sponheimer, *Landesgesch. d. Niedergrafschaft Katzenelnbogen u. d. angrenzenden Ämter auf dem Einrich* (1932), and also the studies of E. Anhalt on the district of Frankenberg (1928) and of K. Buchmann on that of Eschwege (1931).

Wildgrafen and their various branches, Eppsteiner, Nüring, Solmser, Gleiberger, Arnsburger, Büdinger, Isenburger, Hanauer, and from the. neighbouring districts we can mention the Katzenelnbogen, Arnstein, Diez, Nassauer, Merenberger and others. The oldest properties of all these families lay in the land which was settled early, but they lay on the outskirts of this land: from here the families in question made their start, but their principal holdings were in the newly colonized territories. It was in the newly colonized land that they established their *Bann-bezirke* or " jurisdictions "; in the newly colonized lands arose the great lordships and among them an occasional sovereign principality.[52] In contrast to this it is a remark-able fact, and one which demands full emphasis, that not one single family among the high dynastic nobility estab-lished a lordship for itself within the whole of the area which had been settled at an early date. On the contrary, the area of early settlement is found to be inhabited ex-clusively by innumerable branches of the lesser nobility or knightly class, whom we find in almost every village. Only in quite exceptional cases, where royal demesne, for example, has passed into private hands, do we find proper-ties of any importance in the possession of " dynasts ". Finally, we must draw attention to the fact that far from

---

[52] A good example is provided by the work of Sponheimer on Kat-zenelnbogen; cf. also G. Simon, *Gesch. d. reichsständischen Hauses Ysenburg u. Büdinger* (1865). See further the map in Fabricius, *Erläuterungen z. gesch. Atlas d. Rheinprovinz* VI (1914), and G. Bernard, *Das nördl. Rhein-hessen* (1931), 77 sq.—Aubin, *Landeshoheit*, 401 sqq., discusses the forest counties, without however carrying his observations to their logical con-clusion.—J. Friedrich, *Burg u. territoriale Grafschaften* (1907), offers a penetrating examination of the questions at issue, with particular reference to the Middle Rhine district, and his conclusions are in part most valuable. But although he mentions the forests, he has not investigated their signi-ficance; cf. for example p. 41, where is he speaking of the " judicium apud Reckenforst . . . in generali placito, quod lantdegedinge dicitur, cui comes Gerhardus de Dieso presedit in Reckenforst." He discusses the rise of the comital families, but can offer no explanation of the origin of the counts' rights or more generally of the growth of dynastic lordships. What he has to say of single families is not beyond criticism, and in any case he only offers a general survey of the various houses. The systematic con-struction of castles and fortified places, with which his work is mainly concerned, is nevertheless a very important factor in constitutional history, and well worth emphasizing. In this respect Germany was, in point of time, very far behind France.

all of the high nobility, whose lordships were centred in the newly colonized lands, were in a position to rely on or to bring forward royal privileges as a legal basis for the powers which they were exercising. The picture which we obtain from other German territories is similar. A map of the princely fiefs in Württemberg shows that they were confined almost exclusively to the newly colonized lands and were absent in the area of ancient settlement.[53] In Bavaria there was a series of families belonging to the high nobility, and their property lay similarly in the newly colonized districts, particularly north of the Danube.[54] If we examined other provinces, examples could be multiplied.[55] When these privileged families attained their position, we do not know; but FABRICIUS has stated that in the district round the middle Rhine they were established about the turn of the twelfth century.[56] In these circumstances it is not difficult to conclude that the families which distinguished themselves

[53] The map of enfeoffed property in Württemberg was published by the statistical office of the state in 1920.

[54] Cf. Doeberl, *Entwicklungsgesch.* I, 136, 141, 143, 146, 152, and E. Wallner, *Altbayrische Siedlungsgeschichte in den Ortsnamen der Ämter Bruck, Dachau, Freising usw.* (1929).

[55] For Upper Austria, cf. the studies of J. Strnadt on the historical geography of the district in the *Archiv. f. österr. Geschichte*, together with the recent and very instructive investigations of F. Brosch, " Siedlungsgeschichte des Waxenbergischen Amtes Leonfelden," *Jahrbuch d. ober-österr. Musealvereins* LXXXIV (1932). For Hesse and Thuringia, cf K. A. Eckhardt, *Politische Geschichte der Landschaft an der Werra u. der Stadt Witzenhausen* (2nd ed., 1928), and H. Eberhardt, *Die Anfänge des Territorialfürstentums in Nordthüringen* (1932). For Alsace, cf. the *Elsass-Lothringischer Atlas* (ed. G. Wolfram and W. Gley, 1931), especially maps VII and IX.

[56] Fabricius, *Erläuterungen* VI, 21. Cf. Seelinger, *Staat u. Grundherrschaft*, who writes (p. 28): " When the individual jurisdictional districts arose, we do not for the most part know. Perhaps they derive more frequently than can yet safely be conjectured from Frankish formations, from ancient *potestas* districts." This means that Seelinger also can make no definite statements, and what he has to say beyond this refers practically exclusively to ecclesiastical lordships. H. Witte, in his article on the older counts of Spanheim, *Zeitschr. f. Gesch. d. Oberrheins, Neue Folge* XI (1896), 228 sq., says: " it has not been possible to apportion any definite county to the Spanheimer; for those counties which immediately come to mind, were one and all definitely in the hands of other families. It is a question for the most part of allodial property, to which were added a few fiefs, specifically such as were held from the bishopric of Speyer. This whole property-complex broke away, as early as the first half of the eleventh century, from the hundred organisation under the *Gograf*, and thenceforward its holder himself exercised count's rights."

in the work of reclamation and colonization acquired not only more extensive demesnes but also the special legal position and prerogatives of the high aristocracy. This conclusion is supported, also, by the fact that " ministerial " families with considerable estates in the newly colonized lands, such as the Bolanden, Hagen and Erbach families in Hesse, were very quickly assimilated to the higher nobility and actually obtained the right of *connubium*,[57] though their rise occurs in a later period. Nevertheless, there must be some support in the written authorities for our conception of the rise of the high nobility and the source of its privileges, for changes so fundamental in character cannot have occurred without leaving some traces. What, then, is the attitude of our historical authorities to colonization and the clearing of waste ? Is there any evidence that it was regarded as a source of public rights ?

Among economic historians LAMPRECHT in particular drew attention to the importance of essarts or clearings of forest and waste,[58] but without pushing his ideas to any definite conclusion. More recently there have been a number of historical and legal studies dealing with the forests.[59] In the middle ages, it has been shown, the term " forest " signified the exclusion of a particular district from general use, but also—and in our connexion this is the more important factor—its exclusion from the general administrative organisation of the state. In origin, no

[57] Cf. the index in v. Dungern, *Herrenstand, s. v.* Bolanden, Erbach, Hagen.—The conclusion which has been reached above, it may be added, is of general importance. The issue is whether historical conclusions may be drawn *a posteriori* from a complete and absolutely unambiguous geographical picture, or whether, because in certain cases another explanation (e.g., origin in a state office like the office of count or particularly that of warden of the forest) is possible, such individual cases are to be generalized. In my view conclusions arrived at by generalisation from single cases— cases which in themselves are perfectly understandable as resulting from special historical circumstances—are dangerous and even inadmissible, since the uniformity of the whole picture can never be explained on this basis. Cf. *infra*, n. 63.

[58] K. Lamprecht, *Deutsches Wirtschaftsleben* I, 426.

[59] H. Thimme, " Forestis. Königsgut und Königsrecht nach den Forsturkunden vom 6. bis 12. Jahrhundert," *Arch. f. Urkundenforschung* II (1909); K. Glöckner, " Bedeutung u. Entstehung d. Forstbegriffes," *Vierteljahrsschr. f. Sozial- u. Wirtschaftsgesch.* XVII (1924); O. Bethge,)ber ' Bifänge '," *ibid.* XX (1928).

doubt, the conception denoted by the term " forest " referred primarily to woodland and chase, but it soon came to comprehend all usufructuary and other rights in and over the woodlands, and included particularly the rights of clearing the waste and colonizing. This idea is expressed already in a charter of Sigibert I, and in the charters concerning the Spanish *apprisiones* it is made clear that forest and rights of forest also comprised powers of jurisdiction.[60] In a formula from St. Gallen immunity is explicitly designated by the term *forestis*, and the situation at Fulda also indicates that *forestis* had the same meaning as immunity.[61] But the most instructive instance of all—apart from exactly parallel cases in Hesse—is supplied once again by the archbishopric of Salzburg. The archbishop had commenced reclamation without any charter at all, as very frequently happened; but he wished, of course, to safeguard his occupancy, and for this purpose, shortly before 977, he had an imperial diploma forged, which he then succeeded in getting confirmed.[62] And nothing can be more significant than the fact that, although the archbishop exercised all rights of government in the colonized district, what was forged was neither a grant of count's rights nor a grant of jurisdiction nor even a charter of immunity, but a forest privilege.[63] That a forest privilege was regarded as a

---

[60] MG. *Dipl. Merov.*, 22 (No. 22); cf. Thimme, 131.
[61] In this regard cf. especially the interesting charter of Otto II (DO. II, 221), to which Thimme has already drawn attention.
[62] *Salzburger Urkundenbuch* II, 34, 57.
[63] E. Richter, MIÖG. *Erg.-Band* I, 617. The fact that the archbishop forged a privilege at all might be supposed to force us to the conclusion that a privilege was fundamentally necessary for colonization. But, as Glöckner (*op. cit.*, 27) has shown, colonization and afforestation occurred also without any privilege, and are in no way to be considered as illegal. A royal privilege was certainly desirable as a final safeguard. Such privileges were particularly sought after when the district in question had already been settled, and what it was particularly desired to obtain through the acquisition of rights of forest was therefore plenary governmental rights over the district and its inhabitants. Fulda offers an excellent example of this, and the position in Salzburg was no doubt similar, for as early as the ninth century the very wide area which the archbishop claimed in the forgery was already beginning to be inhabited. At the same time it becomes clear that the sovereign rights which the crown claimed in theory over the forest, were far from always asserted in practice, and that numerous woodlands existed to which they did not extend. If such an extension was thought desirable, there is not much doubt that it was

sufficient title for the exercise of the archbishop's extensive rights of jurisdiction and government is therefore an excellent illustration of the wide significance of the juridical conception denoted by the term *forestis*.

It is well to guard against too far-reaching generalization, and we have therefore no intention of maintaining that the whole of the high nobility owed its position and rights simply to its work of colonization. Before this could be said a detailed investigation of each single family would be necessary. But it is nevertheless certain that colonization on a large scale led to the acquisition of the rights denoted by the term *forestis*—which, as we have seen, amounted to full rights of government in the colonized woodland—and for the very reason that, throughout such extensive districts, we find no " dynasts " who were not settled on newly colonized land, it is fair to say that the privileged position of the high nobility was derived from the *forestis*. The area reclaimed in Germany after the Frankish period was very extensive, as place-names and field-systems alone are sufficient to show;[64] and from this evidence we can obtain some idea of the date at which the lordships in the hands of the high nobility arose. We see also that public rights were far from rigid or inelastic, and that they could be created and acquired by the exercise of particularly important functions, by achievements such as the extension of the area of land in human occupation. This took place both with and without royal privilege. The conclusion to which we are led is, therefore, that public rights in Germany were far from always derived from the central authority of the state, but were also indigenous, and that consequently

effected by an explicit declaration that a certain district constituted a royal forest.

[64] Cf. the maps in O. Schlüter, " Deutsches Siedlungswesen," *Reallexikon d. germ. Altertumskunde* I (after p. 424); A. Bach, *Die Siedlungsnamen des Taunusgebietes* (1927); F. Langenbeck, " Beiträge z. elsäss. Siedlungsgeschichte," *Elsass-Lothringisches Jahrbuch* VI (1927), the map to which is very instructive.—The significance of colonization in general constitutional history is still by no means adequately appreciated. Many of the controversies concerning the mark, the village community, etc., are due to the fact that one historian is thinking of newly colonized land, another of districts of early settlement, with the result that argument is often at cross purposes.

from the very moment at which public rights arose, a pronounced dualism was in existence.

But there is yet another significant conclusion which follows from what we have said. It is well known that the early mediaeval state is to be regarded as an association of persons, in which lordship over the land was merely of secondary importance. When Tassilo swore fealty, his oath signified the incorporation into the Frankish empire of the district over whose inhabitants he exercised sovereign rights.[65] Similar transactions occurred often thereafter. The idea of government as rule over persons could scarcely be displaced in practice in the early period of German history, since the scattered and divided nature both of landed property and of sovereign rights, which then predominated, made it far from easy to construct a territorial basis for the state. There are many serious difficulties to be met in explaining the change over to the later conception of a uniform territorial state. Immunity, which broke up the old county organization, has often been regarded as the decisive factor; but on account of the extraordinarily scattered character of ecclesiastical holdings, it has become increasingly clear that immunity cannot have been decisive. ROSENSTOCK traces the process back to the constitutional situation in the marcher lands; but on the face of it this is a very improbable explanation, for it is difficult to see how the situation in the eastern marches can have affected the position in old west Germany.[66] In the forests, on the other hand, we have found a natural starting-point, because in the forests sovereign rights were derived not from rights over persons but from rights over an area of land.

Let us again return to the comparison with France. There also much reclamation and colonization was carried out between the eleventh and thirteenth centuries,[67] but not to the same extent as in Germany. In France the

---

[65] Cf. supra, 14.

[66] Rosenstock, Königshaus u. Stämme, 116 sq., 133 sq. Nor can I agree with Rosenstock in his exaggerated estimate of the racial units and in his supposition that they possessed legal personality; cf. supra, n. 28.

[67] Cf. M. Bloch, Les caractères originaux de l'histoire rurale française (1931), 5.

districts brought under cultivation were not, as in Germany, large and consolidated. Moreover, in France public authority, although it was far from necessarily the authority of the king himself, was stronger; and consequently colonization could never result in the creation of new districts, separate and distinct in public law. The structure and constitution of the state were not, in mediaeval France, determined by internal colonization. In this respect reclamation and colonization had in France the same significance as in those parts of the German east where strong territorial lordships were already in existence at the time when reclamation was begun.

Once again, therefore, the result was an important difference between France and Germany. In France one could, in the very nature of the case, only become a possessor of public rights—what VON BELOW terms a person in authority[68]—either through the conferment of those rights by the state or through illegal usurpation: in Germany one could legimately acquire those rights from another source. There precisely lay the constitutional and political significance of the *forestis*, which was thus a logical supplement to the ancient particularist rights and claims of a seignorial and tribal character. When the French king was strong enough to enforce his rights, he was the veritable source of all rights: in Germany, on the other hand, the king could only force the persons with indigenous rights of their own to become dependent on the crown. If he wished to declare justice as a whole to be derived from royal authority, he had no alternative except to encroach on and interfere in the autogenous legal competence of others. Thus we see that there were differences between Germany and France which were due not only to the effects of the Italian policy of the German emperors or to the fact that France had undergone a five centuries long process of levelling and blending under Roman rule. There were more important differences still, which resulted from the fact that the development of France and Germany in the middle ages

[68] " Obrigkeitliche Person "; cf. G. v. Below, *Der deutsche Staat*, 220.

was conditioned by fundamentally different factors. The inevitable consequence was that the strengthening of the movement to indigenous development, which was so characteristic of German political life, never made headway in France.

Since the high dynastic nobility of Germany owed its position for the most part to its own efforts, it is comprehensible that it was jealous of its rights. It is a noteworthy fact, which SCHMEIDLER has pointed out,[69] that the German nobility was often unruly and even treacherous under a strong and politically active king, but remained loyal to a weak ruler. The explanation lies in the fact that the strong rulers sought to extend the central power of the monarchy, to make public governmental rights dependent on royal authority, to transform them into real state rights. The underlying meaning of political development was, after all, the formation of larger states and the strengthening of the central power. To this tendency royal policy responded, and the aristocracy came into conflict with the crown precisely because it did not wish to subordinate its own interests to this development; because it opposed its own particular rights, historically well-founded and for the most part legitimately acquired, to the right of the whole nation to fulfil its historical development.[70] Often enough racial passions were awakened, where the real issue was simply an aristocratic struggle for power; often enough tribal particularism was evoked where really there was a one-sided and unreasonable extension of the dualistic conception of constitutional rights. Again and again it was possible to depict representatives of particularism, like Duke Ernst of Swabia, as representatives of liberty.

The whole meaning of Henry IV's attempt at constitu-

---

[69] B. Schmeidler, *Franken u. d. deutsche Reich im Mittelalter* (1930), 3, 4, 6.

[70] When Schmeidler (p. 7) raises the question whether certain German rulers may not have carried centralization too far " without need," he seems to me to do scant justice to the import of the general development of the German folk and state as a whole. Nor can I agree with him when he speaks of the " justified reaction " of the lay nobility to the favouring of the church, for, thus formulated, the whole question is put in a false perspective.

tional reform, about which HANS HIRSCH has recently enlightened us,[71] lay in his efforts to make the exercise of criminal justice, the most important of all public rights, dependent on royal authorisation, on the grant of the " ban " by the king, and thus to transform it into a function of state. There is no doubt that, in pursuing this object, Henry IV really did interfere with the rights of the high nobility, substantial rights which they were actually exercising; and owing to this attempt the king was overthrown. With his fall the first effort at reform was frustrated. The second attempt, which was designed to follow the path along which the French monarchy had already travelled, was made by Frederick I, who not only constituted a ministerial administration and a territory directly under the crown, but also wished, in his relations with the princes, to apply the principles of feudal law, to make the *Heerschild* or military hierarchy, and the system of military tenure bound up with it, the basis of the system of public law, and thus to introduce the " monistic " conception of the state into Germany.[72]   But this endeavour, in spite of excellent prospects at the beginning, was brought to nothing by political circumstances, particularly the early death of Henry VI, the effects of the right of free election and the subsequent troubles and disorders.   In consequence of this chain of events the territorial princes became so strong that a generation later, when feudal law really came to prevail, although the royal authority was formally the pivot of the state and the king the fount of all justice, although he still retained the power of conferring public rights, he could himself only exercise such rights where he himself was the territorial prince, in other words on his royal and family demesnes.   During the intervening period the territorial principality had triumphed over the

---

[71] In his illuminating work, *Die hohe Gerichtsbarkeit im deutschen Mittelalter* (1922); cf. particularly p. 232 sqq.   And cf. Dopsch, MIÖG. XLVI, 36.
[72] Cf. von Dungern, *infra*, 203–233, though v. Dungern is concerned in the first place with the introduction of *ministeriales* into the administration.   This process related for the most part to the family property of the king and to the imperial demesne, and thus to the creation of a consolidated royal territory.   Cf. Hampe, *Hochmittelalter*, 217.

idea of one united realm and over royal authority. Germany, which in the central period of the middle ages had been in a commanding position as a political power and in this regard had surpassed France, now fell behind France as a political force. The dualism in law, which we have already observed, crystallized into a political antithesis between the realm and the single principalities and thereby lost the greater part of the usefulness it might have possessed as a constructive force, capable of building up a German nation.

It would, however, be false to trace the formation of the sovereign principalities exclusively to the usurpation of royal rights. The territorial princes rather built up the modern state by assuming the undischarged tasks of government, by developing their own rights, and not least of all by subjecting the local " dynasts " to their territorial authority. This positive achievement still deserves full recognition. The principalities established the principle of the uniform territorial state in the face of the disorganisation due to the existence of innumerable immune authorities and franchises; the princes restored calm to the land both by taking control of the movement for establishing public peace and by giving substance and purpose and practical justification to the varied functions united in the ducal office. How markedly the rise of the territorial powers depended on this achievement, and how clearly the movement for establishing a *Landfrieden* reflects the growth of the state, in the sense in which we are now using the word, is shown by the history of the central German lands within the boundaries of the old Frankish duchy. In this district there was no superior power and no single ruler capable by himself of establishing a general peace for the whole land: voluntary unions were therefore formed with the object of restoring peace,[73] but a great territorial unit did not arise.

[73] Cf. H. Vielau, *Beiträge z. Gesch. d. Landfrieden Karls IV* (1877); E. Fischer, *Die Landfriedensverfassung unter Karl IV* (1883); J. Schwalm, *Die Landfrieden in Deutschland unter Ludwig d. Bayer* (1889); W. Fabricius, " Die älteren Landfriedenseinungen der Wetterauer Grafen," *Arch. f. hess. Gesch., Neue Folge* III (1904).

Next to the movement for instituting public peace and
the formation of the territorial state, the most important
movement directed towards achieving the complete pre-
valence of state authority was absolutism, which led to
unification and uniformity of public life. In Germany,
however, there was no imperial absolutism, only the absolutism of the single principalities, through which the
fantastic map of German localism and particularism, dependent often on the accident of marriage or inheritance,
was finally settled, and the idea of dualism in public law was
grotesquely distorted. BISMARCK himself said that " the
unlimited sovereignty of the princes . . . was a revolutionary
acquisition, won at the expense of the nation and of its
unity."[74] Actually dualism ceased, for the empire itself
had no power left, and a state without power is a bloodless
system of legal regulations without political effectiveness.
In the principalities, on the other hand, a new dualism of
a particular sort gradually developed with the growth of
a system of estates and of a constitutional law based on
estates.

We have followed the development of the German state
in its main stages and return once again to the question of
the constitution of the German state as contrasted with
that of the Romanized lands. It is a question to which
we can give no easy answer. The Roman state, also, was
a product of historical development; but it made its appearance at the beginning of German history as a centralized, monistic state, and it was as such that it remained
alive and effective in the Romanized parts of Europe. We
come face to face with it in France, where it was not itself
an indigenous growth, but an importation. In the German
state, on the other hand, the persistence of Roman institutions was not of decisive importance. Only isolated elements were introduced there, and the system of centralized
government as a whole had not sufficient strength to take
root. This is shewn under Conrad I and under Henry I.
Development in Germany was consequently indigenous,

[74] *Gedanken u. Erinnerungen,* 338.

autogenous, and started with the idea of small political formations, each with its own rights and competence, which were only held together by a system of government based on allegiance. This idea of the autogenous rights of the smaller political units found powerful support in the rights derived from reclamation and colonization, which we have emphasized. The *forestis*, the forest in its legal aspects, was both an effect and a cause of the dualistic conception of the state. In the German state, therefore, there were always rights which were not derived from the central power. The subordination of these powers under the centralized authority of the crown, had it been possible, would accordingly have been an immeasurably greater achievement in Germany than in France. In Germany the " state " as such had first to be created, and this was hardly to be done without the co-operation of the local powers. In Germany there was no monistic basis of law, and the central power was politically too weak to be able simply to trample over the rights of the constituent members of the body politic. The incorporation of these rights and of their holders into the state does, indeed, constitute a large part of the mediaeval constitutional history of Germany; but it was carried into effect by the princes within the limits of the territorial principalities, and not by the empire. The territorial principalities themselves were the result of the dualism in German law, though they eventually managed for the most part to surmount, if not entirely to suppress it: within the empire, on the other hand it was carried to absurd extremes.

The question is now whether German constitutional development will and must take the same path as that of France, whether the difference between the two countries is only a difference in time or whether it is fundamental. There can be no mistake that in many facets of public life German development stands, in point of time, far behind that of France. But we have seen that the basis of development in the two countries was in no way the same, that it was often radically different. Many similarities have been introduced in recent times, particularly in the nineteenth

century, by the importation of French institutions in no
way suited to the German character or to the German state.
Once again we must emphasize the fact that it is a specifically German legal conception that every organism within
its own sphere of interests, be it an individual, a corporation,
a community or a land, has a right to far-reaching, inalienable independence, proportionate to the functions it fulfils.
By the side of, and above, all individuality, however, a
strong central authority is necessary, which can guarantee
in all main questions the power and unity without which
no state can live.   That the middle ages did not allow the
state, in this respect, as much power as was essential if it
were to thrive, was a misfortune for the German people.
On the other hand, though unceasing centralization may
be possible in states formed by conquest, although it may
be necessary when a disintegrating empire has—as under
Diocletian—to be held together, a people which stands
culturally at its height cannot in the long run be ruled
absolutely.   At a time of crisis a system can be justified
which makes it possible to exercise all the powers of government without friction, but in the long run no centralized
state with its bureaucracy can call forth that power which
is decisive both in state and in nation, in politics and in
culture: the creative initiative of the individual in his own
small sphere of activity, through which in the final analysis
the greater edifice is built.   The maintenance of this initiative is part of the whole German conception of the state,
a state which is constructed not on obedience but on the
voluntary co-operation of each individual.   The German
state is based on a system of service,[75] in which each takes
part.   Whosoever contributes has rights; but whosoever
has rights has also duties and responsibility.[76]   Rights,

[75] When Aubin, *Landeshoheit*, 238, writes: " Economic development
was the motive force, which brought about the transformations of the
idea of immunity, and of the institutions in which it was embodied, and
which drove territorial lordship onwards towards its final completion,"
he also is expressing the idea that the historical development of the law
and of the constitution depends on services performed.   For my part,
however, I would in no way limit the idea of service to the economic sphere,
but would extend it as generally as possible to all services important in
the life of the people.
[76] Cf. W. Merk, *Vom Wesen u. Werden des deutschen Rechts*, 78.

duties, responsibility, each must always balance the other. Responsible performance of duties eliminates compulsion, safeguards the private rights of the individual and of smaller circles, and maintains the state. That is the meaning of the dualism in German constitutional law, as it appeared, grew to maturity and established itself in a development of ten centuries, and as it permeates the work of the greatest German statesmen from the Carolingians onwards. to Stein and Bismarck.

THE PROPRIETARY CHURCH AS AN ELEMENT OF MEDIAEVAL GERMANIC ECCLESIASTICAL LAW[1]

By ULRICH STUTZ

THREE different positive conceptions of law and of the state have faced the Christian Church in the course of its history in Western Europe; three different legal and political systems have ruled the West during the period of its existence.

It was under the rule of Roman law and of the Roman Empire that the Church came into existence. Then followed one of its outstanding achievements, the conversion of the Germanic invaders; and under the rule of Germanic law, in close connexion with the Germanic and Frankish monarchy and with the feudal society which followed, it attained new strength. Yet the Church was not so closely bound up with this society that it could not outlive it. As, with the revival of Roman law, a new society took shape and the mediaeval was slowly transformed into the modern state, the Church developed with it, passed over into the newer system, and continued to fulfil its sacred mission within modern society. At no stage has the Church identified itself fully and finally with the one or the other of the temporal systems with which it has found itself in contact: none has proved itself essential for the Church's stability and permanence. On the other hand, none of the temporal systems has passed without leaving its mark on the Church. For the Church's sphere of activity is in this world, though its purpose is supernatural; and it is therefore dependent to a greater or lesser degree on

[1] *Die Eigenkirche als Element des mittelalterlich-germanischen Kirchenrechtes* (Inaugural lecture in the University of Basel, delivered on 23 October 1894). Berlin, H. W. Müller, 1895. Thanks are due to the publisher's successor, Ferdinand Enke in Stuttgart, for permission to translate.

its worldly environment. In particular it needs, in fulfilling its purpose, a legal organization; for without this no society can maintain itself. The Church has therefore a law. This Church law is, however, only one branch of general law. Ecclesiastical and temporal law are nearly related, and influence each other in their development. For this reason, each of the three systems of social organization which we have named has powerfully affected the law of the Church, each has been of fundamental importance for the canon law.

No one would deny the accuracy of this statement as far as the first and the last of the three epochs, ancient society and modern society, are concerned. The influence exerted by the Roman Empire and by Roman law is a commonplace, and it is already necessary for scholars to guard against an exaggeration of their importance. Equally undeniable is the basic influence of modern law and political organization on the law of the Church; it is sufficient, in this regard, to point out that scientific treatment of the canon law as a whole belongs to this period, that it was at this time that the law of the evangelical churches was established and marriage law received a stable form—all under the most far-reaching influence of secular law. On the other hand, not every one would be in agreement, if a parallel significance in the history of Church law were attributed to Germanic law and to the Germanic states of the Middle Ages.

Such a view has, at all events, little support in modern legal literature. There are still no thorough and comprehensive studies of the interaction of Germanic and ecclesiastical law. In the past there has been general agreement that the Church, as a child of the ancient world, only accepted the ancient—that is, the Roman—law, and looked down with something like contempt on the law of the barbarian peoples. The Germanic nations, it is maintained, took over a Church which was already perfected, and did practically nothing to develop Christian dogma: how could they have achieved pioneer work in the sphere of Church law ? Considerations such as these seemed to render a painstaking survey of the mutual influence of the two legal systems unnecessary. In certain particulars, of course, Germanic influences were recognised; not a few abuses, for instance, were attributed to them; but that Germanic society had any really fundamental importance for the law of the Church was tacitly denied. Such is the impression to be gained from modern literature and research.

But an appeal lies from the modern literature to the original authorities. And the original authorities prove with singular clarity, for any one who studies them carefully from this point of view, both the actual existence in an earlier age of a body of Germanic Church law, and the fundamental significance, in the historical development of canon law, of Germanic law and custom. It is out of the question to prove this here for all spheres of legal activity. Even a general survey of Germanic Church law as such would not achieve this end. A comparison with the law of the Church before and after the Germanic era would still be necessary: starting with the ecclesiastical law expounded for example, by Hincmar of Reims, we should have to compare, on the one hand, that of Gregory I, on the other, that of Innocent III or Gregory IX. Could this be done, the result would astound anyone who still maintained the accepted view. The similarity between the legal systems of the earlier and the later periods would still be obvious at first sight. The Church law of the Germanic period, on the other hand, would have a completely unexpected appearance. For Germanic influence over the Church and its law was so strong, that it left its own imprint on both, an imprint which differentiates Germanic Church law as decisively from the preceding system as from the formulation of ecclesiastical jurisprudence in classical canon law, which was to follow. Only closer inspection would make clear the connexion with the law both of the past and of the future, and would shew that considerable Germanic, as well as Roman, elements maintained their place in the canon law of later days and thus were handed down to us. But these general implications, as has been said, must be ignored here. On this occasion, it will be enough to single out one particular element of Germanic Church law, to trace its history and to try to explain the part which it played in the formation of Germanic Church law as a whole. In this way the existence of such a body of law will be proved, and one way at least will have been indicated, in which Germanic conceptions were absorbed into the Church and its jurisprudence.

Every historian and particularly the legal historian has a larger task before him than that of merely setting down what has occurred or taken shape within any particular epoch: it is equally part of his work to make clear which of the events of the future were not undergoing preparation in the period with which he is dealing, what future facts were not yet actualities. This is particularly necessary for the historian of Church law, because of the recurrent tendency to push back the origins of single ecclesiastical institutions to the very beginnings of Church history. In this tendency one explanation can be found of the neglect of the share taken by the Germanic peoples in the development of church law: much has been attributed to the Roman epoch which was really due to the Germans. For this reason, we must attempt to discover what was still lacking in the law of the church in pre-Germanic times, which were the spheres in which it had no application: this is the surest way to discover the points at which Germanic 'development could begin.

At the end of the Roman epoch the main bodies were already in existence: the Church as a whole and the single churches.

The organization of the Church, considered as one body, was near to completion. It was still no unified monarchy, ruled by the bishop of Rome, but it was already a federation of more or less sovereign episcopal churches. This federation had a constitution. There were meetings of the federation, Synods; high officials of the federation, the Metropolitans, Exarchs and Patriarchs; and a federal

administration, modelled on the administrative organization of the Roman state, with its own administrative
districts. An elaborate federal law regulated the relations
of the individual churches and their bishops to one another
and to their superiors. Among its more important sections
we may notice the rules about Synods, about the position
and rights of Metropolitans and about episcopal elections,
which at an early date had been transformed from a concern of the individual churches alone into a concern of the
whole federation. All these matters had been regulated
by the law of the pre-Germanic period, and for the most
part the rules of pre-Germanic law have retained their
influence throughout subsequent centuries.

In regard to the single churches, also, legal organization
had long been in existence. One rule of law equated the
secular and the ecclesiastical unit, the *civitas* and the
ecclesia in its narrower meaning, made the civic boundaries
the bounds of the bishopric, and the body of citizens the
episcopal community. It was another legal rule that each
individual church must have a bishop as head, and that
membership of the church depended on connexion with a
legally appointed bishop. In virtue of a legal ordinance,
there was in each church a body of lay members—to all
intents and purposes a passive body—and a priestly class,
set apart for the government of the church, just as in civil
society at that epoch there was the body of Roman citizens,
whose civil rights were of a passive nature, and side by
side with it a ruling bureaucracy. The ecclesiastical
hierarchy, also, was legally constituted, and in spite of the
Greek names which they bore, the heads of each official
class were more or less the equivalents of the officials of
the secular bureaucracy of the Roman state. Even the
beginnings of an ecclesiastical law of property were in
existence. A customary prescription ordained that all
ecclesiastical wealth was the property of the episcopal
church, and a rule expressed in both secular and ecclesiastical legislation hindered or even prevented the alienàtion
of church property, the administration of which was otherwise left to the discretion of the bishop.

What was lacking, however, was legal co-ordination, legal organization within the structure of the single church. It would be mistaken to regard the episcopal church of pre-Germanic times as similar to the ordinary modern bishopric; rather it was like a modern missionary bishopric. In it the bishop was everything. His relations with the outer world, with other bishops and their churches, were ruled by law; but internally, within his own church, he was master and ecclesiastical interests and opportunity alone determined his actions. There were no legal checks on him in this regard, either in favour of persons or in favour of things. The laity had no word; rights of the church communities had fallen into desuetude. The clergy lived at the bishop's behest and held office *ad nutum episcopi*; they depended on him in spiritual matters, for they officiated in the bishop's name and at his order, and they were economically dependent on him, for he paid each a *stipendium* at his own discretion and could unconditionally grant out landed property in the form of the revocable *precarium*. There were already, of course, many churches in existence, particularly in country districts, besides the episcopal church; but in spiritual matters they were simply subordinate chapels of the episcopal church, and from the point of view of the law of property they were owned by the bishopric and were subject, together with the revenues derived from them, to the bishop's arbitrary administration, limited only by the prohibition of alienation. The episcopal church, in short, was ruled as a whole by the bishop, not in accordance with legal principles, but at his own free will. It was still not legally organized, still essentially without an ecclesiastical law of its own.

This conclusion appears astounding at first sight; but it becomes comprehensible on closer examination. Law can only arise where two or more powers contend for conflicting interests. In the ancient church, as we have seen, there was but one power, the bishop: a second, which might have engaged with him on a struggle of interests, was lacking. The clergy sank too soon and too completely into dependence on the bishop to be able to impose legal checks on him; they had carried out in the earliest centuries not their own, but the bishop's business and so became an instrument, not an opponent of episcopal power. And the laity, also, with the emergence of the principle that laymen have no active share in ecclesiastical affairs, lost the opportunity to establish their rights against the bishop. They might have obtained a certain independence of the bishop for the churches they founded and the clergy employed in them by imposing conditions and tributes, but little was made of this possibility: even for churches founded by private persons the principles we have traced on the whole remained in force.

With the entry of the Germanic peoples into the Church, however, this situation was completely changed. Immediately the episcopal power found itself faced by a dangerous opponent. This opponent was the Germanic conception of territorial or manorial proprietorship (*Grundherrschaft*). And the object over which bishop and territorial magnates struggled, the point over which episcopal and seignorial interests conflicted, was the " proprietary church "[2].

On the lands of a prosperous German stands a church. It is in no wise a juristic personality, the subject of legal rights: it is a thing, an object.[3] But it forms the centre of a separate property-complex. The focus of the whole is the ground on which the altar stands: there has been no delivery of it at the time of consecration, it has remained the property of the lord of the land. On it is built the altar, with the relics of the saint to whom it is dedicated: the name of the latter is the title under which the lord acts as owner of the church's possessions and takes part in business concerned with church property.

The altar-ground and the altar together are the principal:

[2] Cf. the revised and extended edition of the author's article, " Eigenkirche, Eigenkloster ", in the *Real-Enzyklopädie für protestantische Theologie und Kirche* (3rd ed., Leipzig 1913) XXIII, 364 sqq., where full references to the literature on the subject will be found.

[3] On the following, cf. the author's essays, " Das Eigenkirchenvermögen. Ein Beitrag zur Geschichte des altdeutschen Sachenrechtes auf Grund der Freisinger Traditionen ", *Festschrift zu Otto Gierkes siebzigstem Geburtstag* (Weimar 1911), 1187 sqq., and *Ausgewählte Kapitel aus der Geschichte der Eigenkirche und ihres Rechtes*, I—III (Weimar 1937), and in the ZRG. LVII, *Kanon. Abt.* XXVI (1937), 1 sqq.

all the rest is merely an adjunct. The church building with its fixtures, vestments and utensils, books and bells, is therefore an adjunct. Whatever real property and usu-fructuary rights and income the church possesses is also an adjunct. The domains which the founder and others have made over to the altar, and which lie, perhaps scattered, round the church, are adjuncts. Adjuncts also are the offerings, the first-fruits, the dues levied by the priest for his services, and later the tithe. But the subordinate, accessory character of all these elements is not limited to the mere fact that, in the event of an alienation of altar and church by the lord, they follow or accompany the principal object. The chief effect of this relation of adjunct to principal, as of all similar relationships in Germanic law, is that the dependent or accessory objects only continue to yield a profit or a benefit to the owner by and through the principal object itself. All accessories are directed to the principal object and its central focus, the proceeds of the whole are consolidated in the principal. From this revenue the territorial lord must defray, in the first place, the upkeep of the whole establishment. He has to maintain the fabric of the church. He is bound to keep divine service going, and for this purpose, if he is not himself ordained, must employ and pay a clerk. Furthermore, he has to provide for charitable works, and allow the church the means with which to help and protect the poor. Only if these claims are satisfied, and if there remains (as is usual) a profit, is the lord empowered to take the latter for himself, whether in the form of a direct impost, or of the services and dues of the clergy. Because of its character of a mere appurtenance to altar and church, the property of the latter stands, not in a direct, but in an indirect relation to the owner: the single elements are still in the ownership of the lord of the altar, but only indirectly, as accessories or adjuncts of the altar.

The acceptance of this whole conception or institution by the Church brought about a further development. The appurtenant relationship, of which we have spoken, became indissoluble, permanent. This was the effect of the ecclesiastical prohibition of alienation. In its true meaning the prohibition was, of course not applicable in this connexion: since no ecclesiastical ownership existed, alienation of the property could not be forbidden. But it was applied by analogy: what had once been granted to the church by the territorial lord or others was not to be taken away again, the dependent relationship, once set up, was not to be revocable. Church property was to be capable of growth, but not of diminution.

For the rest, the lord of the land retained full control over the church. From a modern point of view, his power can best be regarded as flowing from two legal sources: the law of property and public law.

From the point of view of property law, the proprietor had full civil rights over the church and its possessions, except for the stipulation that the church was not to be diverted from its purpose. The lord of the land could, therefore, sell, exchange or bestow it freely as a whole, give it as dowry or otherwise alienate it; he could devise it, grant it as a fief or lease it: he could also mortgage it. On the other hand, he could no longer, in Christian times, turn it into a barn, a house a wine-press or a smithy; for this would be secularization of ecclesiastical property, and therefore an offence against the Church's prohibition of alienation.

The powers derived from public law, on the other hand, gave the manorial lord full direction and control over the church: he appointed and dismissed the priest, and the latter administered the church and exercised his office on the lord's behalf.

And finally the legal form in which this control was exercised, was that of ownership. Ownership in its Germanic form is, and has always been, more comprehensive than Roman ownership; it has always had the tendency to incorporate within itself elements of public law. In the sphere of secular affairs it has, as time has progressed, developed into seignorial lordship (*Grundherrlichkeit*)—that is to say, has usurped a share of the powers of government. In the sphere of activity with which we are dealing, where an ecclesiastical institution was at stake, we see it take the form of lordship over single churches, and attract to itself a share of church authority. Yet it did this without changing its legal character. It remained a manifestation of ownership (*Eigentum*), of proprietary rights; and I have for this reason designated the church subject to such ownership as the proprietary church (*Eigenkirche*).

About the origin of the proprietary church nothing certain can be said. In my view it derives from the priesthood with which the head of the Germanic household was invested.[4] As the Germanic family group grew in size through the addition of numerous free, dependent and servile members who were not related to the head of the family, and as the progress of civilization began to make itself felt in the domestic life of the Germanic peoples, the more prosperous individual built for the worship of the household deities a special temple, which in the course of time was no doubt used by his less wealthy neighbours as well. The priestly quality of the head of the Germanic household, which was based on his patriarchal authority, and which the coming of Catholicism would in any case have destroyed, thus passed out of existence, and was lost for centuries, until the Reformation brought it to life again in a new form. In its place, however, there appeared the right over the private or proprietary church, constructed on the basis of ownership and seisin.

Whether or not this explanation of the origins of the institution is correct, it remains certain that the private church was an institution common to all Germanic peoples. From the very moment when a Germanic tribe enters the Catholic Church and thus becomes more accessible to historical investigation, the private church is found to exist among its institutions. The *Suevi* in Spain had it, and also the Visigoths and the Burgundians. Clearly, therefore, it must have permeated and outlived the ecclesiastical régime of the Arian period. On the other hand, it is true in the

---

[4] Further discussion in the author's study, " Arianismus und Germanismus ", *Internationale Wochenschrift* (1909), coll. 1561 sqq., 1615 sqq., 1633 sqq., and previously in the *Geschichte des kirchlichen Benefizialwesens* I, i (Berlin 1895), 89 sqq.

case of all these races that the proprietary church eventually disappeared from among their midst: the Catholic episcopacy became too strong among them for an institution to which the prelates were so violently opposed, to take permanent root. The Lombards, on the contrary, thanks to their exceptional tenacity and ruthlessness, were able to maintain their private churches. And—even more important—the Franks also, and the other German races, who had possessed private temples while still heathen, and had brought them into the Church on conversion, held fast to their institution. Particularly after the beginning of the seventh century the new element is noticeable within the Frankish church. The episcopacy, desirous of regaining its ancient omnipotence, bitterly complained, about 650, in a synod at Chalon-sur-Saône, that the territorial magnates were withholding from the bishops the property of their domanial churches, and withdrawing their clergy from the disciplinary authority of the archdeacon. After the end of seventh and the beginning of the eighth century the victory of the proprietary church régime within the Frankish Kingdom was decisive, and this victory assured its entry into the legal system of the Western Church.[5]

Private or proprietary churches now sprang up everywhere, like mushrooms in the night. All the numerous places of worship erected on the royal demesne by the king himself or with royal permission were private churches. The churches of monasteries, moreover, both those which they themselves built, and those which they acquired by bequests or otherwise, were private churches. For as yet there was no spiritual relationship between a monastery and its church. " Incorporation ", which created such a relationship, was itself an offshoot of the *Eigenkirchenrecht*, and belongs to a much later period: what bound together monastery and church was still, in the early period, solely the fact of ownership. Finally, all churches founded by private persons, whether clerks or laymen, and all places

---

[5] On the proprietary church in England, cf. H. Böhmer, " Das Eigenkirchenwesen in England ", *Festgabe für Felix Liebermann* (Halle 1921), 301—353.

of worship which fell into the hands of laymen in virtue of
the extensive secularizations of church property which
occurred from time to time, were private churches. Compared with the number of such proprietary churches the
number of episcopal churches was insignificant. In the
bishopric of Chur, for example, at the beginning of the
ninth century, the bishop possessed thirty-one, the king
and other laymen more than two hundred churches.[6] Nor
must it be supposed that the important parish churches
were left to the bishop and only the smaller titular churches
subjected to the private church régime. The completion
of the network of ecclesiastical organization, which took
place precisely during the centuries in question, and which
could never have been carried out without the co-operation
of the territorial lords, together with the recurrent confiscations of church property, had the result that numerous
parish churches became proprietary or seignorial.

The dangers with which the private church system
threatened the episcopal government of the Church and
the ancient ecclesiastical order are self-evident. In every
proprietary church the episcopal authority over the church
and its ministers was radically challenged. Whose influence would predominate with the clergy of the proprietary church—that of the bishop, who attempted to exercise
control from a distance by means of spiritual admonition
and the threat of ecclesiastical penalties, or that of the
territorial lord, who had the minister in his household, gave
him his daily bread, and, if necessary, would not shrink
from teaching him obedience with the whip—this question
could never for one instant be open to doubt. In a very
short time the consequences of the " Private Church "
régime became fully evident. It is well known, for example,
that the reign of Charles Martel ended in a sort of ecclesiastical anarchy, that the Frankish church was at that moment
near to dissolution. The responsibility for this state of
things has hitherto been attributed to the confiscations

[6] Further information in the author's essay, " Karls des Grossen
divisio von Bistum und Grafschaft Chur ", *Historische Aufsätze Karl
Zeumer zum sechzigsten Geburtstag dargebracht* (Weimar 1910), 101 sqq.
(and separately).

carried out by the "major domus" and to his practice of filling bishoprics and abbeys with warlike laymen. Yet these measures could only affect the proprietary rights and the discipline of a few cathedrals and monasteries. What brought about the general collapse of ecclesiastical government, on the other hand, particularly in country districts, was the proprietary church. It was not without reason that the *concilium Germanicum* of 742, the decrees of which were confirmed by a capitulary of Carloman, issued an edict ordering that every priest within a diocese should be subject to his bishop—an edict which would have been incomprehensible, since it was a matter of course, from the point of view of the ancient canon law, but is comprehensible enough if we consider the devastations which the proprietary church régime had caused in the intermediate period within the established ecclesiastical order. The immediately preceding decades had, in fact, seen the bishop lose his influence in country districts almost completely; faced by the Germanic proprietary church, the old Roman ecclesiastical law had withdrawn into the cities.

Not the least therefore among the tasks with which the Carolingian reform movement had to grapple, was the solution of the problem of the proprietary church. Yet a solution on the lines of the abolition of the whole system of proprietary churches was out of the question, if only for the reason that the Carolingians themselves, who were the directors of the reform, were vitally interested, as the largest possessors of private churches, in the maintenance of the system. Thus the only practicable course was a compromise between the old and the new orders.

Such was the direction taken, the object pursued, by the extensive legislation dealing with the proprietary church, which began under Carloman and Pepin and outlived the Frankish Empire. Its history is of the greatest interest. The magnates sought to use the legislation for the maintenance and even the extension of their rights, the bishops to achieve through it as full a limitation of seignorial power as was possible. The interests of the monarchy were divided: as owner of numerous churches it stood on the side of the magnates, as protector of the civil and ecclesiastical order it inclined to the bishops. A detailed examination of the course of the whole movement would, however, be out of place here. It is only necessary to say that, in the first period, which extends from the middle of the eighth century until the first half of the reign of Ludwig the Pious, the tendency of legislation was to assure as far as possible the stability of the proprietary church and its property in face of the territorial lord, to improve the position of its ministers and to bring them in some degree into subordination to the bishop. With the first of these objects in view, the partition of private churches among co-heirs was forbidden; they were to have a regular endowment; and the bishop was given powers to see that they were maintained in good condition. From the second point of view, the manorial lord was deprived of the power of dismissing the clergy in the private church or of appointing them without the bishop's assent; the filling of private churches with unfree clerks was checked; and the territorial lord was obliged to give the ministers in his private churches, together with the church, at least one freehold *mansus*. The third consideration led to the decree that every priest in a private church must annually give the bishop some account of his administration, that he must attend synods, and take part in the meetings of the bishop's court. As contrasted with all this, the second period of legislation regarding the proprietary church brought nothing new: as the episcopate could only maintain with difficulty what it had won in the first period, the subsequent age was content on the whole simply to repeat the older decrees.

Under Ludwig the Pious and Lothar I attempts were nevertheless made to abolish the proprietary church completely. Agobard of Lyon, Jonas of Orleans, and a synod, full of the spirit of Pseudo-Isidore, which was held at Valence in 855, declaimed against the system; and glosses to the authorities of ecclesiastical law gave vent to clerical anger at the proprietary church régime. But all was without effect. Even in Rome the system made headway, and proprietary church law was of dire necessity given explicit recognition. Subsequently, even the Church party assimilated it. The bishops came increasingly to treat those churches which remained in their hands as private churches. And Hincmar of Reims, the expert interpreter of the Church law of the Frankish period, in his treatise *De ecclesiis et capellis*—only recently discovered[7] and as yet not adequately interpreted—characteristically attacks only the unauthorized encroachments of the territorial lords and their greedy exploitation of their churches. The legal system centred round the proprietary church, in the form in which it was established by Carolingian legislation, he defended with remarkable determination, for he was completely dominated by the conception of the proprietary church and by the legal construction built up on this basis. In this, as in much else, he represents the standpoint of the Church law of the Germanic period which was in its prime in his own day, and of which therefore he is outstandingly the most valuable witness.

We must now try to understand what were the consequences within each single diocese of the acceptance of the proprietary church régime.

The main result was undoubtedly a complete revolution in the division of ecclesiastical power. Instead of the thorough-going centralization of the Roman period complete decentralisation took place. In the first place, the ownership of church property was decentralized. Instead of there being one single subject or possessor of proprietary rights, the Cathedral or Diocese, such rights belonged now to an unlimited number of possessors, ordinarily laymen— namely, the territorial lords; each church with its possessions had now in principle a particular owner; in principle, there were now as many owners of church property as there were churches within the bishopric. But the administration, also, and the use of church property was decentralized. Whereas, in the Roman period, a single person—namely the bishop—had disposed of ecclesiastical revenues, and

[7] It was edited in 1889 by W. Gundlach in the *Zeitschr. f. Kirchengeschichte* X, 92 sqq.

allowed clergy and poor to partake of them as seemed to
him best, now it was a number of persons—and again of
territorial lords—to whom the disposal of church revenues
belonged, and who passed on a share of them to the clergy
and to the needy; and once again the number of those in
control of church income corresponded in principle to the
number of churches in existence. Even ecclesiastical
authority itself appeared now to be decentralized—or so,
at least, if considered from a popular, secular or Germanic
point of view. We have already remarked that lordship
over the Church included complete powers of direction and
control, as opposed to which the bishop's rights were no
more than a subsequently added limitation. In full agreement with this is the fact that, according to the legal
conceptions of the day, the territorial lord nominated the
priest with or even without the assent of the bishop—the
bishop did not, as might be thought, fill the living on the
presentation of the lord. But although the Church suffered
these results on the whole patiently enough, they were
never given formal recognition. For the Church, the bishop
remained as he always had been, the sole possessor of administrative authority, church government continued to be
regarded as centralized in character. Yet even if we accept
this clerical point of view, it still remains undeniable that
the church's unity, even in matters of ecclesiastical government, was by this time seriously menaced.

This situation was not without influence over the course
of legal development. The bishop, had he retained his
former omnipotence, would never have considered the possibility of regulating his legal relations with the subordinate
clergy; for that would have been tying his own hands.
For the bishop who was almost powerless, on the other
hand, it was of the highest importance to know that his
position in relation to the single churches and their ministers
was legally safeguarded. For this reason, the period in
question saw the beginning of a process which had been
hitherto neglected: the systematic, legal construction and
delimitation of the diocese. This process was, indeed, not
completed during the Germanic period; for a decentralized

organisation, based on the multiple control of the laity over the Church, could under no circumstances be the object to which the development was directed. Lay domination was only justified as long as it was necessary in lending support to the local churches and local clergy against the bishop, and in teaching them to become the independent upholders of their own rights. As soon as each particular subordinate office was adequately strengthened, the office-holder himself could be depended on to maintain and further his own rights, and lay support and control then became unnecessary. From that moment the time for the final shaping of the structure of the diocese had arrived; for a bishopric was now possible in which a balance of power between a legally controlled central authority and a number of local authorities with many guaranteed rights could be maintained by purely ecclesiastical means. Such a bishopric was created in post-Germanic times. But the diocese of classical and modern canon law is nevertheless the daughter of the Germanic diocese. Whereas a revolution, rather than a mere evolution, led from the Roman to the Germanic bishopric, the Germanic diocese was the immediate, evolutionary basis of the later form. For this reason it can rightly be maintained, that the consolidated bishopric of modern times is essentially a product of Germanic society; the Germanic races transformed the episcopal church into a *Rechtskirche*, built up on a careful partition of rights, just as they transformed the State into a *Rechtsstaat*, the basis of which again was a balance of rights.

This is perhaps all that need be said about the general effects of the proprietary church régime. But, besides its more general consequences, it led also to the creation of a number of particular legal institutes and legal rules, through which the law of the Church was enriched.[8]

In this connection, the particular law dealing with private churches itself calls for first consideration. Pre-Germanic

---

[8] In this connexion, cf. the author's " Kirchenrecht, Geschichte und System ", in F. v. Holtzendorff und J. Kohler, *Encyklopädie der Rechtswissenschaft* V (7th ed., Leipzig 1914), 288, 301 sqq., 307 sqq., 313 sqq., 335, 347, 376, 384.

times had nothing similar to show, since the intervention
of the founder or of his heirs in the administration of his
foundation was not tolerated. In post-Germanic times
there sprang up, on the basis of the right over the private
church (*Eigenkirchenrecht*), not only the legal institute
known as incorporation, but also the advowson or right of
patronage which is still effective to-day. As early as the
sixth and seventh centuries, indeed, a form of lay dominion
over churches very similar to patronage, made its appearance
in Visigothic law. It was the result of a compromise
between the bishops, who were using their influence for
the suppression of the dangerous proprietary system, and
the territorial lords, who were unwilling to surrender all
their former rights in the churches they had founded.

The institute known as the *ius regaliae* was, again, only
a particular form of the exercise of plenary rights over the
proprietary church. In ordinary circumstances the lord
had granted the church and its possessions to a clerk, and
any benefit he derived from the church property was
derived indirectly through the latter. When, however, the
concession came to an end through the death of the grantee,
the lord recovered the immediate enjoyment of his property;
but he was naturally obliged to provide for divine service,
until the vacant living was filled, either through a vicar or
another clerk, employed at his own expense. As the institution of private ownership of churches gradually fell
into decay, particular attention was given to the corresponding rights exercised by the crown over royal churches,
and from this particular exercise of a normal element of
the *Eigenkirchenrecht*, a special right was created and called
the *jus regaliae*.

Similarly, the so-called "right of spoil" stood in the closest
relation to the private church. It was, indeed, no part of
the oldest law. In the earliest times, the ministers in
private churches were predominantly bondmen of the lord:
anything they earned during their lifetime, therefore, went
to swell the *peculium*—that is, the property invested in
the domanial church—anything they left at the time of
death was acquired wholly or partially by the lord. From

the beginning of the ninth century onwards, however, as a consequence of the Carolingian legislation we have mentioned, unfree priests became increasingly uncommon in private churches: a free clergy came to be the rule. Their profits of office were divided into two parts. In virtue of a customary law which had been established at an early date on the basis of repeated contractual agreements, real property fell to the church, as did moveables which were by their nature intended for the church itself and not for the minister. All other moveables, on the other hand—and their total increased continually—belonged to the clerk, and formed, after his death, his unimpeded estate. If the territorial lords did not wish to lose this completely, they must therefore find a special legal title by which it could be claimed. Such a title they found in the rule of Church law which stated that every clerk must leave to his church the whole, a third or a quarter of what he had earned in its service. This rule they applied, sometimes in virtue of contractual arrangements with their clerks, to their private churches and ministers, and seized the moveable estate of the latter in whole or in part. In this way there arose, about the second half of the ninth century, the *jus spolii*, which appears to have been used by the lords in actual practice not so much for the benefit of their churches as in their own private interests.

To the private church is due also the institution of the right to take fees for the performance of religious ceremonies. Such charges had, indeed, long been demanded and paid; but the only reason for them was the avarice of the individual members of the clergy, and they were therefore more or less effectively suppressed as abuses. Only with the arrival of the proprietary church régime were they systematically developed and consolidated. The proprietary church was the private undertaking of the lord; the priest was a private official of the lord's demesne. Yet others besides the lord used the church, particularly when it was at the same time a parish church, and others laid claim to the services of the minister. It was therefore only natural that the lord of the church should demand from other users a contribution to the upkeep of church and clergy, and that he was not satisfied with voluntary offerings, but charged, through the minister, a fee for every important service rendered by the latter. Thus a burial fee was demanded and paid, as had already been the case in pagan times, and other specifically Christian dues were added: the fees for baptism, consecration of marriage, holy communion, confession and extreme unction. The struggle of the Church against such a sale of spiritual offices, utterly opposed though it was to its basic principles, was henceforward of no avail. It could put no check to the abuse, which rested on the interests and power of the territorial lords, and in 1215 at the Fourth Lateran Council Innocent III had to approve the payment of dues as a *laudabilis consuetudo*.

The territorial magnates, however, did not stop there. They wished not only to obtain an established income for their private churches, but also to get some guarantee of its permanence. This led to the further development of parochial rights and parochial law. Purely ecclesiastical and public considerations had led to the introduction of the parish system. For the purpose of ecclesiastical organisation smaller cures of souls had been set up within the bishop's sphere of action; for the sake of ecclesiastical order the faithful had been urged, if possible every Sunday and at least on the main festivals, to attend divine service in the parish church. Now, however, under the domination of the proprietary church régime, fiscal and private considerations came to the fore. In the course of time the lord was able to enforce the monopoly of his mill; by means of the jurisdiction placed in his hands the wielder of secular authority, who was often the local lord himself, could prohibit the inhabitants of a particular district from taking their corn to be ground in any but the seignorial mill. In exactly the same way, however, it was posssible to get the bishop to use his administrative authority to forbid the parishioners to go for their spiritual needs to any but the domanial parish church. And this was what happened. The parish churches, at first the proprietary ones and then those under the bishop's control, acquired a monopoly, and so there arose a body of parochial law, which in its legal character was—and where it has persisted until to-day, still is—neither more not less than a mediaeval, Germanic assumption of the right of jurisdiction.[9]

More important and less unsatisfactory than the consequences so far described, was the final achievement of the proprietary church conception and of Germanic church law as a whole: I refer to the ecclesiastical benefice.[10]

It has been the accepted doctrine since the days of THOMASSIN, that the system of ecclesiastical benefices was derived from the *precariae*, which were from time to time bestowed on clerks by bishops of the Roman and Merovingian period. This theory is nevertheless untenable. Contemporary authorities offer no indication of such a development; and if the facts are examined at all closely, a development of this sort is seen to be unthinkable, for not only were the driving forces and interests which might have brought it about absent at the time in question, but it is clear also it could never have resulted in the situation which actually came to obtain. The point of departure of the movement towards ecclesiastical investiture was, on the contrary, the proprietary church. The system of proprietary churches prepared the way for the movement in so far as it created within the diocese small independent church properties, the focal point of each of which was a church and a clerical office. And it was in the private church that ecclesiastical investiture was first put into use. As we already know, the territorial lord had the duty of making provision for the spiritual ministration of his church. Unless he personally performed service there, he had therefore to appoint a minister. This could be done in a number of ways. The lord could have one of his serfs ordained priest and let out the church and its property to him as a

---

[9] Cf. the author's article, " Zur Herkunft von Zwing und Bann ", ZRG. *Germ. Abt.* LVII (1937), 289 sqq., 333 sqq.

[10] Cf. the author's articles, " Lehen und Pfründe ", ZRG. *Germ. Abt.* XX (1899), 213 sqq., and " ' Römerwergeld ' und ' Herrenfall ', zwei kritische Beiträge zur Rechts- und Verfassungsgeschichte der fränkischen Zeit ", *Abhandlungen d. preussischen Akademie* (1934), *Hist.-phil. Klasse*, No. 2, pp. 52, 60 sq.

peculium; but this method of filling the living, as we have seen, was proscribed by the Church, and rendered increasingly difficult. Alternatively, the appointment of the clerk might take the form of a covenant for service which could be dissolved at any time; but this again was a method opposed by the Church, for ministers without any permanent title, who normally worked for a starvation wage, and who were known, in Biblical phraseology, as hirelings, *mercenarii* or *conducticii*, were untrustworthy and all too dependent on their lord. Most frequent—and from the point of view of the Church, most desirable—was a permanent appointment in the form of an investiture. Any type of investiture would serve this purpose, and in fact we read in the authorities of churches which were granted to clerks in the form of a libellary contract, *métayage* or *Teilpacht*, a *precaria*, and even for the duration of a number of lives. But since the *beneficium* was the most popular and most widely disseminated form of tenure at the period at which the free investiture of churches made its appearance—that is to say, in the eighth century—and since it was .furthermore the form favoured by the law of the Frankish Kingdom, it was natural that it should have been employed for preference in the conferment of churches.

The benefice which in this way took its place among the legal institutions of the Church, was moreover the pure Frankish *beneficium*, not the *feudum* or the fief, which had yet to be created out of a combination of benefice and vassalage. Its basis, north of the Alps, was normally an orally concluded agreement followed by a formal act of investiture. Through the oral agreement, the conclusion of which was usually marked by the payment of an *exenium*, a gift, to the party making the grant, the clerk obtained a possessory right in the church, its property and revenues, which was just as stable and an indivisible as the proprietary right of the lord, and which continued in existence for the duration of the clerk's lifetime: for this reason it was not subject to the incident of renewal on a change of lord. Corresponding to this contractual right, however, there was a contractual duty: namely, the duty of keeping the church in good condition and in proper use, and of paying dues and performing services. But it is easy to see that, under this system, the holy office was not likely to receive due consideration. It was reduced to a private tenurial service, became indeed a purely routine duty. The clerk no longer administered the church in virtue of a commission from his ecclesiastical superior, but because he had agreed, as one of his terms of tenure, to maintain it in its stipulated use. In other words, he read mass here for the same legal reason as another tenant ploughed his lands or tended his vines. This attitude is very evident in Italian documents dealing with church tenure. Not only do they place service in the church on the same footing as the rearing of the cattle belonging to the church and the management of church lands, but they make characteristic distinctions according to the churches circumstances. In a city church, for example, more services must be held than in a suburban or country church: each church has its own particular routine, and this the clerk promises to maintain.

The investiture itself was a symbolic act, carried out by the handing over of a book, a staff or another token, and through it the grantee acquired seisin (*Gewere*). A *renunciatio*, a surrender by the party making the grant, did not take place any more than commendation or an offer of homage on the part of the clerk. Only in a later period, and, so far as I can see, only in France, was an attempt made to turn the *beneficium presbyterale* into a *feudum* or *fevum presbyterale* with *hominium* and tenurial services, just as there was an attempt to extend hereditability of fiefs to church benefices. But both tendencies were successfully resisted by the religious movement which came to a head in the days of Gregory VII, and were finally defeated.

On the other hand, the *beneficium ecclesiasticum* underwent, in the course of time, other radical transformations. Where previously it had extended both to the church and to all its property, investiture came to be limited to only a portion of the latter, the lands attached to the benefice; the ownership of the beneficial lands passed to the church itself as a legal personality, and in consequence the right of conferment was transferred from the territorial lord to the bishop or one of his officials, usually the archdeacon; and finally the *officium* itself, as opposed to the *beneficium*, received more adequate recognition. The result was that the benefice, in modern times, took on an appearance which it did not have in the Middle Ages: it came to be regarded as the established income of the holder of an ecclesiastical office, permanently united with the office, and derived from property which was in the full sense church property. Intrinsically, therefore, it became radically different from the Frankish *beneficium*, although its external appearance remained much the same, and it retained the old name. Its acceptation by and incorporation in the legal institutions of the Church, in fact, kept the *beneficium* alive, and saved it from the fate of its derivative, the fief.

Such were the effects of the proprietary church régime within the structure of the single diocese. But the system also showed signs of penetrating into the higher spheres of ecclesiastical organisation. Some consideration of this development is necessary in conclusion, because it was in this way that the whole proprietary church system was brought to its downfall.

The conception of the proprietary church, in point of fact, was not confined to the lesser churches, but attacked also the greater ones, the bishoprics and the abbeys. Of the latter, indeed, some considerable proportion need no consideration in this connexion—those, namely, like Prüm, Echternach, Hersfeld and others, which were founded on secular or monastic property according to the established rules of the law governing the proprietary church. From the very beginning, these were proprietary monasteries, and were subject to substantially the same régime as the ordinary proprietary churches, except that the community itself, which in this case took an active place beside the legally passive church, was able in the course of time to control the territorial lord in the exercise of certain of his rights—for example, in the nomination of the abbot or other superior. Apart from the bishoprics, therefore, we need only in this place take notice of those abbeys which like the bishoprics themselves, were free from any form of secular domination in Roman times and at the time of the Germanic invasions, and remained in this condition under Germanic rule, and which indeed showed a tendency to increase in numbers through the foundation of new houses on the model of the old.

Both groups, free abbeys and bishoprics, were first of all brought into a certain degree of dependence on the secular power through the protection which, in Merovingian and Carolingian times, they sought from the King or from powerful nobles. Protection was only accorded to a monastery, if, in the person of its momentary superior, it entered into the *mundium* of the lord; the abbot, in other words, had to commend himself to the protector. In the case of the bishopric, however, an effort was made to avoid personal dependence of this sort, and therefore we do not find, in this case, any mention of royal *defensio* and royal *mundeburdium* until, under Ludwig the Pious, a less personal, more objective form of protection was devised, which could be obtained without the commendation of the church-superior. Even so, it was impossible to exclude the element of dependence completely. And the grant of immunity, which was from this time normally combined with the new form of protection, not only did nothing to weaken the relationship with the secular power, but actually strengthened it, since it exempted the immune church and its territories from the already fairly independent ordinary administration, and placed it under the rule of the lord of the immunity, with which it was less difficult for the crown to interfere. Nevertheless the significance of all these forms of dependence was chiefly evident in the sphere of public law, particularly of constitutional and criminal law. From the point of view of private or civil law, the individual personality of the religious institution obtaining protection remained unaffected. Although the concrete but transcendental personality of the patron saint was substituted for the abstract, legal personality of earlier times, the practical situation remained the same, and as long as this state of

things persisted, there was no alteration in the legal position
of the churches in question.

In post-Carolingian times, however, changes began to
take place. More or less unconsciously, the dependence
of bishoprics and abbeys was increased and extended also
to their position in private law. In other words, the conception of the proprietary church, with which the minds of
contemporaries were permeated through and through, and
which has done such good service to the interests of crown
and magnates in the case of minor churches, was to be
applied to bishoprics and abbeys as well: bishoprics and
abbeys were to be reduced to the position of private
churches.

In the case of the abbeys, a certain proportion of which,
as we have already said, had been private monasteries from
the very beginning, this process met with small resistance.
For this reason, I shall take no account of them in the remarks which follow, and shall limit myself to sketching
the developments in regard to bishoprics. And here the
law governing the filling of vacant sees seems to have been
the point at which the penetration of proprietary church
doctrine began. It is well known that, although episcopal
elections were originally free, the secular power came in
course of time to exercise increasing influence over them.
The chief person in the state reserved for himself the power
to confirm the bishop-elect or to designate the person to be
elected; indeed, from the Frankish epoch onwards, the
king actually nominated the bishops. The original reason
for this attack on the liberty of the Church was solely that
of public interest; the bishops were much too influential
dignitaries and played far too important a part in secular
affairs for it to be a matter of indifference to the secular
authority, who became a bishop. The matter was therefore essentially one arising out of the relations of church
and state; but gradually another point of view came to
predominate. The king had the same freedom in appointing his bishops as in appointing the clergy in his private
churches: was it, therefore, surprising that in course of
time an identical power came to be explained through an

identical legal theory ? Moreover, the king exercised
certain rights of supervision over the administration of the
property of the Church of the realm—his assent was necessary, for example, if any of its lands were alienated—and
these churches, the *Reichskirchen*, owed him important
servitia; in fact, he enjoyed similar rights and profits from
them as from his own proprietary churches. It was,
therefore, not surprising that contemporaries increasingly
came to regard the relation of the king, or of the magnates,
to the bishoprics as one of full dominion, the cathedrals
themselves as important royal proprietary churches, and
their lands as the property of the crown, invested in the
church (*Reichskirchenvermögen*). Already in the days of
Hincmar of Reims this attitude is apparent—he calls the
bishoprics benefices which the bishops receive from the
king's hand—and in post-Carolingian times it became the
ruling conception.

It was not long before practical consequences began to be
drawn from this new conception. In other words, the
endeavour was made to bring the legal position of the
greater churches into full agreement with the law governing
the proprietary church, and to add to the authority exercised over the bishoprics what was still lacking if it were
to be transformed into a true dominion over a proprietary
church.

It was in this way that, in the tenth century, the practice
grew up of clothing the conferment of bishoprics and
abbeys in the form of an enfeoffment, and carrying it out
in a solemn act which was known, from the end of the next
century, as investiture. The distinction between this act
and that used in the conferment of smaller livings was only
formal, and consisted in the fact that it was combined in
the former case with the taking of an oath of fealty and
the performance of homage. The material position was
fully equivalent to that created by an investiture in a
minor church; for in both cases the person invested received both church and office for the duration of his life,
in return for tenurial services.

The same conceptions led also to the extension of the

jus regaliae and then of the *jus spolii* to bishoprics and abbeys. As the application of these rights to th⹂ churches in question was both gradual and to all appearance without ulterior motives, modern historians have sometimes found it difficult to explain. And it is true that it remains inexplicable, if it is supposed that the legal basis of the relations between the crown and the church of the realm remained unchanged from Frankish times onwards, or that the king had already in Frankish times possessed the rights —whether we describe them under the heading of ownership, of protection or of a general power of disposal, is a matter of indifference—which he claimed over the *Reichskirchen* in the tenth, eleventh and twelfth centuries. The whole development becomes clear, on the other hand, if we recognize that it was the gradual advance and penetration of the idea of the proprietary church in post-Carolingian times which created the basis from which little by little such rights could be put forward and developed.

Certainty that this is the correct method of interpretation is provided by such cases as that of the bishopric of Béziers, which Viscount William gave his daughter as dowry in 990, just as he left the bishopric of Agde to his wife as her jointure, or that of the bishopric of Albi, which the lord, a count of Toulouse, offered to his bride in 1037, together with half the bishopric of Nîmes, as a *donatio propter nuptias*, or finally by the case of the bishopric of Carcassonne, which Ermengarde and her husband, Viscount Raymund of Albi and Nîmes, sold in 1067, together with the town and county, to Count Raymund of Barcelona. In these cases and others, which both FICKER and IMBART DE LA TOUR have already brought forward as evidence of the existence of proprietary rights over bishoprics, the conception of the private church is seen in full application to episcopal churches; or at least, it is difficult to see what element which goes to make up a full proprietary right over a church is wanting.

These examples serve nevertheless to prove that it was only in unusually favourable circumstances that it was possible to reduce bishoprics to the position of real private

churches—in fact, only when they were forced out of direct
or immediate connexion with the crown, and fell into dependence on a neighbouring magnate, for whom matters
of public law were of secondary importance and the more
private aspects of seignorial dominion, implicit in the proprietary church system, predominated. In Germany,
however, the immediacy—that is, the direct relation with
the crown—of the bishoprics was almost fully maintained:
not one bishopric fell into permanent dependence on a
secular magnate. Consequently the conceptions bound up
with the proprietary church only progressed very slowly
within the German boundaries. Nevertheless, it is probable
enough that there also they would have made further
progress, if at the decisive moment the Papacy had not
intervened.

The Church of Rome was itself in the same position as
every other bishopric. Originally filled by canonical
election, to which at a later date imperial confirmation
came to be added, its relations with the Empire in no way
differentiated it from other bishoprics: from the time of
Charlemagne it was simply the first of the metropolitan
churches of the realm. Because, however, of the strength
of ecclesiastical traditions—which naturally were particularly pronounced at the seat of papal power and were
maintained there with extraordinary tenacity—and also on
account of the weakening of relations between Rome and
Germany characteristic of post-Carolingian times, methods
of appointment to the Holy See did not develop in the
same way as the modes of election to ordinary bishoprics,
and the appointment was not so quickly brought into
strict dependence on the crown. The first emperors to
claim a right of appointment to the Roman Church were
the Saxons and the Salians. What led up to this, however,
even more than had been the case with other bishoprics,
were considerations of public interest and of public law.
The Emperor received his crown from the Pope, and that
in itself was reason enough for the former to regard the
filling of the Holy See as a matter of more than ordinary
interest. On the other hand, the belief that the exercise

of seignorial lordship over a private church was the issue
in this case also, could not arise until the time of Henry III
and his utterly unrestrained disposal, his domination and
control, of the See of St. Peter. Once that moment arrived,
however, the conception of the proprietary church was
near to embracing the Papacy as well; a few more emperors
like Henry III, and the mother-church of Western Christendom would become the private church of the German ruler.

There is a certain attraction—and perhaps also a key
to the understanding of subsequent developments—in
supposing for an instant that such a transformation had
taken place, and that in the case of the Papacy no less than
in that of the other churches, the victory of the proprietary
church idea had been complete. Would there be any
denial, if such a process had occurred, of the existence of
a positive body of Germanic church law ? So complete
would the " Germanization " of the Church have become
that, at every stage of the hierarchy, from the throne of
the vicar of St. Peter down to the most insignificant chapel,
it would have been dominated by the legal forms and conceptions, which in an earlier period the Germanic races,
still directly conscious of the domestic priesthood of their
pagan religion and of its attendant institutions, had built
up to suit the simple circumstances of their native land
and had brought with them into the Christian Church on
their conversion. Such a victory of Germanic church law
would, however, have been combined with a quite unparalleled enslavement of the Church and its exploitation
for secular objects, and would have resulted in a practically
complete exclusion of all public considerations from church
law. Thus there would have been no question of the growth
of a body of constitutional law within the Church, the
relations between the different churches and ecclesiastical
organs would not have been built on a common constitution,
secular control and in the last analysis secular ownership
would have been the only bond holding them together.
And finally, it is hard to think what would have been the
fate of a church so circumstanced in the event of a collapse
or even of a thorough-going transformation of this Germanic

conception of ownership; without doubt the break-up of its secular foundations would have involved the collapse of the Church itself.

If such were the prospects involved in a complete victory of Germanic law within the Church, no one to-day will regard the powerful counter-attack which followed rapidly on the death of Henry III and led to a century-long struggle between Church and State, as anything but a historical necessity, in spite of the fact that it shook the foundations of the German Empire and injured German law and legal institutions more than was ever needful. Once, moreover, it is realized that the monarchy was forced by the logic of earlier historical development to maintain claims which seem, if viewed in the remote perspective of history, to be merely excessive and pernicious, there is every reason to be more cautious in judging the first German king to be involved in the struggle; for Henry IV, although he was not blameless, was also unfortunate in the heritage to which he succeeded, and showed real greatness in more respects than one. And finally, it is fair to maintain that a correct judgment of the greatest of Henry's adversaries is only to be obtained, when we realize what actually was the state of affairs in his day. Through an examination of the actualities of the situation, it becomes evident, on the one hand, that Gregory VII did not lightly seek a pretext for a struggle, was not urged on solely by specious hierarchical ambitions, but acted because the continued existence of the Church was threatened by Germanic conceptions and Germanic forces—he acted, in other words, in self-defence. And on the other hand, it becomes evident that the success which the Church ultimately obtained in the struggle, was as much the consequence of the intrinsic rightness of its cause as it was due to the personal merits of its first or of any of its later champions and leaders.

But to Gregory VII there still remains the peculiar honour of having recognized, with remarkable clarity of vision, the dangers which faced him.

Much was thought and much was written throughout

those years about papal elections and about episcopal elections and about the rights of the crown over episcopal churches. Many illustrious persons dealt with the investiture question at that time, from Humbert, cardinal-bishop of Silva Candida, down to abbot Godfrey of Vendôme. But it is only relatively late that there is any recognition, among these writers of the fact that the problem as it affected the higher churches was at bottom no different from that affecting minor churches, and that both the investiture of and rights over the bishoprics must be dealt with in direct connexion with the investiture of and rights over ordinary churches; to the best of my belief, no publicist of the age comprehended this before the end of the eleventh century, when Cardinal Deusdedit lightly touched on the relation between investiture and the proprietary church problem in his *Libellus contra invasores et simoniacos*, and the first writer to put the issues clearly was Placidus of Nonantula in the treatise *De honore ecclesiae*, which he wrote in IIII.

In contrast with this lack of insight, ecclesiastical legislation showed no hesitation, as far as it originated in Rome and was filled with the Hildebrandine spirit, in proclaiming, from the very beginning, the watch-word : away with lay investiture of every sort and description, away therefore with every sort of lay domination and lay ownership of churches ! Already in Nicholas II's great Roman synod of 1059, it was determined that a clerk or priest might under no circumstances receive a church from a layman, and in regard to lay ownership and lay lordship over churches— although we are unfortunately only imperfectly informed about the earliest legislation of Gregory VII—we know that both were already condemned as sinful usurpations in the two Roman synods of 1087.

Once the true nature of a danger has been recognized, the danger itself is half overcome. In the mere choice, on the part of the Church, of the tactics to be followed in the struggle which was beginning, it was of inestimable value that it was fully understood in Rome what the final objective must be—namely, to put a definite end to every sort of private lordship, whether over major or over minor churches. The whole of this programme, of course, could not be realized at once. Thanks to the political situation and to the fact that what was at issue was a legal relationship which was still in process of formation, the prospects were favourable for an attack on the royal power of investiture and on the lordship exercised by the king over the greater churches. On the other hand, there was at the beginning small prospect of success in the far more difficult problem of the minor proprietary churches, for here not the crown alone but the whole lay aristocracy was the adversary; as early as 1078, therefore, shortly after the opening of the dispute, a synod assembled at Gerona enunciated the view that it would be difficult to do away completely with the rights of the laity over their churches. In any case, by raising at one and the same time the question both of minor and of major churches, the Gregorian party would only have offended the magnates, who were urgently needed as allies against the crown, and would have driven them into the royal camp. Therefore it was decided at Rome—but without any surrender on the matter of principle—to postpone the struggle against the system of the private ownership of lesser churches, and to concentrate in the meantime on convincing the faithful of the spiritual dangers attendant upon the exercise of lordship over churches, in the hope that the laity would thus be induced to hand over spontaneously to the bishops a large number of their private churches.

What was immediately begun and carried through, therefore, was the struggle against the rights exercised by the crown over the greater churches: the Investiture Contest in the narrower sense, which we may regard after what has already been said, as the reaction of the ancient church law of the Roman period, now awakened to new activity, against the Germanic church law, which firmly rooted in the proprietary church, was overrunning all ecclesiastical institutions. The progress and the issue of the struggle is well known. After the failure of the convention of Sutri, provisional agreement on lines proposed

by a royalist party of reconciliation was achieved in 1122
in the Concordat of Worms. But later, during the troubles
which followed the death of Henry VI, the Empire lost even
the influence over episcopal elections which it had kept in
1122, and in the end it retained nothing but the purely
secular investiture with the sceptre, by which the king
bestowed the *regalia* on the bishop-elect before his consecration, and in return received fealty and homage, and
with them the assurance of feudal service.

Before this point had been reached, however, the church
party was ready to take up the further task which had
previously been adjourned: the struggle for mastery of
the minor proprietary churches. In the meantime, however, changing circumstances had done much to prepare
the way. Ownership of churches had suffered the fate of
all Germanic land ownership: in the course of time it had
become satiated. Above all, the numerous private churches,
which little by little had obtained the right of levying
tithe, were producing a quite exceptionally high income for
their lords and an income which, moreover, grew continuously with the increase in population: the foundation of
churches was probably the most profitable investment of
the early Middle Ages, and innumerable churches were
built as much from motives of speculation as of piety.
The result of this high productiveness was that the ownership of the church itself and of the church lands, which
yielded the lord practically nothing in comparison with
tithe and other revenues, fell into insignificance, and ceased
to be considered the basis of the lord's rights as a whole.
The consolidated, undivided right over the proprietary
church broke up into as many particular rights as there were
possibilities and means of exploiting the church: henceforward we hear of a *jus fundi* or *fundationis*, a *jus peti-
tionis*, or *patronatus*, of a *jus conductus*, a *jus praesentationis*,
a *donum* or an *investitura ecclesiae*, of a *jus regaliae*, a *jus
decimationis*, and so forth, but there is increasingly in-
frequent mention of *proprietas* in the sense of the old col-
lective right over the whole complex.

This development, which, though hitherto overlooked,

proves once again without ambiguity that the old lordship over the private church was nothing but Germanic land ownership applied to churches, was used by Gratian and by pope Alexander III with great skill for the Church's ends. The former, in the first place, completely obliterated from canonistic doctrine the basic conception of ownership,[11] which had itself already fallen into decay. The latter then set up in its place another conception: the gratitude of the church, and on this basis he built up the so-called right of patronage.[12]

As far as its contents were concerned, the right of patronage was not, indeed, so very different from the older right of church proprietorship: in a spirit of careful moderation, many of the powers which had formed part of the old were incorporated in the new law, and many powers which were not included, but which were of great financial value to the territorial lords, were tolerated for the time being.[13] On the other hand, the differences established in form and in essence between the new law and the old were for this very reason all the more far-reaching. Where private or proprietary church law had been characterized by the subordination of the spiritual and public elements, which formed part of its legal content, to the one purely temporal element of ownership, patronage could be, and was, defined as a *jus temporale spirituali annexum*. The implication of this definition was twofold: in the first place, the interests and welfare of the church were the primary consideration, and a right of the patron over the church was only to be countenanced so long as it endangered neither the one nor the other; and secondly, this right was subject to ecclesiastical control and appertained henceforth, in case of controversy, to the jurisdiction

[11] Cf. the author's article, " Gratian und die Eigenkirchen," ZRG. XXXII—XXXIII (1911—1912), *Kanon. Abt.* I, 1 sqq. and II, 342 sq.
[12] On this aspect of the subject, cf. the recent essay by the author, " Papst Alexander III gegen die Freiung langobardischer Eigenkirchen ", *Abhandlungen d. preussischen Akademie* (1936), *Hist.-phil. Kl.*, No. 6.
[13] Cf. the author's articles, *Das Münster zu Freiburg i. Br. im Lichte rechtsgeschichtlicher Betrachtung* (Tübingen 1901), and " Das Habsburger Urbar und die Anfänge der Landeshoheit ", ZRG. *Germ. Abt.* XXV (1904), 227 sqq.

of the church courts. Finally, and most important of all, the complete freedom from ecclesiastical control which had been a feature of proprietary church law, had no application in regard to the law of patronage: patronage depended utterly on the goodwill and recognition of the church. In this way the Church secured for itself the possibility, as time passed, of becoming less grateful and less accommodating: it could simply allow to fall into disuse those of the powers of patronage which no longer suited it.

And this is precisely what occurred. Slowly and without upheaval the most valuable rights of patrons were reduced or brought to an end, until finally, after centuries of slow decline, nothing more remained than the modern canon law of patronage, the paltry contents of which are set out in the no less paltry rhyme:

Patrono debetur honos, onus utilitasque,
Praesentet, praesit, defendat, alatur egenus.

In this way, thanks to the adroitness of the Curia, there disappeared the old proprietary church law, which for some five centuries, in spite of bitter enmity and persecution, had maintained its position and extended its sphere of influence. With it disappeared also a large part of the Germanic church law, to which it had given life; but a certain proportion proved its vitality and its value for the Church, and this part, as we have already indicated in greater detail, has endured into our own day. Whoever looks with open eyes at the mighty structure of canon law to-day will see not only elements which reflect the style of Byzantium and of Imperial Rome or are executed in Renaissance manner: he will find also considerable parts which bear the mark of the Gothic of mediaeval Germany.

III

FRANCONIA'S PLACE IN THE STRUCTURE OF MEDIAEVAL GERMANY[1]

BY BERNHARD SCHMEIDLER

THE structure of mediaeval Germany, as it was constituted until about 1200 or at latest 1250, may be compared with a soaring modern construction in steel or iron, such as a majestically spanned bridge. A number of major parts, each separately moulded, are bound together by rivets and ties which skilfully balance tension and pressure, and the appearance they present is that of one single edifice, as powerful as it is light and free. The map of Germany in the later middle ages and in modern times with its multitude of petty territories, principalities, imperial fiefs and free cities, reveals the confusion and disorganization of the later Empire and presents a vivid contrast to its earlier condition. It is as if the lofty structure had collapsed and the ruins and battered parts lay strewn on the ground. The difference in this regard between the earlier and the later middle ages is, however, in itself well known. What the internal structure of the edifice was in the earlier centuries of the middle ages, on the other hand, by what balance of tension and pressure it was held together and preserved from collapse and destruction, is another question, and this question has still not been sufficiently thoroughly investigated and elucidated. It is therefore my intention to say something of this problem here.

The existence of a balance between tension and pressure in the structure of the mediaeval German state has, of course,

[1] " Die Stellung Frankens im Gefüge des alten deutschen Reiches bis ins 13. Jahrhundert," *Franken und das Deutsche Reich im Mittelalter, Erlanger Abhandlungen zur mittleren und neueren Geschichte*, Vol. VII (Erlangen: Palm & Enke, 1930), pp. 46–64.—Thanks are due to the publisher for permission to translate the essay which, based on a lecture delivered in 1924, was originally published in 1925.

been observed by earlier writers. But the specific incidents in which this balance was revealed, have usually been considered in a very one-sided way as " revolts " of the local authorities against the state or of the princes against the emperor. It is to GIESEBRECHT and his conception of the mediaeval Empire that this attitude is due; and even to-day it is safe to say that historians as a body are still much too strongly under GIESEBRECHT's influence. In the seventeenth and eighteenth centuries and even in the first half of the nineteenth century the conception which he represented was far from obtaining exclusive predominance; but since his time it has scarcely been recognized as one-sided or criticized from a methodological point of view.[2] If GIESEBRECHT's view is accepted, practically the whole internal history of Germany from the tenth to the thirteenth century is reduced to a long, uninterrupted series of rebellious attempts by irresponsible princes against the sovereignty and authority of the whole community, and one is almost forced to ask in amazement how the Empire managed, in spite of this attitude on the part of its most outstanding members, to remain for so long so powerful a state—the most powerful state, indeed, in the whole of Christendom.

It is necessary, I believe, to replace this obsolete point of view, explanable in its own day by contemporary events and tendencies, by a less one-sided, more scientific and objective approach to the problem. The moments of tension and friction, which were no more lacking in the period between the tenth and the thirteenth centuries than at any other time in German history, cannot be traced in this exclusive way to the ill-will of single individuals, and specifically to the ill-will of the German princes. A wider basis must be sought for this process of pressure and counter-pressure: instead of attributing decisive importance to individuals, we must consider the greater forces which were fused together in the structure of the German state. It was from their relations among themselves and their separate aims and endeavours that those moments of internal

---

[2] Cf. Schmeidler, *Franken u. das deutsche Reich*, 1–4.

friction arose which are known to us in the history of mediaeval Germany as " revolts " and " insurrections ".

These greater forces—at any rate in the earlier mediaeval period with which we are here concerned—are the German " stems " or races, and anyone who desires to understand the occurrences of which we have been speaking must proceed by considering how the German races, above all the Franks, the Bavarians, the Swabians and the Saxons— the Lotharingians, on account of their particular situation, may best be omitted—pursued within the territories of which they had taken possession and within the compass of the Empire their permanent and unchanging policy of expansion, and how each strove to maintain its own particular position within the state. And since, in the course of the centuries, we can trace behind the sporadic activity of the " stem " units and their leaders a series of unchanging and constantly recurring motives or objectives, the merely accidental and singular elements in each incident in the chain of events fall into the background, and the way is prepared for a proper understanding of the system which underlies the whole process. This system, as indicated, is of a geographical and racial or tribal character. Among its numerous aspects or divisions we shall, in what follows concern ourselves particularly with the duchy of Franconia and its place in the structure of mediaeval Germany as a whole; but we may start, as a means of obtaining a more incisive comprehension of the problem, with a survey of the separate political life of the other racial divisions of mediaeval Germany.

Saxony[3] had always been a potent centre of separate political life. Incorporated with the greatest difficulty and after violent struggles into the Frankish empire by Charles the Great, in the first place as a subject race, the Saxons had already in the course of the ninth century obtained an increasingly important place in the East Frankish dominions, and at the beginning of the tenth century they

---

[3] For further detail, cf. the essay " Niedersachsen u. das deutsche Königtum vom 10. bis zum 12. Jahrhundert," *Franken u. d. deutsche Reich*, 25–45.

assumed for three generations the leadership of the newly
established German kingdom. From the beginning the
centre of gravity of Saxon tribal life lay on the Elbe. Here
was settled the strongest element in the Saxon folk, the
Nordalbingians, whose destruction and transportation had
been necessary before Charles the Great could regard himself as real master of Saxony. Here also was concentrated
the landed property and power of the warlike aristocracy
of the land, from whose midst the Liudolfinger or Ottonian
family rose to predominance in the course of the ninth
century, although other noble families still remained strong.
From the Harz and the Bode to the Elbe and the Saale
stretched the possessions of the Ottonians: Quedlinburg,
Gandersheim, Magdeburg, Merseburg are among the centres
of their power. Their attention, like that of the whole
Saxon aristocracy, was turned to the east, their vision
directed across the Elbe. To the west and to the south-
west lived Frisians, Rhinelanders, Franconians, members of
the German state with equal rights: in this direction friction
and quarrelling was plentiful enough, but there were no
prospects of large-scale acquisitions. To the south-east
lived the Thuringians, and in this direction the Saxon
duchy, from the beginning of the tenth century, sought
to expand. In the east, on the other hand, across the Elbe
were the Slavs, split into many small tribes, a scorned and
hated people, and here were possibilities of fame and gain.
A bloody, pitiless, unbelievably gruesome border struggle
between Slav and Saxon fills the years between the ninth
and the twelfth centuries, until finally the united Saxon
forces break through the frontier, cross the Elbe under
Lothar and Henry the Lion, and carry out the great
mediaeval task of the colonization of the German east.
This was the direction in which the Saxon border nobility
had always looked, and this fact must always be remembered
if the political attitude of the Saxon " stem " is to be
correctly interpreted in the framework of German history.

Two other great centres of political concentration and
political self-will lay in the south in the tribal units of
Swabia and of Bavaria. Both tribes had, at an earlier

date, from the third and fourth until the seventh and eighth
centuries, had a separate political existence, and had only
been brought into subjection to the Merovingian empire
after a series of struggles.   But they retained an independent political consciousness for long enough after this—in
Bavaria, in some respects, down to modern times.   This
separate consciousness found its chief expression in passion-
ate enmity between the two neighbouring powers.   There
are scarcely two German tribes between which there was
greater hatred and less esteem than the Swabians and the
Bavarians.   Many times during the eleventh and twelfth
centuries the Swabian frontier city on the Lech, Augsburg,
perished in border warfare.   The opposition of Welf and
Hohenstaufen, one of the main factors in German politics
in the twelfth and at the beginning of the thirteenth century, is to be explained in no small degree by the too rarely
noticed fact that, from the end of the eleventh century,
the Welfs were the Bavarian, the Staufen the Swabian
ducal family, and that behind their dynastic struggle for
ascendency in Germany lay the long-inherited enmity
between the two peoples.   Of all the objects of mutual
contest and rivalry, however, none was more important
than the struggle of each to secure domination over Italy.
As early as the sixth century, at the time when the Lombards were in control in Italy, we find not only political
marriage ties but also military invasions by both Swabians
and Bavarians.   In the first half of the tenth century, with
Italy utterly weak and disorganized, a prey to its neighbours,
this connexion increased enormously, and in the twenties,
thirties and forties of this century one expedition followed
another from Swabia or Bavaria to the western or eastern
sector of the Po valley.   One of the first great shocks to
the newly founded Ottonian Empire, the " rebellion " (as
it is called) of Liudolf in the first half of the fifth decade
of the century, is to be explained in the main as a consequence of this Swabian-Bavarian rivalry for control of
Italy.[4]   At that time Liudolf, the eldest son of Otto the

[4] The traditional attitude of the older German historians to Liudolf's
revolt is, however, essentially different: they sift out the ostensibly per-

76   B. SCHMEIDLER

Great, was duke of Swabia, whilst his uncle, Henry, the younger brother of Otto, was duke of Bavaria. Both were intent on an extension of their power beyond the Alps and both were checked and frustrated by the crown which itself reached out to Italy and seized for itself authority over the

sonal motives of those involved, and on these they lay the whole emphasis. The classical formulation is that of Köpke-Dümmler, *Kaiser Otto der Grosse* (*Jahrbücher d. deutschen Reiches unter der Regierung Ottos d. Gr.*, Leipzig 1876), 212: "Only accidentally and indirectly was Otto's expedition for conquest beyond the Alps the occasion of such a serious disaster. In itself it had evoked neither the opposition nor the antipathy of Liudolf or of anyone else in the realm; the discontent of the heir to the throne and his confederates was due rather to changes which had made themselves felt at Court, particularly among the leading members of the government. But other quite different interests, very varied in character, were rapidly involved in the revolt, once it had begun, and the representatives of those interests used Liudolf's cause as a cloak for their own activities. There can be no question of an opposition of ideas or of conscious principles: rather it is a question of a combination of highly personal passions, which— without producing one constructive thought—were extensive enough to cause serious ravages and to convulse the structure which had been so firmly established . . ." The positive, impersonal elements in the struggle are hardly mentioned, except for the remark (p. 193): "Incidentally, no doubt, he (i.e. Liudolf) hoped to extend the circumference of his duchy, which bordered immediately to Italy"; cf. also p. 209 sq. Nor is the emphasis on the concrete objectives much stronger in Ranke, *Weltgeschichte* VI, ii (1885), 185 sqq. And Dümmler's point of view is expressed even more vigorously and in more general terms by Otto Rommel, "Der Aufstand Herzog Liudolfs von Schwaben in den Jahren 953 u. 954," *Forschungen z. deutschen Geschichte* IV (1864), 121–158, who follows up his thoroughly justifiable refusal to accept the theory of Sybel and Maurenbrecher, according to which the revolt was a national movement against Otto's universal policy, with the following remarks (p. 149): "In none of the numerous rebellions of the tenth century was there any question of the defence of high political principles . . . And yet each of the revolts, in spite of the fact that it was undertaken solely for the furtherance of personal interests, found partisans among the warlike tribes of Germany, where both greater and lesser nobles were jealous of their personal liberty . . . It was, therefore, not a question of Liudolf summoning the duchies of Swabia and Lotharingia to fight for ther independence from the crown, for such was not the issue, but merely the defence of personal interests; and the insurgent force which was collected for this purpose was made up also of partisans from the native lands of Liudolf's opponents." And Rommel expresses the same attitude once again in his summary (p. 157), when he writes: "Even careful criticism of the authorities leaves us with the conclusion that the inmost motives of Liudolf's revolt were essentially personal in character, though of weighty consequence: its political significance lies not in the sphere of foreign, but in that of internal politics, and is bound up predominantly with the question, who shall carry weight at court." Then he goes on, with an exaggeration of the possible consequences of isolated events which is characteristic of the historiography of his day, to express the view that "as a consequence of the coincidence of the revolt with Otto's intervention in Italy the whole future of the German monarchy and of the Empire itself was placed in question. Had the revolt succeeded, it is impossible," he says (p. 158), "to decide whether the unity

whole land. In the course of this process, however, Otto gave certain immediate advantages to the greater duchy and to his brother, handing the marks of Aquileja and Friuli to Bavaria and thus placing the most important passes over the Alps and the eastern half of the Po valley under Bavarian control. Swabia emerged empty-handed, confined within its old boundaries. The reply to this was Liudolf's unsuccessful revolt. And soon the German crown followed this first limitation of the Swabian duchy by limitation on still another side. On the south-east of the duchy lay the kingdom of Burgundy, settled far beyond the confines of Alsace by kindred *Alemanni*. More than once in the tenth century the Swabian dukes tried, by war and marriage alliances, to gain influence in this neighbouring land and even to take possession of it. At the beginning of the eleventh century, however, the German

of the kingdom could have been preserved." Similarly F. Jung, *Ruotger u. der Aufstand Liudolfs v. Schwaben* (Schwerin 1901), who sees the main cause of the revolt in the antithesis between Liudolf and Henry of Bavaria, Otto I's brother, and conceives of this antithesis in almost exclusively personal terms; cf. p. 23 sqq.—For a narrative which gives more prominence to objective, impersonal causes, we have to turn to L. M. Hartmann, *Geschichte Italiens im Mittelalter* III, ii (Gotha 1911), 246: " The two German princes with the most immediate interest in Italian policy were naturally Henry, Otto I's brother, who had been invested with the Bavarian duchy in 948 after his reconciliation with the king, and Liudolf, the young and high-spirited prince, who had shortly before received the duchy of Swabia. To them, as to their predecessors, it seemed that the geographical position of their territories gave them a right to the leading place in every invasion of Italy. Henry had, indeed, not many years earlier led an expedition on his own initiative to Trent and occupied Aquileia. The favourite of Matilda, the queen-dowager, he was perhaps the scheming opponent of the heir presumptive, Liudolf, and the driving personality behind the Italian policy, from which he rightly expected great personal profit. In view of this situation, and in order to keep abreast of his uncle (p. 247) and to create a *de facto* position which could not easily be unmade, Liudolf determined to anticipate Henry, and when the decision to invade Italy had been taken, he suddenly crossed the Alps, without asking the king's permission, supported only by the quite insufficient forces which he had assembled in Swabia . . . ".—Here the real connexions and motives behind the revolt are much more firmly brought out, but even here the whole situation is neither seen nor expressed. And this one incident may be taken as a characteristic example of the whole tendency and method of German mediaeval studies in the nineteenth and at the beginning of the twentieth century. In every connexion the generation of Giesebrecht and of the *Jahrbücher* emphasized as strongly as possible the non-recurring and personal elements in the formation of events, and consciously aligned itself against more general associations and wider causes: only with difficulty and still within narrow limits is a wider understanding of the underlying coherence and continuity gradually being built up.

monarchy under Conrad II (1024—1039) once again stepped
in, united Burgundy with the Empire, and thereby deprived
Swabia of its second opportunity of expansion—the only
opportunity left to it after the initiation of an Italian
policy carried out by the German peoples as a whole.
Once again the reply was a Swabian revolt, led by the young
duke Ernst II against Conrad II, his step-father, which
ended still more unhappily than Liudolf's insurrection with
the complete destruction of the self-willed leader.[5] Twice,
therefore, in the early middle ages was Swabia checked and
its ambitions prejudiced by the power of the crown. But
the accession of the Hohenstaufen saw a Swabian dynasty
on the throne, and with this event the period of Swabian
glory and external prosperity commenced. The Hohenstaufen pursued their Italian policy from Swabian soil,
favoured and improved the western passes over the Alps,
the Septimer, the Splügen and the St. Gotthard, and made
Chiavenna into a Swabian city. Frederick I married the
heiress of Burgundy, Beatrice, and as lord of Swabia and
supreme authority in the Empire, exercised power and
influence in that land. Through the Hohenstaufen, therefore, Swabia obtained tardy compensation and freedom of
movement in both the directions in which previously it
had been held in check by the monarchy.

Saxony, Swabia and Bavaria are thus three of the most
important political bodies, each with a separate existence
and will of its own, which were bound together in the
German kingdom and which had to learn to take their place
within the state. Already a brief survey has indicated
how this necessity might lead to difficulties and to friction.
If, however, the relations of these three bodies among
themselves are to be fully understood, still another political
entity, a fourth centre of power, must be included in the
survey. This fourth centre is Bohemia.

As a racially distinct, self-contained land bordering on
Bavaria, Saxony and Franconia, Bohemia had long been

---

[5] Here again earlier writers have emphasized the personal element
in the revolt to the detriment of its real causes; cf. Schmeidler, *Franken
u. d. deutsche Reich*, 11 n. 6.

a threatening salient reaching out into the provinces
populated by the German peoples. Protected from Germany by a mighty range of mountains, it was more likely
to engage on incursions itself than to stand in fear of
attack. Shut in on three sides by German races after the
German colonization of the ninth and tenth centuries and
the creation of the Ostmark (Austria), penetrated to some
degree by German colonists, but still maintaining coherence,
solidarity and a strong political organization within its
own boundaries, it could not remain indifferent to the
political life of the neighbouring kingdom and was forced
by its position to bring its influence to bear in German
politics. It was a fourth centre of power, similar to the
centres of which we have already spoken and necessarily
connected with them, another political entity which the
German king had to take into account, with which he must
come to terms. What, then, must be the procedure of the
German monarchy which found itself surrounded by these
powerful political groups and which desired to assert its
position and to prevail over them ? What means had it
at its disposal ?

With this question our attention is naturally turned to
Franconia, the central land, the nucleus in the midst of
these politically powerful outer provinces. In Franconia
no native ducal power comparable in strength to that of
Saxony, Bavaria or Swabia, had arisen. Two great families,
the Conradiner and the Popponen or Babenberger, engaged
in the ninth century in a struggle for predominance, a
struggle which ended in 906 through the intervention of
the monarchy with the destruction of the Babenberger;
and this led also to the elevation, on the death of Louis the
Child in 911, of the leader of the victorious party, Conrad I,
to the German throne. Even these early incidents
are not without interest and significance. In no other
German land had the Carolinigan monarchy or its guide
and adviser, the Archbishop of Mainz, intervened so firmly
in party warfare or punished the hostile party with such
merciless extermination; and it is hard to believe the contemporary tradition according to which personal enmity

and perfidy alone led the archbishop of Mainz to execute his opponents in this Franconian struggle. It is more probable that he was thinking, already at this early date, of the particular interests of the monarchy in this central region, and such ideas were certainly in his mind in 911 when he had the duke of Franconia elected to the German throne in the first royal election of German history at Forchheim. But the new king wore out his energies in unsuccessful struggles with the powerful duchies which surrounded him, particularly Saxony in the north, and then on his death-bed—with a statesmanlike realization of the hopelessness of his endeavours—designated his chief opponent, the duke of Saxony, as his successor. Henry I, against whom the Bavarians had set up their own duke, Arnulf, as king not only in Bavaria but over the whole realm of Germany,[6] established the kingdom on another more federal basis, and accorded far-reaching recognition to the independence of the racial divisions, particularly of Bavaria. But this settlement was in large measure revoked by his son, Otto I,[7] who pursued from the beginning of his reign a systematic policy of centralization which proved to be the real foundation of the strong German monarchy of the period between about 955 and the end of the twelfth century. And the means which he employed in the furtherance of this policy once again throw vivid light

---

[6] Cf. MG. *Scriptores* XXX. 2. i, p. 742: " Bawarii sponte se reddiderunt Arnolfo duci et regnare eum fecerunt in regno Teutonicorum."—This fact, which has still hardly obtained the recognition it deserves, was brought to light in 1923 by H. Bresslau, " Die ältere Salzburger Annalistik," *Abhandlungen d. preussischen Akademie d. Wissenschaften*, 1923, *phil.-hist. Kl.*, No. 2, pp. 57 sqq.

[7] The last ten to fifteen years have seen prolonged discussion among German historians regarding the question of centralization and federalism in mediaeval German history, the attitude of individual rulers to these problems and particularly the significance of Henry I and Otto I. As far as Henry I is concerned, the one safe conclusion which can now be added to what is written above is, in my opinion, the fact that the old king had decided and even begun in his last years to adopt the policy which his son was to follow, i.e., expansion into Italy externally and greater centralization at home. Indeed, it is possible that Otto I, so remarkably certain of his objectives from the very beginning of his reign, was only carrying out his father's programme. Cf. among others, M. Lintzel, " König Heinrich I. u. die Gründung des Deutschen Reiches," *Thüringisch-Sächsische Zeitschrift für Geschichte u. Kunst* XXIV (1935), 25–42.

on the special features of the position of the Franconian duchy.

It is well known that Otto I obtained much help from the church in his struggle against the long-standing efforts of the duchies to gain independence, and that he relied on bishops, archbishops and the abbots of imperial monasteries against counts, dukes and margraves. Less noticed is another expedient which really made possible the subsequent exploitation of the resources of the church: this expedient was the permanent union of the duchy of Franconia with the German crown. Otto came into conflict at one time or another with every German duchy and in most cases removed not merely the actual occupant of the ducal office but also the ducal family as a whole, replacing them by new men who were for the most part members of his own family. But the duchies themselves were left standing. Neither Otto nor his successors shewed any tendency to keep the ducal office vacant when forfeiture had occurred: nothing was done to prepare the way for the eventual " mediatisation " or suppression of the duchies themselves. The sole exception was Franconia. When duke Eberhard, the brother of Conrad I and his successor in the duchy, was killed in the rebellion of 939, together with the duke of Lothringen, and when the third confederate, the duke of Bavaria, had been driven out of the land, it was in Franconia alone that Otto appointed no successor.[8] Instead he reserved the land permanently for the German crown. And this must have been done fully consciously and in the most solemn form, for no future German ruler, in the whole period until the fall of the Hohenstaufen, from whatever land or duchy he sprang, did anything to change or modify this settlement—a

[8] This fact has once again been demonstrated by A. Karnbaum, "Die Aufhebung des Herzogtums Franken," *Neues Archiv* XXXVII (1912), 786–790, against the views of P. v. Winterfeld, " Die Aufhebung des Herzogtums Franken," *Neues Archiv* XXVIII (1903), 510 sqq., who maintains that Otto I's son, Liudolf, succeeded after Eberhard's death and that the duchy only passed to the crown after Liudolf's downfall in 954. That the Franconian duchy, particularly in its eastern division, was in a weak position even earlier, under Eberhard himself, has been observed by E. v. Guttenberg, " Die Territorienbildung am Obermain," *Bericht d. historischen Vereins zu Bamberg* LXXIX (1928), 49 sq.

settlement which was obviously connected indissolubly with the other rule of German constitutional law according to which the German king must be a subject of Frankish law[9] and was *ipso facto* placed under Frankish law by his election, if he was not already subject to it by birth. Both arrangements clearly gave Franconia a special place in the constitution, but of the two the permanent union of the duchy with the German crown was clearly of the greater material importance. The demesnes, towns and strongholds of this prosperous region were in this way placed at the disposal of every German king by the mere fact of his election, and thus contributed directly to strengthen the power of the crown. This was, from a purely geographical as well as from a political point of view, a fact of the greatest moment. From whatever duchy the king originated, his own sphere of influence combined with Franconia, the land of the centre, always formed a preponderant block, from the pressure of which no other single duchy could permanently free itself. If he started from Saxony, like the three Ottos, Saxony and Franconia together formed a mighty northern territorial agglomeration, and Bavaria and Swabia, tightly pressed in between this region and Italy, the most distant of the German monarchy's sources of power, could not hope to put up successful resistance. If, like Henry II, his primary base was Bavaria, he was able to cut off Swabia, habitually hostile, both from Bohemia and from Saxony, and to take up a controlling position which ran through the very centre of the land. If, however, the king was originally in possession of Swabia, like the Hohenstaufen, his territory, combined with Franconia and extended towards Thuringia and the lands along the middle reaches of the Elbe, formed a broad barrier between Bavaria and Bohemia on one side and Saxony on the other. Under all circumstances and at all times, therefore, the king stood firm on a broad, central base between his possible opponents, dividing them automatically through the mere facts of geography and in a position to meet each one of them with superior force and overcome them with-

---

[9] Cf. E. Rosenstock, *Königshaus u. Stämme*, 10 sqq.

out difficulty. For one German duchy alone was such a combination with the centre impossible and never seriously attempted: this was Lotharingia, and it is characteristic that the sole attempt at establishing a monarchy with Lotharingia as its basis, when Count Hermann of Salm was set up as anti-king against Henry IV, was a miserable failure.

The central position of Franconia and its significance for the German monarchy at all periods is a fact so unquestionably illuminating that it is almost incredible that it has never, so far as I know, been properly discussed or appreciated as a factor in the general development of mediaeval Germany. Otto I has been praised, and rightly, for fitting the church into the German governmental system, for subduing the duchies, and for many other deeds of war and peace which make him the real founder of the great and durable state of the period between 950 and 1200. He is one of the most gifted statesmen of all time, at any rate in German history. It is, however, precisely the resumption of the Franconian duchy for the German crown, an achievement still too generally neglected, which proves his genius and clearsightedness and which was one of the most durable and influential of the means which he employed in the foundation of the mediaeval German state.

Franconia itself derived profit enough from its position as the special land of the German crown, and developed as a consequence a tendency to steady expansion. In its original form it consisted only of Rheinfranken (the western or Rhenish division of the province, partly included in the modern Palatinate) and of Ostfranken, the present Lower Franconia with its centre in Würzburg. The modern provinces of Central and Upper Franconia, around Nürnberg, Bamberg and further along the Main, were still in the tenth century distinct from Ostfranken, and formed the Bavarian Nordgau. This latter district remained under the direct administrative control of the duchy of Bavaria until the death of duke Arnulf in 937; but Otto I withdrew it in 938 from the direct administration of the duke, without completely severing its association with Bavaria, and

placed it under a certain Berthold of the family of the
counts of Schweinfurt—a family which, in another branch,
rose to importance in Austria after 976 as the later Babenberger dynasty—who was already administering the East
Franconian hundreds of Radenzgau and Volkfeld.[10]
Through this change the province was detached effectively
and permanently from its association with Bavaria, and
tended more and more to attach itself to the more westerly
districts on the Main and around Würzburg.   Already in
the eleventh century the name Franconia was rapidly becoming usual for this district, to which it had originally
been in no way applicable.   Thus an important region
between the lower Main and Bohemia was early incorporated
into the Franconian province.   And from this Franconian
base the German monarchy sought also to get possession
of the adjoining districts of Thuringia and of the region
centred round the middle courses of the Elbe.   The rulers
of the eleventh, twelfth and thirteenth centuries gave
constant attention to the Thuringian county of Weimar,
the Saxon mark of Meissen and the bordering districts.
And their object is clear: to make their hold on their
central territories secure they were necessarily compelled
to separate the two important political centres, Saxony
and Bohemia.   The history of Thuringia and of the land
along the middle Elbe as a territory sought after by the
crown for its own, would therefore make a separate chapter
of mediaeval German history:[11] in conjunction with an
extended Franconia these districts would have supplied
the German crown with an almost unshakable material
basis for its power.   In spite of propitious beginnings,
however, the monarchy was unable to achieve permanent
success in this direction.

[10] Cf. M. Doeberl, " Die Markgrafschaft u. die Markgrafen auf dem
bayerischen Nordgau," *Programm des k. Ludwigs-Gymnasium in München*
(München 1894), 7 sq.   The view expressed by Giesebrecht, *Jahrbücher
Ottos II* (1840), 32 sq. and App. V and VI (pp. 131–138), namely that the
Nordgau was first separated from Bavaria in 976 in consequence of the
revolt of Henry the Wrangler, is incorrect.   Cf. K. Uhlirz, *Jahrbücher d.
deutschen Reiches unter Otto II* (Leipzig 1902), 52; von Guttenberg, *Die
Territorienbildung am Obermain*, 57 sqq., 68 sq.

[11] For a few indications, cf. Schmeidler, *Franken u. d. deutsche Reich*,
12–18.

A brief survey of German history in the period between Otto I and Frederick II reveals again and again the permanent importance of Franconia and the significance of its central position, and shews how its influence was felt at each stage of development. Under Otto I himself, internal conflicts ceased after the last great struggle between Bavaria and Swabia for domination in Italy. Germany was so powerful a block during the lifetime of its founder and to all appearances so firmly welded together that there were no subsequent attempts at internal reaction. But under his son, Otto II, the old struggles immediately started again, and their result was a strengthening of the process, already under way in the previous reign, by which the Nordgau became independent of Bavaria. We have, indeed, already seen that the reign of Otto II did not mark the establishment of the Nordgau as a province separate from Bavaria; on the contrary, the situation created by Otto I in 938 and the years which followed seems to have remained unaltered.[12] But the Bavarian Ostmark—later to be transformed into the duchy of Austria—now received a ruler of its own in Luitpold, the brother of the very Berthold who was in control of the Nordgau. The house of Schweinfurt was thus once again advanced at the expense of the Bavarian ducal line, and the result was necessarily a growth both of their actual independence and of their efforts to obtain further independence in the Nordgau as well as in Austria. Under Otto III, however, no further developments took place, and we can therefore leave the reign without further consideration; but Otto's death and the succession of the founder of Bamberg, Henry II (1002—1024), led to a series of events which are highly instructive.

At the very beginning of Henry II's reign the margrave of the Nordgau, count Henry of Schweinfurt, rose in revolt on the apparently not altogether unjustified ground that the king had promised him the duchy of Bavaria which he had himself vacated on his elevation to the throne, and had then refused to concede it or had at least used every possible excuse to postpone the fulfilment of his promise. What is

[12] Cf. Uhlirz, *op. cit.*, 79 sqq.

most evident, however, is the growth of the pretensions of
the house of Schweinfurt, which now dares to reach out
after the duchy of Bavaria, one of the highest positions in
the realm, second only to the royal office. Like Henry the
Wrangler before him, the count of Schweinfurt allied with
Bohemia and Poland, which had at this very moment
become a dangerously strong power under Boleslav Chrobry.
In these circumstances Henry II determined to erect a
firmer defence for the heart of the kingdom on both sides
of the Main than Otto I and Otto II had succeeded in creating in the margravate of the Nordgau. He destroyed the
power of the Schweinfurter family and set up in its place
on the upper Main the bishopric of Bamberg,[13] which, as
one of the many clerical supports of the monarchy and
the royal demesne, was intended to provide a more trustworthy defence for the duchy of Franconia than could be
expected from what many rulers of that age—and particularly Henry II with his strongly religious disposition—
considered to be the untrustworthy and egotistic attitude
of the secular princes. Würzburg and Bamberg were
thenceforward the two great bulwarks on the river Main,
dominating the most important routes connecting north
and south, and as such they more than once played an
important part in the subsequent history of Germany.
But the new organization meant a strengthening of Franconia, and with the districts now attached to it Franconia
stretched out as far as the north-west corner of Bohemia,
completely separated Bavaria not only from Saxony but
also from central Germany, and was in a position to keep
a close watch over any hostile intrigues which might arise

---

[13] This view of the foundation of the bishopric of Bamberg—namely,
that secular and political motives (rather than the missionary and spiritual
objectives emphasized by earlier historians) were highly important, if not
decisive, for Henry II—was put forward independently and approximately
contemporaneously by Erich Freiherr von Guttenberg in his frequently
cited book: *Die Territorienbildung am Obermain* (*Bericht d. hist. Vereins
zu Bamberg* LXXIX, 1928), 72 sq. (and in articles a few months earlier).
The starting point, in v. Guttenberg's case, was the local situation at
Bamberg, whereas for me it was the general political and constitutional
situation in Germany: our points of view may therefore be considered to
supplement and confirm each other. Cf. also A. von Hofmann, *Das
deutsche Land und die deutsche Geschichte* (1923), 523–526.　　·

between Bavaria and Bohemia and, if necessary, to frustrate them.

Under Henry II's powerful successor, Conrad II, we hear at the beginning of the reign of many far-reaching conspiracies and alliances: from Poland to Lotharingia, across the whole of Germany from furthest east to furthest west, hostile movements were in combination. But Conrad had no difficulty in mastering his enemies. Himself by origin a count in Rheinfranken, sprung from the neighbourhood of Worms, he had full control of the central territories of the crown; but in no other duchy had he either landed property of his own—his inheritance also was small—or undoubted influence which could be combined with and made to supplement the royal lands of Franconia. In such a position he made use of a better method than mere force to maintain the allegiance of the secular lords. Depending less exclusively than any other king from Otto the Great onwards on the far from necessarily unswerving allegiance of the ecclesiastical princes, himself a lesser secular magnate in origin—small in landed property although descended from the Ottonian house—Conrad gave the lay princes their due and interfered with none without reason. The consequence was that, like Henry I who had founded the kingdom in peaceful agreement with the temporal lords, Conrad II raised it in equal concord to the height of its power, and scarcely ever needed to use force in internal affairs. But his son, the melancholy, fervid, ascetic Henry III, was of another temperament. Strongly religious by upbringing, he again increased the power of the ecclesiastical princes beyond all measure and made plain his mistrust of the temporal lords at every turn of events. In Lotharingia, as in Thuringia and in Italy, he attempted to diminish their power, and the result was perpetual revolts during his own reign and a general attitude of hostility to the crown when he died and was succeeded, in 1056, by his six year old son, Henry IV. During the subsequent fifty years of a life which was as stormy in its private as in its public aspects, this unfortunate prince had to atone not merely for his own but also for his father's sins and mistakes. The alliance of the princes with the papacy was a direct consequence of Henry III's exaggerated centralizing policy. But in the numerous disorders of Henry IV's reign—disorders too manifold to be surveyed at one glance—the significance of Franconia as the principal seat of the German monarchy is once again clearly evident: the struggles fought out during the Investiture Contest, looked at geographically from the point of view of internal German politics, have the appearance of a straightforward fight for Franconia as the last sure basis of Henry IV's government. In the north, Saxony had deserted him completely and would have nothing further to do with him for a decade and a half: in the south, the dukes of Bavaria and Swabia were frequently in rebellion. They were, indeed, unable to carry their whole people with them into revolt: but again and again they managed to cause Henry the greatest difficulty and to involve him in bitter warfare. His journey to Canossa, also, was particularly endangered by the fact that the hostile dukes held all the passes over the Alps, so that he had almost to steal like a fugitive through a hostile land to obtain reconciliation with Gregory VII. Again and again northern armies from Saxony and southern armies from Swabia in particular threw themselves against the central line of the Main and against Franconia: separated by the crown land and thus reduced in power, Henry's opponents tried to unite on royal soil and so to bring about the king's destruction. In the Saxon and Thuringian passes which led from north to south, those by Melrichstädt and Flarchheim among others, Henry more than once engaged the advancing Saxon host, and in spite of many defeats in battle was ultimately successful in preventing their entry into Franconian territory. He had repeatedly to contend with Swabian and Bavarian forces for possession of Würzburg, but this stronghold on the lower Main remained in Henry's hands until the last months of the reign. Even the last great contest with his son in 1105, which led to Henry's deposition, was from a geographical point of view a struggle for Franconia and for control of the region round the Main. The archbishop of Mainz, the primate of Germany, who had deserted the excommunicated king, was in exile in Thuringia, constantly endeavouring to win back his see. When Henry V himself revolted against his father—thus giving resistance and rebellion of every kind a legal standing—he was successful in capturing Würzburg, in imposing cautious neutrality on bishop Otto of Bamberg, whose predecessor, Rupert, had for many decades been one of the firmest supporters of Henry IV's government, and finally in taking Mainz. With this success the whole line of the Main fell into the son's hands, and Henry IV suddenly found himself driven from the principal basis of his power and relegated to the north-west corner of his realm, the district of the lower Rhine. From this point he once again, after the unhappy incidents of his deposition,[14] attempted an almost hopeless resistance, cut short in his fifty-seventh year by the early death which was the result of the long exertions of a difficult life. In this last struggle by the emperor to retain his hold on Franconia the stronghold of Nürnberg for the first time played a great part in history: after long and honourable resistance to siege the garrison finally surrendered to Henry V in the late autumn of 1105.

Under Henry V himself the struggle between crown and princes, far from dying down, became even more bitter and deep-rooted. The hard, dispassionate figure of this cold, calculating monarch was designed rather to awaken antagonisms than to calm them. Henry's endeavours, considered from a geographical point of view, were a continuation of the old attempts, working from the base in Franconia, to obtain power and possessions in Thuringia and in central Saxony, to annex them to the crown lands, and to diminish the power of the princes of central Saxony. In pursuing these objects, however, Henry found himself face to face with a similar project on the part of the duke

---

[14] Cf. Schmeidler, " Heinrichs IV. Absetzung, 1105/06. Kirchenrechtlich u. quellenkritisch untersucht," ZRG. XLIII, *Kanon. Abt.* XII (1922), 168–221; and by the same author, *Kaiser Heinrich IV. und seine Helfer im Investiturstreit. Stilkritische u. sachkritische Untersuchungen* (Leipzig 1927), particularly cap. VI, § 6, pp. 315–334.

of Lower Saxony who, as leader of the aristocratic opposition during the reign of the last of the Salian monarchs, was intent on extending his authority in Lower Saxony into the region of the middle Elbe and the Saale, on annexing these districts and making them the most southerly projection of his own sphere of power.[15] It was a project which in an earlier generation had imbued the mind of Henry I, when he was Saxon duke, and had involved him in a struggle with the southern monarchy.[16] Under Henry V a similar struggle was menacing; but it was prevented by the early death of the king, and the antithesis never came to a head for the reason that Henry's successor was his chief opponent, the Saxon duke. The latter continued as king the policy inaugurated when he was duke, but now imbued with a very different conception: the idea of a monarchy based on Saxony. To this end he got control of the important region of the middle Elbe and the Saale and tried also, though without success, to attach Bohemia to his immediate sphere of power. In the south, if he wished to keep free the road to Italy—and he was no less interested in this aspect of policy than any other German king[17]—he had necessarily to choose between Bavaria and Swabia. In fact, he allied with Bavaria as the mightier land, and concentrated his attack in Franconia and Swabia on the heirs of his earlier Salian opponents, the Hohenstaufen. Thus, besides Saxony and Bavaria, he held Franconia, which he had wrested from the Hohenstaufen, and he also acquired considerable landed property in Italy—namely the

[15] Cf. Schmeidler, *Franken u. d. deutsche Reich*, 16–17.
[16] *Ibid.*, 13.
[17] J. W. Thompson, *Feudal Germany* (Chicago, 1928), 261–265, has developed a conception of Lothar's policy and that of the later Welfs (Henry the Proud was Lothar's son-in-law and heir) the main features of which are that they held aloof from Italian policy as a whole and stood out, in internal affairs, as the champions of freedom and legality against the Hohenstaufen. But if Thompson is right in maintaining that Lothar was no weakling, both his other conceptions are fundamentally wrong. It is impossible here to refer to the mass of recent literature on Henry the Lion's career and personality, but respect for law and self-restraint were certainly the last faults which could be charged against him. And Frederick I was not the brutal tyrant whom Thompson depicts. Perhaps the best study of the two men is K. Hampe, " Heinrichs des Löwen Sturz in politisch-historischer Beurteilung," *Hist. Zeitschr.* CIX (1912), 49–82; cf. also *Hist. Zeitschr.* CXL (1929), 591–595, particularly p. 593 sq.

hotly-contested Matildan lands in the centre of the penin-
sula—with which he invested his son-in-law, Henry the
Proud. Once again, therefore, the crown had built up a
powerful, to all appearance irresistible dominion, and although he himself had no son, Lothar could reasonably
hope to found through the Welfs, the Bavarian ducal
dynasty of his son-in-law, a strong new monarchy. But
the German princes, particularly the ecclesiastical princes,
were by now radically opposed to such a development;
and for this reason a small minority, led by the archbishop
of Trier, hastily and with an utter disregard for constitutional forms elected as Lothar's successor the Hohenstaufen,
Conrad III. The latter, like Conrad I before him, wore
himself out in fruitless struggles with the duchies, attempting from his base in Swabia and Franconia to bring force
to bear on Saxony and Bavaria. His nephew and successor,
Frederick I, like Henry I before him, came to terms with
the temporal princes, acknowledged the dual authority of
the Welfs in Bavaria and Saxony, though diminishing its
extent by the creation of the independent Austrian duchy,
and on this basis and thanks to the reconstituted dominion
of the crown over the church, which was a result of this
settlement, was once again in a position to rule effectively.
In this reconstituted government Franconia had its part
as the basis for a repetition of the endeavour, which we
have already had many occasions for mentioning, to reach
over into the Elbe districts of Saxony and Thuringia and
attach them to the crown lands. It is plain enough that
Frederick was trying to build up his power in these regions,
and we find him frequently holding court in Altenburg,
where he rebuilt the royal residence. Ultimately the obstinate resistance of Henry the Lion—a resistance which
may have had its roots in the policy of expansion which
has been sketched[18]—drove Frederick into a direct struggle

[18] The struggle with Henry the Lion was due in part at least to a
territorial question: namely, whether emperor or duke was to have possession of Goslar; cf. Otto of St. Blasien, *Chronica* (ed. A. Hofmeister, MG.
Script. rer. Germ., 1912), cap. 23, p. 33 sq. For Henry the Lion's policy,
which has been the subject of much discussion in recent years, cf. (among
others) R. Hildebrand, *Der sächsische " Staat " Heinrichs des Löwen*
(Berlin 1937)—a work which, however, is open to criticism—and G. Läwen,

with the Saxon duchy, from which he emerged successful.
The result was the disintegration of Saxon power and the
extension of the immediate authority of the crown as far
as the lower Elbe basin, where Lübeck was constituted an
imperial city. His son Henry VI went even further.
When the Mark of Meissen escheated to the crown in 1195
he refrained from granting it out within a year and a day
and proposed to absorb it as an imperial territory—the
first ruler of mediaeval Germany who openly avowed his
intention of getting possession of this region, and the last
who, possessed of Franconia (and Swabia), with a broad
territorial basis on which to depend, was able to contem-
plate its junction with Franconia and the strengthening of
the empire by the addition of a strong new clamp. But
immediately on his death the realm broke apart, and never
again could it be reawakened to its old vitality as an active
political body, dependent on its own resources alone and
developing through its own energies. Under Frederick II
Germany became a mere appurtenance of the empire,[19]
in which the development of the territorial principalities
was everywhere making rapid progress and was actually
accorded constitutional recognition by the ruler himself.
After Frederick's death the whole structure fell to pieces
and became, for a long period at least, the desolate heap
of ruins which was the description I gave, in my opening
words, of the German state of the later middle ages. Only
after painful and laborious preparation could the fourteenth
and still more the fifteenth century erect a new imperial

Die herzogliche Stellung Heinrichs des Löwen in Sachsen (Diss. Königsberg,
Düsseldorf 1937).
    [19] This conclusion must, I believe, still be maintained in spite of the
fact that many recent German historians have expressed divergent opinions
and greater attention has rightly been given to the manifold administrative
activities of the later Hohenstaufen, Frederick II and his son Henry (VII),
in Germany itself. But their main objective and the basis of their policy
was still Italy. F. Schneider, " Kaiser Friedrich II. u. seine Bedeutung
für das Elsass," *Elsass-Lothringisches Jahrbuch* IX (1930), 130–155, tries
to shew that Frederick II really felt at home in Alsace; but cf. Salimbene
(f. 355c, MG. *Script.* XXXII, 350) who quotes Frederick as saying " quod
Deus Iudeorum non viderat terram suam, scilicet Terram Laboris, Cala-
briam et Siciliam et Apuliam, quia non totiens commendasset terram, quam
promisit et dedit Iudeis." Here, therefore, Frederick himself speaks of
southern Italy as *terra sua.*

structure, which finally achieved a certain shape and fixity under Frederick III and Maximilian I.[20] As far as Franconia and the age of Frederick II is concerned, it is worth mentioning that, even at that date, a bishop of Bamberg, Ekbert of Meran, who had been long in office (1203—1237) and who came of a mighty family, was playing an important part in imperial policy as a counsellor of the emperor;[21] even under Frederick II, therefore, Franconia and the bishopric of Bamberg were still regarded, as they had been regarded for centuries past, as particularly useful and important pillars of the German monarchy.

Thus we come to the end of our survey of German history in the earlier centuries of the middle ages. It would be possible to indicate and to prove in detail how, in the same period, other regions and other racial units maintained their own unchanging policies and objectives, how each exercised a permanent influence, geographical as much as political, within the structure of the German realm as a whole; how the history of the whole can only be understood in the light of the co-operation and interrelationship between these component parts. But the close connexion which existed between Franconia and the German crown amply justifies our singling out this region for special attention; and it may be therefore considered a useful addition to our knowledge, if the brief account of Franconia's place in German history which has been given, makes possible a clearer and more vivid conception both of the position of Franconia as the special land of the German monarchy and of the influence which it was in this capacity able to exert over the general course of German development in the middle ages.

[20] For the history of the German state in the later middle ages and particularly for the relations between the imperial government and the nascent territorial principalities, cf. the recent survey in my book, *Das spätere Mittelalter von der Mitte des 13. Jahrhunderts bis zur Reformation* (*Handbuch für den Geschichtslehrer*, ed. O. Kende, IV. i, Leipzig & Wien 1937.)
[21] Cf. the unprinted thesis of E. Hautum, *Ekbert von Meran, Bischof von Bamberg* (Diss.-Erlangen 1924).

IV

THE INVESTITURE CONTEST AND THE GERMAN CONSTITUTION[1]

By PAUL JOACHIMSEN

THE year 1922 marks an anniversary in German history. On 23 September, eight hundred years will have passed since the first great German civil war—the war which we call the Investiture Contest—was ended by the Concordat of Worms. That this anniversary will receive much atten-tion is improbable; but I should like to grasp the oppor-tunity it offers to indicate, in relation to the general course of historical development, the place which the Investiture Contest takes in the history of the German constitution. For this purpose we must direct our attention not so much to the episode of Canossa—which is apt, because of its dramatic, almost legendary, character, to be incorrectly regarded as a climax—as to the proceedings which formed the background to this act, the negotiations of Henry IV with the German aristocratic opposition at Tribur and Oppenheim in October 1076, and Rudolf of Swabia's election as king at Forchheim in March 1077. There can be no question of embarking on a detailed critical discussion of the frequently debated details of these proceedings, though it will be impossible to avoid such discussion en-tirely; but our main purpose will rather be to assign the events of 1076 and 1077 their place in the wider current of German constitutional development.

What, however, was the course of constitutional develop-ment in the period preceding the Investiture Contest ?

The German constitution, as it existed on the foundation of an independent German kingdom comprising the five

[1] " Der Investiturstreit und die deutsche Verfassung," *Bayerische Blätter für das Gymnasialschulwesen* LVIII (1922), 53—75.—Thanks are due to the Verlag R. Oldenbourg in Munich, who have given permission to translate.

races of Franks, Saxons, Bavarians, Swabians and Lotharingians, was a successor of the Frankish constitution. Without the Frankish empire and particularly without the government of Charles the Great, there could never have been a German kingdom. Not merely the conception of one monarchy ruling over all the German races, but also the very organisation of the kingdom, with counts and bishops as its two main pillars, was an inheritance from the Franks. Yet the monarchy which the Saxon dukes took over was in essence no longer the old Frankish monarchy. The Carolingian rulers had, indeed, never forgotten that their kingship was a Germanic and therefore a popular monarchy, that it owed its institution to the will of the people; but the progress of Carolingian kingship had led step by step away from this popular basis and onwards in the direction of an hereditary monarchy with an independent title and rights of its own. Under Charles the Great, moreover, the Frankish conception of the state had developed both a theocratic form and theocratic substance. The decisive factor, however, in German constitutional development was that, on the death of the last of the East-Frankish Carolingians, Louis the Child, the German races themselves—in the first place, the four eastern races without the Lotharingians—had come forward and claimed the right to nominate the king; and at this date each race was a legal, military and at least partially a political unit. Thus the crown passed " from the king who represented the Carolingian monarchy and who was king and nothing further, to the most powerful of the tribal chiefs, for that is what Conrad continued to be, even after he had taken over the kingship."[2] But when, in the end, this last defender of the Carolingian inheritance was defeated by " tribal " opposition to an effective royal authority, he assigned his inheritance to the folk which had most recently joined the old Carolingian empire, and handed over the leadership to the Saxon people, which without doubt still maintained closer connexion than any other racial group with ancient Germanic forms of political life.

[2] Ranke, *Weltgeschichte* VI. ii, 84.

It is well known that, in the proceedings at Fritzlar, the Saxon duke, Henry I, was elected to the kingship by Saxons and Franks alone. Then, through persevering and skilful negotiations, he won recognition from the dukes of Swabia Bavaria and Lotharingia, and with the accomplishment of this task the German kingdom was established. What, however, was the constitutional character of the new state? The meagreness of the information which has come down to us—a meagreness which is to be deplored not only on this occasion but for long enough afterwards, whenever our object is to discover more than the bare facts of history— leaves room for the most varied interpretations. " It was to all intents and purposes a federation of states," says GIESEBRECHT. " Nothing authorises us to speak of a federal constitution of any sort," retorts WAITZ. Nevertheless the contradiction which finds expression in these contrasted judgements is more apparent than real, for behind the contradiction the solid fact is hidden that even here, on the very threshold of German history, two tendencies or conceptions are at grips: the Frankish conception of the monarchy and the older Germanic idea of free union, through which each single " tribal " unit enters into a relationship with the prevailing dynasty which can only be called federal. The question was whether the German constitution was to develop in the direction of real federalism or towards a revival of the Frankish monarchy; but this was a question which Henry I, with a shrewdness and sense of reality won no doubt in his struggles for control of his native duchy, left the future to decide.

The decision was made by his son, Otto the Great; and it lay in the direction of a revival of Frankish monarchical conceptions. This solution was already foreshadowed at the early date when, after " designation " by his father, election by Saxons and Franks and a subsequent more general confirmatory election, Otto had himself solemnly anointed and crowned by the archbishop of Mainz. If we analyse each of these elements separately, we see that designation implied a choice from among the sons and so the acceptance of one single ruler, that election by Saxons

and Franks indicated maintenance of continuity with the
earlier election at Fritzlar, and that the more general
election by the other German peoples confirmed the results
already obtained by the unifying policy which Henry I
had pursued throughout his reign.   In the anointing and
the coronation, however, Otto once again revived Frankish
monarchical ideas in the form which Pippin and his descendants had given them.   In exchanging his Saxon dress for
the Frankish tunic, he became a Frank.   He entered
Frankish territory under Frankish law, like every German
king from that time forward, and by having the dukes
perform the court ceremonies at the coronation-feast in the
capacity of the four great officers of the royal household,
the most powerful of the racial chiefs once again became
a true Carolingian monarch and once again united the
conception of sovereign authority with the idea of personal
service.   In exactly the same way the dynasty of Pippin
had had its beginnings.

    After Otto's coronation there followed in 951 the assump-
tion of government in Lombardy, and in 962 the imperial
coronation in Rome.   Each one of these acts shews that
Otto was following directly in the traces of Charles the Great.
The German monarchy, in other words, was irrevocably
directed along the path of Carolingian theocracy, and from
that time forward—with a single interruption on the death
of Otto III—it was raised higher and higher until it reached
its culmination in the monarchy of Henry III, in which
the theocracy of Charles the Great seemed once more to
become a reality.

    How are we to estimate the importance of this Romano-
German empire in the development of the German people ?
The old controversy about " Italian policy " and its influence on the destinies of Germany, inaugurated some
sixty years ago by SYBEL and FICKER, has once more been
revived in recent years;[3] but, useful as such argument is
for emphasizing the epoch-making character of the great
turning-points of history, it can lead nowhere, if we base

    [3] Cf. for example G. v. Below, Der deutsche Staat des Mittelalters,
vol. I: " Die allgemeinen Fragen."

our judgements on possibilities or alternatives which in
reality did not exist. And it is certain that there was, at
that time, no possibility of a German federal constitution
as an alternative to the imperial structure built up by Otto
the Great and his successors; for the two essentials of
federal cohesion were lacking. Not only was there no
geographical centre within easy reach of all the inhabitants
of this huge conglomeration of territories, but Germany
also lacked anything which might be considered a spiritual
centre, and this was a want which could only have been
supplied by a central shrine, such as certain Germanic
tribal groups had possessed in heathen times. On the other
hand, there was just as certainly no possibility of a German
monarchy after the manner of the primitive Germanic
" folk " monarchies; for here what was lacking was a
sense of German nationality which overrode all tribal
divisions. Instead of a German folk there were simply
the " tribes " or " stems ", in which the dukes had taken
the place of the ancient Germanic popular kings. And
over the " stem duchies " there was, and could be, nothing
except the conception of monarchy handed down from the
Franks.

This conception, however, was clerical and theocratic.
Not merely because the clergy had preserved it and handed
it on as a legacy to the German rulers, but also because
the clergy alone offered the monarchy a means of organizing
its government. Under both the Ottonian and the Salian
dynasties, right down to the beginning of the Investiture
Contest, Germany was ruled through the church alone.

Recent studies have done much to clarify the fundamental
conceptions on which the relations of the German rulers
of this period with the national church rested.[4] The
authority which the German ruler exercised over the German church, it has been shown, was the authority of a protector. It was a form of *mundeburdium*—a type of authority as effective in public as in family relationships—and its
essential characteristic was the power to represent those

---

[4] See the summary of recent research in K. Hampe, *Mittelalterliche
Geschichte* (*Wissenschaftliche Forschungsberichte* VII), 68 sqq.

who were themselves either completely or partially without legal rights or without an independent legal standing. The German king's position as supreme " advocate " over both the national church as a whole and over individual churches rested on this protective power, with which the " immunity " — an institution of Roman origin—was merged. But the king's position as supreme advocate had an even broader foundation in the Germanic system of " proprietary churches ";[5] for on this foundation the idea of the paramount proprietorship of the state over all property in the hands of the national church was built up. Because of this paramount proprietorship the king was entitled to make use of the church and its wealth; and consequently the church provided him with men and accorded him a large part of its income. It is evident that here, as in the development of the mediaeval German constitution as a whole, conceptions of public and of private law were intermingled, and the question whether the public or the private element was predominant is a point which has been widely argued in recent times.[6] In the particular matters which concern us, however, it is safe to say that emphasis of the governmental or public element in the king's position was a legacy from the Frankish period, whereas the powers he possessed as a private person derived from sources common to all primitive Germanic societies. We can say, further, that the conception of public powers, for the very reason that it arose in the closest connexion with the establishment of royal control over the church, will have found expression in both a " realistic " and an " idealistic " form. In the former case, it hardly amounted to more than a justification of the existing constitutional and social order: in the latter, it claimed all the force of a standard of conduct, and its consequences were therefore almost revolutionary.

This difference between a " realistic " and an " idealistic " policy had already served to separate and distinguish the Merovingian from the Carolingian period, and the

[5] Cf. *supra*, 35—70.
[6] Particularly in the work by v. Below which has already been cited.

greatness of Charlemagne is displayed not least by the fact that he was able for a short time to put an end to the antithesis. But it made its appearance again, in the most outstanding way, both as a difference of personality and as a difference of system, in the figures of the first two Salians, Conrad II and Henry III. Of Conrad II's rule BRESSLAU has written: " Never before and never afterwards, so long as it remained a reality, had the Germano-Roman empire so utterly worldly a character." His son, Henry III, was called by HAUCK a model of conscientiousness. And it was this fine, melancholy, lonely man who undertook once again, like Charles the Great, to base his rule on the twin conceptions of *pax* and *iustitia* in the significance which they had been given in Augustine's *Civitas Dei.*

There is perhaps no better way of approaching the problems which necessarily arose with the transference of the theocratic Frankish monarchy into a German environment, than through a consideration of the concepts of *pax* and *iustitia*.[7] When German people spoke of peace and law in the middle ages, they meant by peace either the tribal peace of a primitive age or the king's peace which had developed from it, and thereby they understood the special guarantee or fencing off of one sphere of social life against misdeeds and offences. Whoever committed such misdeeds placed himself outside the " peace " of the community. In the same way the original significance of compensatory payments was that the evil-doer thereby bought himself back into the peace;[8] and it is comprehensible enough that at least a part of the payment fell to the guardian of the peace, who was later the king. By law, on the other hand, the Germanic peoples meant a right, a claim, or in other words what we to-day should call " subjective rights ". When the king at his election

---

[7] In regard to the following, cf. F. Kern, *Gottesgnadentum und Widerstandsrecht im früheren Mittelalter. Zur Entwicklungsgeschichte der Monarchie* (1915), and the translation in this series by S. B. Chrimes under the title: *Kingship, Law and Constitution in the Middle Ages.*

[8] Cf. K. Binding, *Die Entstehung der öffentlichen Strafe im germanischen u. deutschen Recht.*

undertook to vouchsafe each man his rights, or (as was said later) to maintain every man in his law, both parties understood the term in this subjective sense. Objective law in the middle ages was merely " a complex of infinitely numerous subjective concrete rights ". Very different, on the contrary, is the position in regard to the ideas of *pax* and *iustitia*. These were taken over by the church from the realm of classical thought, and were developed from beginnings already apparent in Roman times into fixed moral standards. When Augustine spoke of *pax* and *iustitia*, peace was for him the peace of the Kingdom of God, which excludes war and every form of violence, and justice comprehended the *bonum et aequum* of Ulpian.[9]

From the very hour of his election Conrad II set special store on being a strict and impartial dispenser of justice, and above all on helping the poor and oppressed to obtain their rights.[10] But he understood justice, law and right in an utterly Germanic sense. He had not the least hesitation in enforcing his own or other's claims—for example, against Adalbert of Kärnten—by every means within his power, until his opponent was wiped out, while he took it absolutely as a matter of course that count Giselbert of Loos, after slaying a certain Wikher, should be able to regain royal favour by the surrender of one of his estates.[11] In the legislation which he promulgated, the most evident feature is the endeavour to fix the " condition " of persons and their appropriate rights and duties. For this very reason he shewed no understanding of the great communal movement which was beginning in his day in Italy. His peace was the old German " king's peace ": that is to say,

[9] Cf. E. Bernheim, *Mittelalterliche Zeitanschauungen in ihrem Einfluss auf Politik u. Geschichtschreibung*, part I: " Die Zeitanschauungen: Die augustinischen Ideen—Antichrist und Friedensfürst—Regnum und Sacerdotium " (1918), and the references in Kern, 146 n. 273. Particularly noteworthy in their conjunction of both the clerical and the secular point of view are the words of Gregory VII in his famous letter of 15 March, 1081, to Hermann of Metz: " Honorem Dei [principes seculares] semper suo praeponant; iustitiam, *unicuique suum servando ius*, amplectantur atque custodiant."
[10] See the story in Wipo, *Vita Chuonradi*, cap. 5, and Bresslau, *Jahrbücher des deutschen Reichs unter Konrad II*. II, 375 sqq.
[11] Bresslau, II, 361, n. 3.

the maintenance of order and the repression of rebels and evil-doers.[12]

Wipo, who praises all this and glorifies Conrad as *pacis ubique dator*, nevertheless expresses one further desideratum in his admonitions to Conrad's son, Henry, in whose education he had without doubt played some part. He advises the young king to issue an edict on becoming emperor, obliging the German nobility to send their sons to the schools and to have them trained there in the law; for, he says, the Italians have long studied the law and it has made Rome the mistress of the world.[13]   In these words Wipo touched on the real weakness of the German realm under the Ottonians and Salians: it had failed to take over, from the rich Carolingian inheritance, the legislative activity which had marked the work of the Carolingian monarchs. GIESEBRECHT has emphasized the significance which such legislation, had it been introduced, would have had in stabilising the German constitution, and has shown how it would have influenced German legal development by creating a body of objective law.[14]   NITZSCH, on the other hand, whose works have cast so much new light on the history of the Salian period, sees in Wipo's proposal an expression of opposition to the whole outlook of the German lay nobility, which avoided a written law as long as possible and emphasized in the education of its sons those poetic and ethical qualities which meet us in the national epics and in the lawbooks of the Hohenstaufen period.[15]   Once

---

[12] *Ibid.*, 375 n. 4.
[13] Wipo, *Tetralogus*, v. 183 sqq.
[14] *Gesch. d. deutschen Kaiserzeit* (5th ed.) II, 446, and the summary in the introduction to vol. III.   For the close connexion which this idea had with the Carolingian tradition, considerable importance attaches not only to the relations of the empress Gisela with Reichenau and St. Gallen, which Wipo mentions in this connexion, but also to the utterance of count Udalrich of Ebersberg, cited by Giesebrecht, *op. cit.* II, 686: " Cum Romani terrarum orbi imperarent, ita moderamine legum scripto regebant, ut nulli impune cederet factum, quod lex vetuerat.   Postquam vero Germanum regnum a Romanis recesserat, Sigipertus et Theodericus ac deinde Carolus iura dictabant, quae si quis potens ac nobilis legere nesciret, ignominiosus videbatur, sicut in me coevisque meis, qui iura didicimus, apparet.   Moderni vero filios suos neglegunt iura docere, qui quandoque pro suo libitu et possibilitate mendoso iure quosque iuvant aut deprimunt et per exlegem temeritatem."
[15] *Gesch. d. deutschen Volkes* (2nd ed.) II, 37.

again this difference of opinion strikingly reveals the antagonism of the conflicting forces within the German constitution of the period. For the formation of a body of written law in Germany would have altered not only the character of German law but also the very position of the monarchy within the German state.

But Henry III did not take the step which Wipo recommended to him. When we see him administering the law in Germany, his attitude is precisely the same as that of his father, and shews the same unqualified acceptance of Germanic legal conceptions. On the other hand, he was strongly influenced by the conception of peace, and unlike his father, he understood this conception in the full clerical sense. When in 1043 he entered the pulpit at the provincial synod in Constance as (in the words of the St. Gallen Annalist) a *facundus orator*, preached to the people, forgave all who had trespassed against him, and then urged all present " tum precibus, tum pro potestate " to do likewise —a proceeding which he repeated throughout the kingdom[16]—it is clear that the king, who regarded himself both as holy and as sinful, was using the full force of his profound religious convictions to impose peace on his subjects as a moral duty. Only in this way did he feel he could acquit himself of his duty to himself and to his royal office. He was *sacerdos* and *iudex*, as Alcuin had said of Charles the Great.

His attitude towards the church was similar. His father and his father's predecessor, Henry II, like the Ottos before them, had not hesitated to make use of the church. They had accepted the gifts with which bishops and abbots repaid their election, with the same lack of misgiving which had characterized the Frankish rulers. When Conrad appointed a new bishop of Basel in 1025 after the payment of a huge sum of money, it was represented to him that such an action was simony, according to the new clerical conceptions which were just beginning to make themselves felt. He therefore swore he would no longer accept money

[16] The authorities are quoted by Waitz, *Verfassungsgeschichte* (2nd ed.) VI, 533 n. 2.

for the conferment of bishoprics and abbeys—" in quo voto," says Wipo with a true courtier's diplomacy,[17] " paene bene permansit ". But the son kept the father's oath. More than any other temporal ruler Henry III helped to set the new view, that simony was a heresy, on its feet. With the acclamation of the reform party he went to Italy in 1046 in order to reform the papacy, which was itself under suspicion of simony,[18] and the monarchical theocracy reached its highest point when the king forced the three claimants of the papal throne to resign at Sutri and Rome in 1046, and then received the imperial crown from the hands of his own pope, the German bishop Suidger of Bamberg. For Henry had as little misgiving about ruling as about reforming the church. The three German popes who now occupied the see of Peter are witnesses to the fact that the Ottonian national church, working through the empire, had captured the papal throne. When the emperor appointed Victor II, the last of the German popes, to the duchy of Spoleto and the margravate of Fermo, giving him also the powers of an imperial *missus*, and when on his deathbed, a year later, he enjoined the pope to protect his five year old son, the relation of the " two swords ", as it had been understood throughout the early middle ages from the days of pope Gelasius onwards, received its most perfect expression, and at the same time the theocratic outlook of the Frankish monarchy seemed to have been reaffirmed with new force and solidity.

Not quite twenty years later Gregory VII opened the struggle against the last heir of the Frankish theocracy. The appearance which Germany then presented, in the year 1075, was very different from what it had been on the death of Henry III.[19] All the forces which the first two Salians had ingeniously and laboriously incorporated

[17] Cf. Bresslau, *Jahrbücher* I, 85, and II, 365.
[18] On the question of the "simony" of Gregory VI, cf. Hampe, *Mittelalt. Gesch.*, 64.
[19] For what follows, cf. section 16: " Die Gegensätze im Reiche u. die Umbildung der Verfassung," in Waitz, *Verf.-gesch.* VIII—a section which has still only been superseded in minor details.

into the edifice of the state had turned back in the direction
of independent development, and new forces had made
an appearance—forces which had, indeed, existed previously
but merely as factors in the social rather than the political
situation, and which in any case had been confined within
the limits of single duchies or particular districts. To
the fore were the old seats of racial opposition, Lotharingia
and Bavaria, and with them a new centre of particularism,
Saxony. More important was the increasing opposition
of the lay aristocracy; more important still the clerical
reaction against the idea of theocracy. This had begun
already under Leo IX, the third of the popes appointed by
Henry III—a pontiff still apparently in complete agreement
with the emperor, but showing nevertheless that unmis-
takable tendency towards clerical independence which was
implicit in the Cluniac reform and still more in its manifes-
tations in Lotharingia.[20] Meagre as our information is,
it can perhaps be said of Henry that, the longer he lived,
the more acutely he came to realise how critical was the
situation in his kingdom. In face of clerical opposition,
he seems at least to have wavered, if not to have given way
in his policy of direct dominion over the church.[21] Three
times he forced the nobles to swear allegiance to his son,
and the second time the oath contained the highly suggestive
addition: " si rex iustus futurus esset ".[22] But the most
significant feature of all is his recognition of the fundamental weaknesses of the German constitution: its lack
of fixed revenues, on the one hand, and, on the other hand,
the lack of an official class to serve in the imperial adminis-

[20] For Leo IX and his policy, cf. the new literature summarized by
Hampe, op. cit., 64 sqq.
[21] In this way, it seems to me, we must interpret the hotly debated
question of Henry's " patriciate," which cannot be discussed here; cf.
Hauck, Kirchengesch. Deutschlands III, 621 n. 3.
[22] It is usual to regard these words, which Hermannus Contractus
relates under the year 1053, as a clause introduced by the princes as an
expression of their dissatisfaction; cf. Steindorff, Jahrb. Heinr. III. II,
228 n. 1. But Giesebrecht, II, 485, correctly remarks that it is far from
clear whether the phrase is intended to express a reservation in the true
sense of the word, or a stipulation on the part of the princes. To my mind,
the second alternative is out of the question; the former, on the other hand,
fully expresses Henry's constitutional ideas. Kern, 161 n. 300, appears
to share Steindorff's views.

tration and in the administration of the royal demesne. These deficiencies, however, were a direct result of the renunciation of the revenues which had hitherto been raised by the disposal of positions in the church—a practice which was now regarded as simony. At the time of Henry III's death, therefore, there were already signs that the old Ottonian system was undermined, and both the strength of the German state and the equilibrium of the whole German constitution were left absolutely dependent on the personality of the ruler.[23]

At this critical juncture there followed the minority of Henry IV, and ten years of regency during which the crisis in the German constitution became ever more imminent. It could only have been prevented by a statesmanlike personality of the first rank or by a firmly established administration, capable of functioning by itself. The one came to the rescue of France, the other to that of England, when similar or even more serious difficulties arose; but in eleventh-century Germany both were lacking. The empress Agnes, who took over the government, was anything but a regent of first-rate qualities, such as the great empresses of the Saxon dynasty, Adelheid or Theophanu. She had grown up in Aquitanian piety and aspired to the cloister. And yet she did nothing in the years of her regency which Henry III himself might not have done. If she silenced opposition in Lorraine by considerable concessions to the house of Ardenne and the counts of Flanders,[24] it is possible that she was only carrying out Henry's testamentary dispositions. If she once again placed the duchies of Bavaria, Swabia and Carinthia in the hands of feudatories, she was only returning to the position of the early years of Henry's reign; for she could not guess that in the three new dukes, Otto of Nordheim, Rudolf of Rheinfelden and Berthold of Zähringen, she was helping three future enemies of her son to seat themselves firmly in the saddle. And if, probably at the very beginning of

[23] Cf. Waitz, VIII, 423.
[24] Cf. Pirenne's particularly penetrating description of the situation, *Histoire de Belgique* I, cap. 3.

her regency, she made the princes swear that, in the event
of the early death of her son, they would do nothing to
fill the throne without her consent,[25] her object was probably simply to safeguard her son, and so her action falls
into line with Henry III's earlier proceedings, when he
sought a threefold assurance of his son's succession.[26]
But the abduction of the young Henry at St. Suitbertswert
in 1062 suddenly threw a vivid light on the political situation.   There was no resistance from the empress, and none
from princes or people; and, more ominous still, no representative of the national church was found, who would
maintain, like the great bishops of the Carolingian epoch,
the dignity of the crown.   Anno of Cologne and his successors in the control of the young king were egoists, intent
on territorial expansion either by increasing their spiritual
or by extending their secular authority; and for all of them
the royal child was simply an instrument for furthering
their personal ambitions.[27]

This development was the more ominous, in so far as
these very years saw the final emancipation of the Roman
church from imperial and German influence.   Under
Nicholas II (1058—1061) the papacy drew up a new electoral
procedure, which, although intended in the first place only
to secure the independence of papal elections from the
influence of Roman aristocratic factions, also undermined
the position of the German king.   Through the Norman
alliance it acquired a political counterpoise to German
military power, and the popular movement of the Pataria
in Milan provided a social counterpoise to the powerful
episcopal churches of Lombardy.   And finally it obtained
a programme of reform in cardinal Humbert of Silva
Candida's treatise *adversus Simoniacos*, which in pronounc-

   [25] This fact is only known to us from Gregory VII's letter of 3 Sept.,
1076, which is discussed below; but the contents of the oath are not given
and must therefore be inferred from the context.   As to the date at which
the oath was taken, cf. Meyer v. Knonau, *Jahrbücher d. deutschen Reichs
unter Heinrich IV. u. Heinrich V.* I, 15.
   [26] For the period of the empress's regency, see Appendix I in Meyer
v. Knonau, v. I.   Here also the meagreness of our information is obvious.
   [27] Adalbert of Bremen denied this, so far as he was concerned; but
cf. his attitude towards the expedition to Rome, planned for 1065.

ing every grant of an ecclesiastical office by the laity or to the laity to be simony, declared war both on the theory and on the practice of the Ottonian and the Salian monarchy. If there was resistance to these tendencies at the German court, it is noteworthy that it originated no longer in the German church, but with the " rectores aulae regiae " or " aulici administratores ", a group only known to us from the remarks of opponents and therefore difficult to define as regards either composition or activity;[28] but it is clear that the group was not strong enough to support the Lombard bishops in their resistance to the papacy. On the contrary, the papacy made still further progress during the pontificate of Alexander II (1061—1073), and already there appeared in the background, as the guiding spirit, the monk Hildebrand, who had once accompanied Gregory VI into exile in Germany, and had perhaps imbibed in German reform circles the very ideas which made him a radical opponent of Frankish theocracy.[29]

Such was the situation in 1065, when Henry IV attained his majority and then, a year later—robbed of his adviser, Adalbert, by the jealousy of the princes—began his personal rule. His character has been so distorted by partisan statements that we can no longer delineate it with absolute certainty. But it is at once evident that he was a man who came early to maturity and was endowed throughout his life with extraordinary talents. The violent changes in his upbringing and the humiliations which he then suffered, no doubt taught him to don the " courtier's cloak of invisibility ", which was to serve him well on more than one occasion in his later life; but he brought with him to the throne the firm will of a ruler—a ruler, it may be added, less of his father's build than like his grandfather, Conrad II.[30]

[28] On the events of 1060, which we have here in mind, cf. App. VIII in Meyer v. Knonau, v. I.

[29] There is an admirable survey of the ecclesiastical developments summarized here, in Hampe, *Deutsche Kaisergeschichte im Zeitalter der Salier u. Staufer* (1st ed.), 32 sqq.

[30] For a character-sketch and appreciation of Henry IV, cf. the Appendices in Richter, *Annalen d. deutschen Gesch. im Mittelalter*, part III, v. I (1890): (1) " The character of the king according to the judgement of contemporaries," (2) " Historical and critical appreciation."

KARL WILHELM NITZSCH, to whom we owe not only the most remarkable but also—even in its errors—the most instructive history of the Salian period, described Henry IV's place in German constitutional development in these terms: " he began his reign as a revolutionary, attacking the old constitution: he finished as its last and almost its sole defender." The revolutionising of the old constitution is seen by NITZSCH in Henry's attempts to create in the Harz a permanent centre for his government. From this centre he hoped to use the resources of the silver mines at Goslar; to bring the Saxons into subjection by building castles manned by Swabian *ministeriales*; and finally to increase the immediate demesne of the monarchy by a general resumption of crown lands. " Henry's early plans for the establishment of a stronger monarchy," says NITZSCH in another place, " would almost certainly have been accepted throughout Germany, if they could have been brought to a successful conclusion at the beginning of his reign. In that case," he continues, " continental Saxony would have been defeated in the same decade in which the Normans conquered the insular Saxons in England; and from that time, without doubt, we should also date the beginnings of an improved governmental organisation in Germany and a new concentration of German national powers,instead of their decline and transformation." It is, of course, another question whether Henry really pursued so conscious and systematic a policy, and what his final objects were. About questions such as this argument will always, in our present state of knowledge, be possible;[31] and any judgement will, in the last analysis, depend on acceptance or rejection of NITZSCH's views. NITZSCH, we have seen, regarded Henry's policy as revolutionary: for HAMPE, on the other hand, it was reactionary and directed solely to restoring the ancient rights of the crown. Yet HAMPE himself drew attention to the analogy of the French monarchy, which built up its power from its base in the Ile de France; and Henry IV's object was precisely the

[31] For the different opinions, cf. App. III amd IV in Meyer v. Knonau, vol. II.

creation of another Ile de France in what was later to be the very heart of Germany, though in this case it was not built out of the old hereditary demesnes of the royal family, but was the beginning of a new crown territory in the colonized lands. The position was no different at a later date when the Hohenstaufen linked up their castles and demesnes in a continuous chain from Alsace to the Egerland, and then, not content with this, reached out to Lombardy, Tuscany and finally Sicily, or when the Habsburg and Luxemburg dynasties moved the centre of their power from western Germany to the colonial lands of the east. In each case the basic cause was the same: the poverty of the crown demesnes and the endeavour of the monarchy to provide itself with a ministerial personnel and with a permanent revenue.[32] This presupposes that the Ottonian constitution no longer satisfied either of these needs, but it presupposes also that there was in existence a group which regarded the satisfaction of these needs by new methods as possible. Such a group we have every reason, with NITZSCH, to see in the *ministeriales*.[33] They are possibly the same class as the *aulici administratores* who had loomed so large during the regency of Agnes, and are certainly identical with the *familiares* and *vilissimi homines* mentioned by Lambert of Hersfeld, of whose influence over Henry our authorities complain. They began at this period to play a major rôle in the development of the German state, and were destined to become a decisive factor under the Hohenstaufen.

This first attempt of the German monarchy to stabilize its position, both territorially and economically, only became a really important factor in determining the actual course of constitutional development when it came face to face with the opposition of the Saxon folk—the race which, above all others, still embodied the old Germanic

---

[32] Cf. what I have said in my book, *Vom deutschen Volk zum deutschen Staat. Eine Geschichte des deutschen Nationalbewusstseins* (2nd ed.), 16 sqq.

[33] For a critical survey of the questions regarding the *ministeriales* cf. F. Keutgen, " Die Entstehung d. deutschen Ministerialität," *Vierteljahrschr. f. Sozial- u. Wirtschaftsgesch.* VIII.

spirit of freedom and kept alive the Germanic conception
of law. Incidental though it may be, it is very characteristic of the profound antitheses which were at play that the
crown under Henry IV set out to recover its actual or
supposed rights through the procedure of the Frankish
inquisition, while the Saxons countered royal claims by
their own ancient law of possession, the basis of which
was seisin witnessed by the community.

But the Saxons soon broadened the basis of their opposition. The revolt with which they replied in 1073 to the
crown's threats of confiscation, brought into prominence,
for the first time in German history, the problem of the
ancient Germanic *Widerstandsrecht*, the question of the
right to rebel and of legitimate resistance not merely to a
particular ruler but also to the crown as such.[34] The
significance of this legal concept in the constitutional development of western Europe has recently been brilliantly
explained by FRITZ KERN.[35] In Saxony the immediate
basis of the right to rebel was that specifically Germanic
conception of right which we have discussed above[36]—
the view that a right is a claim which is established either
by the good-faith of the claimant alone or by witnesses
and the general belief of the neighbourhood.[37] A convic-
tion of the legitimacy of their cause was therefore regarded
as in itself an ample justification for the Saxon revolt,
which was simply lawful or even necessary self-help against
wrong. The first object of the Saxons was to regain their
ancient rights; and whether they hoped to attain other
objects by their rising, whether in particular they had
already conceived the idea of deposing Henry, are questions
which remain uncertain in our present state of knowledge.[38]

[34] Waitz, *Verf.-gesch.* VI, 497.
[35] Cf. the translation of his book, *Gottesgnadentum u. Widerstandsrecht*,
in this series under the title: *Kingship, Law and Constitution in the Middle
Ages.*
[36] Cf. *supra*, 101—102.
[37] Cf. Kern, *Gottesgnadentum*, 183 sqq. and particularly p. 346.
[38] I am less inclined than Kern, 198 sqq., to regard Lambert of Hersfeld's narrative as a true expression of Saxon opinion. All Lambert's
references to " regno privare," in particular, are suspect. The outlook of
the Saxons seems to me to be much more clearly expressed in Bruno's
De Bello Saxonico, where even in the famous speech of Otto of Nordheim

For we, like the contemporaries who recorded the events, can only see the Saxon revolt through the medium of the greater struggle with which it was so inextricably bound up: the Investiture Contest. At the very moment when Henry had defeated the Saxons and forced them to come to terms, he found himself face to face with a mightier adversary still, the papacy of Gregory VII, which grasped the opportunity to press its demands on the German church and on the German monarchy.

It is not my purpose to argue the question whether or not the German monarchy was forced to regard such demands at such a time as a declaration of war. That it was possible to come to an understanding on the question of investiture, even with a papacy imbued with Gregorian ideas, was proved by the outcome of the contest. That Gregory, even in 1075, was seeking some such understanding is at least likely. It is possible to conceive of an arrangement by which the German crown, its power based on its newly-acquired demesnes which could be converted to the uses of a money economy, and on the energies of the *ministeriales* and of the urban classes in the towns of the Rhineland, who were just entering into the political field, might have played the part assigned to it in Gregory's wide-reaching programme of world-policy: the German king, in other words, acting as advocate and protector of the church in Germany and Italy, while the pope led the church's *militia* to the Holy Land.[39] If such a plan were to be realized, however, it would have been necessary for Henry to put himself at the pope's disposal in purging the German church of simoniacs and incontinent clerks; he would have had to abandon the Lombard church politically

at Wormsleben (cap. 2), which was composed under the impress of later events (cf. Meyer v. Knonau, II, 243) the old conception of fealty is still allowed to emerge: " Dum mihi rex erat *et ea, quae sunt regis*, faciebat, fidelitatem quam ei iuravi, integram et impollutam servavi: postquam vero rex esse desinit, cui fidem deberem, non fuit." Still more typical, however, is the enumeration of individual grievances which follows in the next chapter.—The *Carmen de bello Saxonico*, v. 30 sqq., no doubt comes nearest of all our authorities to the conception of law actually held both by the king and by the Saxons.

[39] Cf. Gregory's letter of 7 December, 1074, to Henry, in Jaffé, *Bibliotheca rerum Germanicarum* II, 144.

and the German church at least administratively and
probably also financially. If he perhaps considered this
possibility for a moment,[40] there were no tangible results.
Exalted by his success in Saxony, he once again united
his cause with that of the German bishops, whom Gregory
was threatening, and took up arms in defence of his position
in Lombardy. When, on 8 December, 1075, Gregory
threatened him with the fate of Saul, he opened the struggle
by assembling the German episcopacy at the synod of
Worms on 27 January 1076. Then follow like the blows
of a sledgehammer the great manifestos of the two parties:
at Worms, the deposition of Gregory or rather the declaration by the king in his capacity as *patricius urbis Romanae*
and by the assembled bishops that Gregory's election was
invalid; at the Lenten synod in Rome the pope's reply,
the suspension of Henry from government[41] and his
excommunication; then the king's attempt to reply to
this excommunication with the excommunication of the
pope in an assembly of German bishops held at Mainz
on the feast of St. Peter and St. Paul; next the first defections of German clergy and laity from Henry, the junction
of the south German and Saxon oppositions and the forging
of a connexion between both and the papacy; the arrangements between Henry and the German princes at Tribur
and Oppenheim in October, by which the king was enjoined
to free himself from excommunication within four months
if he wished to keep the crown; Henry's journey to Canossa
and success in obtaining absolution; and finally the election of Rudolf of Swabia as anti-king at Forchheim on
15 March, 1077. Within this circle of incidents are enclosed
the events which irrevocably altered the constitution of
Germany for its entire future.

[40] For the negotiations in the summer and autumn of 1075, cf. Meyer
v. Knonau, II, 562 sqq.
[41] It will be seen later why—contrary to the view of the majority of
modern writers—I follow Ranke in maintaining that the words: " Hen-
rico . . . totius regni Teutonicorum et Italiae gubernacula contradico,"
mean suspension and not deposition. For the opinions of historians, cf.
Meyer v. Knonau, II, 640 n. 32, and Richter, 207.

We begin with the document which, according to RANKE,[42] was a decisive factor in the German situation: Gregory's letter of 3 September 1076 to his lay and clerical supporters in Germany.[43] It belongs to the second stage in the German crisis. Four months previously Gregory had still found it necessary to combat the doubts which those to whom this letter was addressed had felt as to the legality of Henry's excommunication.[44] Now he had to reply to the enquiry of the same parties, asking what was to happen to the excommunicated king. But the letter of 3 September belongs also to the second stage in the development of the ideas with which Gregory himself had entered the struggle. When he attacked Henry at the Lenten synod in Rome, he regarded the king's faults as those of a simoniacal bishop, and so he had suspended him for his attack on Holy Church, just as he suspended bishops who acted contrary to the canons.[45] " Dignum est enim, ut qui studet honorem ecclesiae tuae imminuere, ipse honorem amittat, quem videtur habere." Henry's offence, in other words, was a disciplinary offence, which was met by disciplinary punishment. Excommunication, on the other hand, struck at disobedience against divine law, at the abettor of simoniacs, the obstinate violator of the moral code. It was only this second part of his sentence which Gregory had thought it necessary to justify in his first letter to his German supporters. For him also, in this first stage, the only question was to secure Henry's repentance—" si voluerit resipiscere " — and if this could be obtained, the suspension of the

[42] *Weltgesch.* VII, 274.

[43] *Reg. Gregorii* IV, 3 (ed. Jaffé, *op. cit.*, 248 sqq., and re-edited in 1920 by Caspar, *Das Register Gregors VII*, 297 sqq.). Like most of the other documents to which we shall refer, this letter is also printed by E. Bernheim, *Quellen z. Gesch. d. Investiturstreits*, part I.

[44] Jaffé, 535 sqq., Bernheim, 73 (No. 20); cf. M. Doeberl in the *Programm d. Ludwigsgymnasiums München*, 1890–1.

[45] Cf. for example the proceedings against Otto of Constance (Meyer v. Knonau, II, 642): he is suspended in 1075 because he has maliciously acted against God and apostolic precept, and is deposed and excommunicated at the Lenten synod in 1076 on account of his participation in the synod of Worms.

king from his royal office would, we may conclude, be raised.[46]

By September things had changed. The political effects of the sentence of excommunication had immediately become manifest. The south German dukes and a number of bishops broke away from Henry. Gregory's prohibition of intercourse with an excommunicated person, which released the princes from their oath of fealty and from all duties to the king, was a sufficient excuse for princely egoism as well as for Christian conscientiousness, and the Saxon revolt burst out anew, led by the Saxon nobles who had been freed from the custody of the bishop of Metz, and by Otto of Nordheim, whose reconciliation with Henry had only been superficial. And in this revolt the Germanic conception of the right of resistance was combined with the incomparably more fully developed ecclesiastical theory.[47] Ecclesiastical theory had a definite name for the ruler who had overstepped the law: he was the *tyrannus*. Such is the attitude to Henry which is predominant throughout the historical work of Lambert of Hersfeld. Against the tyrant, however, there was not merely the old remedy of a withdrawal of obedience and self-help, but there was also a formal judicial procedure which, like all ecclesiastical proceedings, was purely declaratory in character:[48] it imposed neither penance nor punishment, but simply declared that the king was no longer king. Though Gregory himself perhaps did nothing directly to spread this view, clerical propaganda and the Gregorian pamphlets which suddenly appeared in ever-increasing numbers familiarized the German princes and bishops with the new conception, and the latter eagerly availed themselves of it. But for Gregory also the whole affair had now assumed a

[46] It is not necessary to conclude (with Meyer v. Knonau, II, 701 n. 129) from the phrase: "semper tamen nos ad recipiendum eum in sanctam communionem, prout vestra caritas nobis consuluerit, paratos inveniet," that the pope had any intention of allowing the German princes to play any part in the matter: it is only an invitation to them to help in converting Henry.—The clearest account of the development of Gregory's designs is that of Rodenberg in his review of the second volume of Meyer v. Knonau's *Jahrbücher* in the *Deutsche Literaturzeitung*, 1895, col. 1289.

[47] Cf. Kern, 65 sqq., 203 sqq.

[48] *Ibid.*, 234.

different complexion: side by side with its ecclesiastical implications, the political aspects had come into the foreground. Henry, he argues, is under the church's ban and thereby he is deprived of his dignity, " anathematis vinculo alligatus et a regia dignitate depositus." Righteousness forbids that he should remain king, " iustitia eum regnare prohibet." The people, on the other hand, which had hitherto been subject to his rule, was now free from every duty towards him, " omnis populus quondam sibi subiectus a vinculo iuramenti eidem promissi sit absolutus "—in other words, the threefold undertaking which Henry III had imposed on the German magnates on behalf of his son, was annulled.

Thus in the proceedings against Henry the immediate question was still to devise measures which would induce him to change his ways and to submit to the church. But the question whether such a submission, if made, could be regarded as sufficiently sincere to justify absolution from excommunication, was reserved by Gregory for his own decision—a decision in which no human considerations, neither hope of advantage nor fear of harm, were to play any part, but justice alone which is divine.[49] If Henry's conversion was not sincere (ex corde), then it would be necessary to elect a Christian king, who would undertake to perform those things for the Christian religion and for the realm which could no longer be expected from Henry; and the way was now prepared for proceeding to this final step, since the German princes were no longer bound by their oath to the king.[50] Such at any rate was the view

[49] Such, I believe, is the meaning of the passage: " De diversorum quidem diversis consiliis dubitamus, et humanam gratiam vel timorem suspicioni habemus." Meyer v. Knonau's translation (II, 722) is no more comprehensible than the text. Giesebrecht (III, 382) considers that consilia may refer to proposals for a new election; but the pope is not speaking of this at this stage in his letter. That the antithesis to humana gratia vel timor is the Augustinian conception of justice (aequum ac Deo placitum) is indicated by Gregory's letter of 25 August to Hermann of Metz (Reg. IV, 2, ed. Caspar, 293 sqq.) where we already read: " Non enim nos latet, quod sint aliqui vestrum, qui . . . timore vel humana gratia seducti presumpserunt eum . . . absolvere. . . . Quibus si aliqui re vera episcopi contradicerent, non eos iustitiam defendere sed inimicitias exercere iudicarent."
[50] For the following cf. K. Brandi, " Erbrecht und Wahlrecht," HZ. CXXIII, 221 sqq.

of the pope. But it was not quite the position adopted
by the German princes. They had not forgotten the
earlier oath which they had rendered to the empress Agnes,
and which defined the position in the event of Henry's
premature death.[51] This oath remained valid, even if the
oatɥs to Henry were relaxed, and it must have disturbed
German consciences seriously, for the pope thought it
necessary to appease them. This oath also, he maintained,
had now no further significance;[52] for whether Agnes
assented to the dethronement of her son or not, the consequences, he said, were clear.[53] What were the consequences,
however ? The pope does not specify them, but they can
nevertheless be defined with some degree of certainty. If
the empress's views played any part in the question of
deposition, then it was clear that the princes' right of free
election was limited by considerations of hereditary right.
In face of the well-established rights of blood, the Germanic
conception of legitimate resistance had, in actual fact,
halted undecided,[54] and we can see that the opposition of
1076 also stopped short at this point. On the other hand,
it was an essential precondition of the papal theory of
royal election that the electors' freedom to depose an unworthy ruler should be unlimited. In Gregory's view,
moreover, the election of a German king was carried out
exactly like an episcopal election, as defined in canon law.[55]
The princes, in his view, had the right of freely electing the
new ruler; but they had then to send the pope official
intimation of the election in order that he might examine
both the electoral proceedings, the person elected and his
moral suitability, and confirm the princes' choice by apos-

[51] Cf. *supra*, 108.
[52] " Non est opus adhuc dubitare." Meyer v. Knonau translates
adhuc as " besides ", but that is impossible: the only doubt is whether it
means " until now " or " from now onwards."
[53] " Quia, si nimia pietate circa filium ducta iustitiae restiterit, vel
iustitiae favens, ut abiciatur a regno consenserit—quid restet, vos ipsi
comprehenditis." For the translation of *restare*, cf. *Reg.* IV. 2: " Nam
qui se negat non posse ecclesiae vinculo alligari, restat, ut neget se non
posse ab eius potestate absolvi."
[54] Cf. Kern, 203.
[55] This is well emphasized by F. Redlich, *Die Absetzung deutscher
Könige durch den Papst* (1892), 21 sqq.

tolic authority. Gregory deduced these rights from the fact that it fell to him to place the imperial crown on the head of the elected king and thus to give permanent effect to the election.[56] In case the electors wished to hear the views of the empress, however, let them ask *both her and the pope* for advice *after* a candidate had been proposed. " Tunc aut nostro *communi* consilio assensum praebebit aut apostolicae sedis auctoritas omnia vincula, quae videntur iustitiae contradicere, removebit." The meaning is clear: hand in hand with the empress, the pope is going to push his way into the electoral proceedings at an even earlier stage than normal procedure would allow. Thus the way is prepared which leads directly to the famous declaration of Innocent III that the disposal of the German throne is *principaliter et finaliter* a matter for the Holy See. The essential presupposition, however, on which this conception is based, is that the German monarchy is a purely electoral monarchy, in which regard is paid neither to rights of blood nor to rights of heredity.[57]

The historical significance of Henry IV's reign lies in the fact that he took up arms against this development. Not merely after Canossa and after the election of the anti-

[56] The important words are: " Ut autem vestram electionem—si valde oportet, ut fiat—apostolica auctoritate firmemus et novam ordinationem nostris temporibus corroboremus, sicut a sanctis nostris patribus factum esse cognoscimus, negotium personam et mores eius, quamtocius potestis, nobis indicate: ut sancta et utili intentione incedentes, mereamini, sicut nobis notae causae, apostolicae sedis favorem per divinam gratiam et beati Petri apostolorum principis per omnia benedictionem."—Meyer v. Knonau's translation is useless at all points, and Giesebrecht also (p. 383) has failed to express the technical terms with precision. For a correct interpretation cf. Waitz, *Verf.-gesch.* VI, 237 n. 2, and Bresslau, " Zur Gesch. d. deutschen Königswahlen," *Deutsche Zeitschr. f. Geschichtswissenschaft, Neue Folge* II, 140 n. 1; cf. also E. Engelmann, *Der Anspruch d. Päpste auf Konfirmation u. Approbation bei d. deutschen Königswahlen* (1886), 9.—I understand *nostris temporibus* by analogy with *suo tempore*, and relate it to the imperial coronation, with which the pope will proceed " at his own time ". In the usual interpretation (*nostra tempora* contrasted with *a patribus factum*) it is impossible to say what *facta patrum* are meant (for the example of Pippin does not correspond), and it is implied that *corroborare ordinationem* is a tautology for *firmare electionem*, which cannot be correct since *ordinatio* and *electio* are not the same.

[57] Cf. Kern, 67 n. 115, on Innocent III's decretal *Venerabilem*: " Change of the ruling line is thereby raised into a principle of the constitution. The entire fate of Germany—to degenerate into an electoral state, instead of attaining, like the monarchies of the west, a stabilisation of the kingship in one dynasty—is implicit in Innocent's words."

king at Forchheim, but immediately. In the manifestos issued at Worms and Utrecht, in his acts of government before the fateful meetings at Tribur and Oppenheim, he defends his inheritance, the Frankish conception of monarchy—the hereditary monarchy,[58] the monarchy by divine right, the monarchy which is consecrated like the priestly office and can therefore rule the latter, which stands in that relation to the *sacerdotium* as a whole which Alcuin once formulated, in the name of Charles the Great, in the famous letter to Leo III. And even at Oppenheim, when the defection of the majority of his supporters, particularly the German episcopacy, forced him to seek an understanding with pope and princes, Henry's pride in his kingship rose up and he made still a further attempt to maintain his position, if not in his relations with the princes, at least in his struggle with the pope.[59] How much of all this is to be attributed to Henry personally, how much to the measures of his advisers, it is no longer possible to decide. Nevertheless we can distinguish three groups in which what we have called the Frankish conception of the monarchy was particularly strong: first, Henry's lay intimates, those very *vilissimi homines* on whom anti-royal writers and even

---

[58] For opinions of writers of the Salian period in support of the view that Germany is an hereditary monarchy, cf. F. Ohly, *Königtum u. Fürsten z. Zeit Heinrichs IV (Jahresbericht Lemgo, 1888–89 and 1890–91) I, 7 sqq. and II, 3 sqq. On the question as a whole, cf. Waitz, VI, 161 sqq.
[59] I refer here to Henry's so-called " declaration of obedience " to Gregory (MG. *Const.* I, 114), regarding which critical and methodical issues are in an almost hopeless state of confusion.—According to the only useful authority, the so-called Swabian Annalist (MG. *Script.* V, 286), this declaration contained in its original form, as defined at Tribur, an acknowledgement of *debita oboedientia, satisfactio* and *poenitentia* (cf. *infra*, n. 61). But this genuine declaration, we are told, was found to have been altered (*alterata et per loca mutata*) on the way to Rome, so that the *materia* was now *longe alia*. The text which we possess falls into three parts: the first contains a promise of *oboedientia* and *satisfactio*, the second of *poenitentia*, but the third demands that the pope also shall purge himself of the accusations levelled against him. It is clear that this cannot be the form agreed on and sealed in Tribur; and if it is that which was read in Rome, it must have been fabricated by changes in and additions to the genuine copy. I accept this view, though without entering into the various hypotheses which have been made as to the nature of the genuine text. The originator of the forgery is certainly not to be sought among Henry's opponents (as Hauck maintains), but was either the king himself or his chancery—or was it, perhaps, the bishop of Piacenza, who held up the imperial ambassadors for so long on their way to Rome ?

the pope himself laid responsibility not only for Henry's obstinacy but also for his moral transgressions, then the Chancery, among the staff of which at least one personality stands out clearly,[60] and finally the Lombard church, which acted while people in Germany were talking. All these forces were to be important in the subsequent course of the struggle, though the first two groups only attained to full significance under the Hohenstaufen. For the moment they were too weak to maintain the monarchical principle, and Henry was therefore forced to enter into the agreement with the hostile princes at Tribur and Oppenheim, by which he promised the pope obedience, satisfaction and penance for his misdeeds, and acknowledged his suspension from government until the pope had made a final decision and he himself was again reconciled with the church.[61]

[60] I.e., the notary "Adalbero C.", whose activities have been revealed by Gundlach's work, *Ein Diktator aus der Kanzlei Heinrichs IV*. It is particularly noteworthy that he worked with Carolingian formulae. The documents attributed to him can conveniently be found by reference to the index in Meyer v. Knonau, vol. V, *s. v.* "Adalbero C.".

[61] Recent research again indicates that the account of the so-called Swabian Annalist can alone be accepted as a sure basis for reconstructing the course of the negotiations at Tribur and Oppenheim; cf. Meyer v. Knonau, *Jahrb.* II, App. 6, Richter, *Annalen*, 220 sqq., Hampe, *Kaisergesch.*, 50. The important words in this account (MG. *Script.* V, 286) are: " rex cessisse se quam vix simulavit, non modo papae, verum quoque regni principibus in cunctis, quaecumque ipsi imponere et observare eum voluissent. Tunc visum est eis . . . ut ab excommunicatis suis se rex omnino separaret nec non litteras papae Gregorio, debitum oboedientiam, satisfactionem et dignam poenitentiam se servaturum firmiter intimantes, absque mora dirigeret, ipse autem iuxta consilium eorum interim manendo responsum apostolicum et reconciliationem illius exspectaret." According to the Annalist's account, the princes acted throughout exactly in accordance with the papal programme of 3 September. They first offered the king a meeting (possibly on the Madenburg near Speyer) in order to negotiate with him on the terms by which reconciliation with the pope might be obtained and his own rule continued. When Henry then appeared with armed forces at Oppenheim, the princes regarded this as *contumacia*, halted on the right bank of the Rhine near Tribur, and took counsel regarding a new election. The agreement between king and princes, which followed, was a result of defections among the royal party and of the mediation of Hugh of Cluny, acting on the orders of the empress and of Beatrix, marchioness of Tuscany. Its contents correspond to the directions which the pope had previously issued: the king was to await the pope's decision whether the royal offer of *satisfactio* and *poenitentia* was adequate. In the meantime, everything else was to remain under reservation. That the princes, because of their distrust of Henry, then decided " ut si in culpa sua ultra annum excommunicatus perduraret, ipsi eum ulterius regem non haberent," no more altered the constitutional situation than the confed-

Such a reconciliation was achieved at Canossa. But Henry obtained nothing further. If he was striving after more—and it seems probable that he wished to combine his absolution with a settlement of political issues[62]—he was unsuccessful. When Gregory, not without very understandable repugnance, granted absolution, he expressly separated from the question of spiritual reconciliation the issues between the king and the German princes. His report to the princes[63] on these matters is diplomatically correct from beginning to end, and his conduct throughout is consistent. He had merely returned to the attitude expressed in the proclamation of excommunication at the Lenten synod at Rome: Henry had promised obedience and done penance, he was thereby reconciled with the church and was again king. But he remained suspended from the exercise of his royal rights until he had afforded *satisfactio* for his transgression of the canons, while the settlement of his differences with the German princes was referred to special proceedings, in which—whether the solemnity of the law or informal arbitration was preferred— the pope himself was to be *cognitor*,[64] exactly as in the procedure for the eventual election of a new king which had been outlined in the letter of 3 September.

What Gregory had now conceded, therefore, was · a judicial enquiry instead of the election of a new ruler— and this, we are justified in believing, with the object of restoring the penitent king. But it was precisely this change which led the German princes to break with the

eracy they entered into as a precaution against royal vengeance or their invitation to the pope to come to Augsburg on 6 January and decide the quarrel—on the contrary, the confederacy points to the conclusion that they were reckoning on Henry remaining king.

[62] There would be no doubts about this, if we possessed the offer which Hugh of Cluny, Adelaide of Turin and Matilda of Tuscany delivered to the pope in Henry's name; but this important document is unfortunately missing.

[63] Jaffé, *Bibliotheca* II, 545; Bernheim, *Quellen*, No. 36; cf. Meyer v. Knonau, *Jahrb.* III, App. 1.

[64] Cf. the *Promissio Canusina* (Caspar, 314—315): " infra terminum, quem dominus papa Gregorius constituerit, aut *iustitiam* secundum *iudicium* eius aut *concordiam* secundum *consilium* eius faciam." The expression *cognitor*, later used technically for the examiner of an election, is in Lambert; cf. Bernheim, 91 (l. 14).

pope. They had regarded Henry's secret flight from Speyer to Italy as a breach of the agreement he had made with them at Tribur, and this alone, they considered, was sufficient legal justification for appointing another prince to the German throne. For this purpose they met, on 13 March 1077, at Forchheim, the traditional Frankish site for royal elections.

We have two principal accounts of the election of the anti-king at Forchheim. The one, which gives the official version of the proceedings and no doubt represents a manifesto of Rudolf of Swabia's party, appears in two derivative forms, the so-called Swabian Annals and Paul of Bernried's biography of Gregory VII; the other is found in Bruno's history of the Saxon war.[65] In the former account the course of events is depicted as follows: those lay and clerical princes who had put in an appearance—they were mainly Saxons and Swabians, in other words, the partisans of Otto of Nordheim and Rudolf of Rheinfelden, together with Frankish, Bavarian and Saxon bishops under the leadership of archbishop Siegfried of Mainz, who had played the part of leader of the clerical opposition since his defection from Henry, and now appeared as the real kingmaker—brought forward and prosecuted an indictment of Henry. To the papal legate, who revealed to them the pope's desire for a postponement of the election, they emphasized the fact that such a course was out of the question. The pope himself, they said, had forbidden them to obey Henry in the proceedings against the king at the Lenten synod,[66] and the situation thus created was in no way altered when Gregory absolved Henry at Canossa; on the contrary, the dissolution of the realm could only be prevented by the immediate election of a new king. A list was also incidentally[67] drawn up of the infringements of the law which private individuals ascribed to the king. The result was

---

[65] Cf. Meyer v. Knonau, *Jahrb.* III, App. 1, and on the authorities, *ibid.*, 628 n. 4.

[66] " Quia papa, ne ut regi oboedirent aut servirent, ipsis iam interdixerit."—The word *servire* is used in a technical sense, and means " to perform the *servitia.*"

[67] The reports leave the chronological order uncertain.

124 P. JOACHIMSEN

that Henry was deposed and deprived of his royal title.
Then followed the preliminary discussions in the palace
of the archbishop of Mainz about the person to be elected
in Henry's place. Clergy and laity deliberated separately;
the clergy directed the choice to Rudolf; the archbishop
of Mainz read the electoral decree;[68] the electors gave their
assent and the people likewise. After he had declared that
he claimed no hereditary right and that the crown was to
remain on his death at the free disposal of the electors,[69]
the assembly swore fealty to Rudolf. This occurred on
15 March; and on 26 March the new king was consecrated
at Mainz.

As contrasted with this report, Bruno is able to add a few
further particulars. According to him, the archbishop of
Mainz's announcement of Rudolf's nomination was followed
by a series of events which he describes in the following
words:[70]

At cum singuli deberent eum regem laudare, quidam
voluerunt aliquas conditiones interponere, ut hac lege
eum super se levarent regem, quatinus sibi de suis
iniuriis specialiter promitteret satisfactionem. Otto
namque dux non prius volebat eum sibi regem constitu-
ere, nisi promitteret honorem sibi iniuste ablatum restitu-
ere. Sic et alii multi suas singulares causas interponunt,
quas ut ille se correcturum promitteret volunt. Quod
intelligens apostolicus legatus fieri prohibuit, et osten-
dens eum non singulorum sed universorum fore regem,
ut universis iustum se promitteret, satis esse perhibuit.
Ait enim, si eo modo, quo coeptum fuerat, promissionibus
singillatim praemissis eligeretur, ipsa electio non sincera
sed haeresis simoniacae veneno polluta videretur. Tamen
quaedam sunt ibi causae specialiter exceptae, quas quia
iniuste viguerant, deberet emendare; scilicet ut episco-

[68] Cf. U. Stutz, *Der Erzbischof v. Mainz u. die deutsche Königswahl.*
[69] " Qui [*sc.* Rudolfus] utique regnum non ut proprium, sed pro
dispensatione sibi creditum reputans, omne haereditarium ius in eo repud-
iavit et vel filio suo se hoc adaptaturum fore penitus abnegavit; iustissime
in arbitrio principum esse decernens, ut post mortem eius libere non magis
filium eius quam alium eligerent, nisi quem ad id culminis aetate et morum
gravitate dignum invenissent."
[70] *Brunonis de bello Saxonico liber*, cap. 91.

patus non pro pretio nec pro amicitia daret, sed unicuique ecclesiae de suis electionem, sicut iubent canones, permitteret. Hoc etiam ibi consensu communi comprobatum, Romani pontificis auctoritate est corroboratum, ut regia potestas nulla per hereditatem, sicut antea fuit consuetudo, cederet, sed filius regis, etiam si valde dignus esset, potius per electionem spontaneam quam per successionis lineam rex proveniret; si vero non esset dignus regis filius, vel si nollet eum populus, quem regem facere vellet, haberet in potestate populus. His omnibus legaliter constitutis Rodulfum electum regem Mogontiam cum magno honore deducunt, et ei, dum consecrationem regis accipiebat, venerabiliter et fortiter, sicut mos apparebat, assistunt.

Historians have cast doubt on this account, and have even wished to reject it entirely;[71] and yet it contains the very information which enables us to comprehend the full significance of the Investiture Contest in German constitutional history. The issue is not merely that the German monarchy now becomes for the first time a purely elective monarchy, and that this, in the view of the electors, is to remain a basic principle of the constitution.[72] What is at issue is rather the whole conception of what constitutes the realm; and here, in this statement of Bruno, a novel conception is formulated through a characteristic combination of Germanic and ecclesiastical ideas.

The combination of Germanic and ecclesiastical ideas had already played some part in Henry IV's deposition by the princes. As the pope, to their astonishment, had kept strictly to the path indicated in his manifesto of 3 September, and had set justice above all else, the princes made good the lack of ecclesiastical grounds for attacking Henry by drawing up a list of the wrongs which they had severally

---

[71] For the views of earlier writers, cf. Richter, *Annalen*, 253.

[72] There is no real contradiction in the fact that the official account, on which Paul of Bernried's narrative is based, announces this as a (voluntary) concession by Rudolf, whereas Bruno speaks of it as a " finding " of the electors, confirmed by the pope (or his representatives); at most it is characteristic that what in reality was a precondition of the election, was made to appear, in the official account, as a concession freely granted by the new king.

suffered at his hands. Henry was no longer their king, because he had assailed the concrete rights of individuals. For he had been king over each individual, bound separately to each as each was bound to him by the bond of fealty, and the breach of this bond was itself a sufficient justification for resistance. In the minds of those whose opinions Bruno airs, Rudolf of Rheinfelden was again to be such a king. Before his election he was to confirm or restore each individual's rights. Without doubt it was the lay princes and secular magnates who forced this consideration into the forefront of the electoral negotiations; and foremost among them were the Saxons who had already declared at the elections both of Henry II and of Conrad II that the elected king would only become their king after he had confirmed their rights.[73] But in 1077 they deferred to the views of the papal legate, and changed their attitude, merely asking for an undertaking that Rudolf would be a just king. Such an undertaking might appear at first glance to be no more than a return to the ancient formula in the oath sworn by German kings at their coronation, or more specifically to the oath of 1053. And yet it was more than a return to the old order. Rudolf's oath in 1077 was not merely an assurance granted by the elected ruler because of his consciousness of his royal duties: instead, it was the condition under which he received his authority from the electors. Twenty-nine years later the archbishop of Mainz declared this without ambiguity, when he handed over the imperial insignia to Henry V.[74] And the undertaking itself, which was now an essential condition of election, was no longer merely an engagement to a number of individuals, but was rather a pact with an *universitas*—an *universitas* which represented the realm, just as the realm was now represented by the princes.[75] Such a development followed unmistakably the lines of ecclesiastical thought as laid

[73] Cf. Waitz, *Verf.-gesch.* VI, 205.

[74] He said: " si non iustus regni gubernator exstitisset et ecclesiarum Dei defensator, ut ei sicut patri suo evenisset " (MG. *Script.* III, 110); cf. Kern. 366, and Richter, III. ii, 720 n. 2, together with the passage from Helmold in Kern, 235.

[75] Cf. the remarks in my book, *Der deutsche Staatsgedanke von den Anfängen bis auf Leibniz u. Friedrich d. Grossen*, xiii sqq.

down by Gregory VII. Gregory's famous letter of 3 September 1076, therefore, does not merely foreshadow the earliest electoral capitulation agreed to by a German king —which was one main innovation introduced by Rudolf's election—but it also contains the germ of the idea that the princes as a body constitute the realm. This conception was the basis of Gregory's attack on the hereditary rights of the monarch; and although it may be said that, for the pope, it was only a subsidiary theory which he adopted in order to secure a victory for the even more far-reaching ecclesiastical principle of *idoneitas* in the ruler,[76] there is no denying the fact that his conception of the realm was definitely a conception of the realm as an *universitas* of the princes. For the future development of the German constitution, however, this latter idea was even more important than the electoral principles enunciated by the pope. The view that the German kingdom was an elective monarchy did not become finally prevalent until some two centuries after the election of Rudolf of Rheinfelden; for Henry IV's struggles against the electoral principle were not in vain. He handed on the ancient theory of hereditary monarchy as an inheritance to his son, and the Hohenstaufen took it over from Henry V and defended it with new weapons. The principle that the princes constitute the realm was, on the other hand, the immediate and permanent result of the Investiture Contest. In their corporate capacity as the realm they ranged themselves between Henry V and the pope,[77] and finally brought about the compromise between the two contending parties which is known as the Concordat of Worms.

The development of the conception of a kingdom represented by the princes was inevitable. The ancient Germanic theory of the state, from which both the Germanic duty of fealty and the Germanic right of lawful resistance

[76] On the conception of *idoneitas*, cf. Kern, 55 sqq., amd also Gregory VII's later discussion of the advantages of an elective over an hereditary monarchy, Jaffé, *Bibl.* II, 464. On the constitutional significance of the election at Forchheim, cf. Kern, 155 n. 292.

[77] Cf. the passages quoted by Waitz, VI, 371, and particularly the *Consilium Wirceburgense principum de restituenda pace* (MG. *Const.* I,. 158, No. 106.)

were derived, had its roots in a primitive conception of law and an equally primitive conception of the constitution, both of which have been very improperly idealized. It was as necessary to supersede such primitive ideas as it was necessary to supersede the Germanic law of the proprietary church, in which churches were treated simply as material objects. In this connexion it is not without significance to recall the fact that the papal legates at Forchheim compared the Germanic conception of law, as expressed in the demands of Otto of Nordheim's party, with simony. Just as it was impossible for the latter to persist unchallenged in the face of a more informed understanding of the meaning of the church, so also it was impossible for the former to persist in the face of a more advanced conception of the state. Nor was it a misfortune that this new theory of the state was established in direct opposition to the older authoritarian principles maintained by the Frankish monarchy. Exactly the same clash of principles led to the growth of the constitution both in France and in England, and subsequent developments in Germany under the Hohenstaufen shew that, even in the twelfth century, there was still a possibility of reducing the relationship of ruler and realm to the concrete form of a coherent, organic association, such as was gradually established in the feudal states of western Europe. If the assembly at Forchheim, far from beginning a new phase of constitutional reorganisation in Germany, proved in the light of later developments to be the first germ of disintegration, it was because of the failure to replace the seignorial connexion between crown and people, which had been so magnificently established by Frankish theocracy, by a new corporate association of a governmental character. OTTO GIERKE has shown us how important a part the corporate association has played throughout the course of German history; but however powerfully it may have affected the social life of the whole community or the political life of smaller units, it proved incapable of creating in mediaeval Germany a general German consciousness of a German state based on the feeling of common responsibility for rights and duties. The political education of the German people, leading to the realization that the German empire, if it is to be a true German state, must be based on such a corporate conception of rights and duties, has been both slow and painful. Even to-day, perhaps it is not quite complete.

V

THE CONSTITUTIONAL HISTORY OF THE REFORMED MONASTERIES DURING THE INVESTITURE CONTEST[1]

By HANS HIRSCH

THE term " reformed monasteries " is used to designate all those monasteries which, directly or indirectly, were founded or reformed by Hirsau and St. Blasien in the last decades of the eleventh and the early years of the twelfth centuries. They were mainly concentrated in Swabia and in the adjoining parts of Bavaria, Franconia and Burgundy, but outposts of the great Swabian reform movement reached east as far as Austria and north as far as Saxony and Thuringia.[2] The colourless designation in the title has been adopted because the various names which have been given to these foundations by earlier writers have been selected to indicate the basis of their legal position, and since this question has given rise to a number of divergent points of view, the result has been controversy regarding the appositeness of the terms used.[3] Writers

[1] " Die Verfassung der Reformklöster des Investiturstreites," *Die Klosterimmunität seit dem Investiturstreit. Untersuchungen zur Verfassungsgeschichte des deutschen Reiches und der deutschen Kirche* (Weimar: Hermann Böhlaus Nachfolger, 1913), cap. II (pp. 26—65).—Thanks are due to the publisher for permission to translate.

[2] Cf. Gisecke, *Die Hirschauer während des Investiturstreites*, 97 sqq., and B. Albers in the *Festschrift z. Jubiläum d. deutschen Campo Santo*, 115 sqq.

[3] Fundamental for the question of the constitution of the reformed monasteries were Ficker's works, *Vom Reichsfürstenstande* I, 324 sqq., and " Das Eigentum des Reichs am Reichskirchengut," *Sitz.-berichte d. Wiener Akademie* LXXII, 444 sq. Then followed two monographs on papal protection by Blumenstock and Fabre (*Etude sur le liber censuum*) and fifteen years later, independent and almost contemporary, my " Studien über die Privilegien süddeutscher Klöster," MIÖG. *Erg.-Bd.* VII, and Heilmann, *Die Klostervogtei im rechtsrheinischen Teil der Diözese Konstanz.* Finally G. Schreiber has given all the attention to the question which is implicit in his subject, in his two volumes, *Kurie u. Kloster im 12. Jahrhundert* (*Kirchenrechtliche Abhandlungen*, ed. U. Stutz, Nos. LXV—LXVI) I, 9 sqq., and II, 254 sqq.—As, in what follows, I shall frequently differ from Schreiber, I should like to take this opportunity of emphasizing the versatility and importance of his work.

have rightly spoken of " Roman monasteries," because the grant of papal protection was the real constitutional charter of the militant abbeys of the Investiture Contest; but even more justified is the designation *abbatia libera*, since this term expresses the fact that the foundations in question arose in conscious opposition to the proprietary rights exercised by the laity over churches and monasteries. SCHREIBER, however, has rejected both these terms,[4] and introduced instead the idea of the " papal proprietary monastery " (*päpstliches Eigenkloster*). We shall see later how far such a designation is justified. For the moment it is sufficient to say that SCHREIBER hardly does justice to the usefulness and significance of the expression *abbatia libera*. The term is found not merely in the narrative sources of the period[5] but also in the more important charters of the reform monasteries themselves. The idea of the *locus* or *episcopatus liber* passed from Cluny to Bamberg, and from there it found its way into German royal charters as early as the days of Conrad II and Henry III.[6] Thus Henry III's charter for Pfävers takes over from the immunity granted to Bamberg the words: "sit vero abbatia illius monasterii libera."[7] And FICKER has not only cited other examples of the use of the terms *abbatia libera* and *monasterium liberum*,[8] but has already drawn attention to the passage in the " Casus monasterii Petrishusani " which proves that these words were, in the twelfth century, the term by which the reformed monasteries were ordinarily designated.[9] The monasteries themselves made use of the designation, and FICKER, WERMINGHOFF and HEILMANN have therefore every reason to call them *abbatiae liberae*.

What the reformed monasteries of the Investiture Contest, the *abbatiae liberae*, understood by *libertas* is indicated

---

[4] *Kurie u. Kloster* I, 10.
[5] This alone is admitted by Schreiber (II, 272 n. 3), following Ficker.
[6] Hirsch, *Klosterimmunität*, 19 sqq.
[7] *Ibid.*, 22.
[8] *Vom Reichsfürstenstande* I, 323 sqq.
[9] MG. *Script.* XX, 636: " Alia nempe monasteria, quae libera vocantur, annuatim Romae aureum nummum quinque solidorum pretium habentem persolvere debent. Petrishusensis autem locus neque Romae, neque Constantiae, neque Mogontiae, neque regi neque duci, set nec ulli aliquid debet, nisi tantum regulari vacare religioni."

without ambiguity by their charters and chronicles. Under the heading: " De libertate monasterii," the chronicler of Petershausen emphasizes the fact that his house owes no one tribute or service, neither pope nor emperor nor diocesan: it claims, in other words, unqualified freedom from everyone, God alone excepted.[10] But if this writer gives a strongly theoretical formulation to the idea of *libertas*, the author of the " Acta Murensia " makes clear against whom the movement for independence is primarily directed.[11] With the introductory words: " Nunc autem qualiter iste locus abbatem vel libertatem consecutus est, explicandum est," he begins his description of the reform of Muri, telling how count Werner of Habsburg responded to the wishes of the abbots of Hirsau and Schaffhausen and released the abbey from his control. But when it soon became evident that this surrender meant nothing more, from the point of view of the monks, than the substitution of dependence on the abbey of St. Blasien for the proprietary rights previously exercised by the Habsburgs, the community declared "locum esse liberum, hic debere esse abbatem." Thereupon the abbey received Lütfried as abbot. Liberty, in the sense of the " Acta Murensia," is therefore independence from any proprietor, clerical as well as secular.

The same conception is found in the charters which tell of the reform of the various houses, and foremost of all in the Hirsau charter of 1075, in which Henry IV confirmed the enactments of count Adalbert of Chalw.[12] Here again the words *libertas* and *abbatia libera* are used more than once, and their sense is in no way ambiguous. Adalbert releases

---

[10] *Loc. cit.*: " Nullum sane servitium neque tributum neque vectigal neque legationem neque alicuius omnino ministerii functionem tam Romano pontifici quam imperatori, set neque episcopo Constantiensi, nec alicui personae cuiuscumque potestatis sit aut dignitatis, de hoc monasterio beatus Gebehardus impendere constituit, nisi soli Deo. Propterea et ipse locus usque in presens inviolabilis perseverat, ita ut nullus eam temerare presumat."—Then follows, under the heading: *De censu aliorum monasteriorum*, the passage quoted in the previous note.

[11] *Quellen z. Schweiz. Gesch.* III. iii, 30 sqq.; cf. MIÖG. XXV, 257 sqq., and Steinacker, *Reg. Habs.*, nos. 19—21.

[12] *St.* 2785; cf. also the passage in the *Vita Willihelmi*, MG. *Script.* XII, 212.

the abbey from his proprietary control, places the monastic lands at the free disposal of the abbot, guarantees freedom in electing the abbot and regulates the *advocatia*. The *libertas* of Hirsau is, therefore, its independence, which could only be obtained through a formal act of manumission or delivery by the count of Chalw. As at Bamberg, so at Hirsau, the prototype is the foundation charter of Cluny. NAUDÉ has already pointed this out: in a whole series of important phrases the Hirsau diploma runs parallel with William of Aquitaine's charter for Cluny.[13] The connexion between the Cluniac movement and the reform tendencies of Hirsau was therefore direct. " Cluniacum villam de propria trado dominatione," says duke William:[14] " omni potestate, servitio, iure et proprietate predicti monasterii . . . sese omnino feliciter abdicavit," is the Hirsau charter's account of Adalbert of Chalw's action.

When royal charters of the pre-Gregorian period spoke of *libertas* or, as at Pfävers, of an *abbatia libera*, what was meant, therefore, was that freedom which was provided and guaranteed by membership of the national German church. The *libertas* of the reform monasteries is the conscious negation of the secular *Eigenkirchenrecht* and of all lay domination within the church. The *libertas* of the Hirsau foundations is independence from every secular power. For that reason the owner or founder had to surrender all his hereditary and proprietary rights over the abbey. The surrender took the popular legal form of a delivery of the landed property over the relics of the patron saint in the presence of witnesses.[15] In order to assure the permanence of these renunciations, the opportunity presented by such events as assemblies of lay or clerical

---

[13] *Die Fälschung d. ältesten Reinhardsbrunner Urkunden*, 93 sq.
[14] Cf. also Fabre, *Etude*, 53 sqq.
[15] It is only necessary to cite the most important references. For Hirsau, cf. *Wirtemb. Urkundenbuch* I, 276: " ex toto super altare sancti Aurelii reddidit, delegavit et contradidit domino deo . . . in potestatem et proprietatem." For Alpirsbach, *ibid.* I, 315: " accessit ad reliquias sanctorum et . . . tradidit imprimis super illas ipsum locum." For Muri, cf. *Quellen z. Schweiz. Gesch.* III. iii, 33: " accessit ad primare altare et dimisit locum liberum penitus ac perfecte."

magnates was frequently used to read over and explain the charter of the former proprietary lord or the monastery's own privileges,[16] and even to get a renewal of the declaration of surrender.[17] To put an end to the system of proprietary churches is the prime consideration of the reform movement: in this way the earlier proprietary monasteries were transformed into *abbatiae liberae*— monasteries independent of every form of secular authority.[18]

The liberty of the reformed houses would, however, have been based on a weak foundation, if the monasteries' only safeguard had been the charters announcing the former owners' renunciation. A more effective guarantee was necessary, and this was provided by placing the houses under papal protection. In the form which it had gradually assumed since the ninth century—in Germany since the pontificate of Leo IX—the institution of protection was particularly suited to this purpose. During late Carolingian times, the period of the decline of royal power, papal protection had not only increased in use and in importance, but had also, through conscious imitation of royal forms of protection, been extended in legal scope and effect. The connexion of papal and royal protection is evident in two respects. In the first place, the institution receiving protection entered into a proprietary relationship with the protector and had to pay an annual or periodical tribute as a token of dependence. And in the second place, both royal and papal protection had, by the tenth or eleventh century, the same legal result: each was intended to give the protected house the privilege of immediate dependence, but the grant of the one in no way excluded the grant of

---

[16] Cf. *Quellen z. Schweiz. Gesch.* III. i, 16, for Schaffhausen; *ibid.* III. iii, 33, for Muri; MG. *Script.* X, 82, for Zwiefalten; *Wirt. Urk.-Buch* I, 316, for Alpirsbach.

[17] Cf. MIÖG. *Erg.-Bd.* VII, 487, 523, 532.

[18] Notices referring to renunciations by founders or owners of monasteries have been collected by Fabre in his *Etude*, 76 sqq., and partly also in his edition of the *Liber censuum.* Cf. also Heilmann, *Klostervogtei*, 42, 56 sq., 62, 107 sq. and my studies in the MIÖG. *Erg.-Bd.* VII, 604, where I have described the significance of this first step in the abolition of the *Eigenkirchenrecht* with special reference to St. Georgen in the Black Forest (p. 487), Schaffhausen (p. 521 sqq.) and Alpirsbach (p. 530 sqq.).

the other—in fact, papal protection was intended to supplement and strengthen royal protection.[19]   But it is clear
that, once the church were to set about the task of separating its rights and privileges from secular rights and privileges—once it set out, in other words, on the path of
" Gregorian " reform—papal protection would play a very
different rôle.   By the middle of the eleventh century the
view had already been formulated that the pope was the
ultimate proprietor of all the protected houses.   When
this stage was reached, papal protection at once became
the most effective means of combating the proprietary
rights of the laity within the church; and by suppying a
large number of monasteries with letters of protection,
the Curia created a body of papal monasteries, under its
own direction, which as a group formed an active counterpart to that other body of proprietary monasteries which
depended on the crown and constituted what we to-day
know as the *Reichskirche* or the national church of
Germany.

It was Leo IX who gave this new direction to papal
policy in its relations with the monasteries of southern
Germany.[20]   Under his immediate successors, however,
little further progress was made in the use of papal protection, and Gregory VII's pontificate in particular was too
full of external struggles for him to find time to further
the ecclesiastical cause in this particular sphere of legal
development.[21]   Urban II, on the other hand, shewed
extraordinary skill in making the most, in the practical
field, of the great victories which the papacy had already
won under his immediate predecessors.   The formula in
which his chancery drafted its letters of protection remained the standard for a century; and he issued charters
to a number of south German monasteries[22] which not only

---

[19] We owe these important conclusions to E. E. Stengel, *Immunität
in Deutschland bis Ende d.* 11. *Jahrhunderts* I (1910), 383 sqq.; cf. also,
Brackmann, *Studien u. Vorarbeitungen z. Germania pontificia* I (1912), 7 sq.
[20] Cf. Hirsch, *Klosterimmunität*, cap. I.
[21] Only two privileges for south German monasteries are known to
have been issued by Gregory VII: JL. 5279 for Hirsau, and JL. 5167 for
Schaffhausen.
[22] Cf. the list in Hauck, *Kirchengesch.* III, 871 n. 7.

shew a marked advance in the formulation of papal protection, but also gave the legal position of the protected houses its characteristic and definite form.

The acquisition of papal protection was thus one of the most important points in the reform programme, and the steps necessary to obtain protection were nearly always taken in direct connexion with the secular owner's renunciation of his proprietary right. The pope, as ultimate proprietor, took the place of the earlier proprietary lord, and it was therefore a very obvious step for the commendation or " oblation " of the monastery and its property to the Holy See to be carried out at the moment when the earlier owner surrendered his proprietary rights. Frequently enough we possess the names of those deputed as agents of the retiring owner to complete the assignment at the papal court in Rome.[23] And the payment of tribute was often arranged, prior to the issue of a papal privilege, at the time of renunciation by the secular owner.[24] It is possible, therefore, in at least a majority of cases to postulate as the most important aspect of monastic reform the change in ownership, by which the proprietary monastery of a secular magnate became a proprietary monastery of the papacy. But the question still arises, whether it is permissible to generalize from such cases and to single out the question of ownership as the outstanding feature of papal protection. To this question SCHREIBER has replied in the affirmative, and with this affirmation he has introduced into ecclesiastical history and ecclesiastical law the idea of the " papal proprietary monastery."[25]

It must immediately be admitted that papal letters of

[23] Cf. for Zwiefalten, MG. Script. X, 79; for Muri, Quellen z. Schweiz. Gesch. III, iii, 36 sq.; for Engelberg, Urk.-Buch v. Zürich I, 146, 150; for Lorsch, Wirtemb. Urk.-Buch I, 334; for St. Paul, MG. Script. XV. ii, 1058; for Baumburg, ibid., 1064; for Berchtesgaden, ibid., 1066; for Reichenbach, ibid., 1079; for Klosterneuburg, Fischer, Gesch. v. Klosterneuburg II, 125. Abbot William himself obtained the privilege for Hirsau in Rome; MG. Script. XII, 213.
[24] Thus at Muri (loc. cit.), at Alpirsbach (Wirt. Urk.-Buch I, 315), at Lorch (ibid. I, 334), at St. Georgen (MG. Script. XV. ii, 1008), and at St. Paul (ibid., 1058). In the Hirsau charter, and dependent texts, there is (Wirt. Urk.-Buch I, 278) the explicit statement: " comes . . . constituit, ut aureus . . . singulis annis Romam . . . persolvatur."
[25] Kurie u. Kloster I, 9 sqq.

protection, both before and after the Investiture Contest, very frequently mention the act of commendation or oblation; they speak of a protected house as the *proprietas* or *allodium* of the Holy See, and it is probably correct, with SCHREIBER,[26] to give the frequently used word *ius* the meaning *proprietas* rather than the more colourless sense of *protectio*. The tribute, also, which the protected houses had to pay, though merely a nominal payment, was a sure sign of dependence. But it is noteworthy that, in an overwhelming majority of cases, the payment was discharged *ad indicium libertatis*, and very rarely *ad indicium proprietatis*. Thus even in papal privileges an expression was chosen which indicated the liberty of the house receiving protection, and not merely its connexion with its papal proprietor.[27] Without doubt, the word *libertas* was introduced into the papal charters by the beneficiaries themselves, whose main object was to emphasize the cessation of lay lordship. If a connexion with the property question is sought in the conception of *libertas*, it must be found in the negative sense, as signifying the end of secular proprietary rights.[28] It would perhaps be correct to say that the monasteries understood *libertas* as meaning independence, but the Curia used it as an expression of its proprietary rights. The legal situation created by the papal privilege could, however, be regarded as *libertas* by the Curia, not only because the pope was guarantor of the monastery's freedom, but also—and here I am in full agreement with SCHREIBER—because " submission to Roman ownership meant a secure and advantageous legal position."

[26] *Op. cit.*, I, 39 sq.
[27] Schreiber (I, 10, and II, 272 n. 3) has clearly recognized the difficulty of correctly interpreting the *libertas* idea; but he goes too far when he sees in it (I, 40) " merely an expression of the proprietary connexion." Very pertinent, on the other hand, are his judgments, *op. cit.*, I, 43, 65.
[28] There is a precise interpretation of the idea of *libertas* in one of Gregory VII's political letters (JL. 4944), where the pope maintains regarding Hungary: " regnum Ungariae, sicut et alia nobilissima regna, in proprie libertatis statu debere esse et nulli regi alterius regni subici, nisi sanctae et universali matri Romanae ecclesiae; quae subiectos non habet ut servos, sed ut filios suscipit universos." Thus Gregory VII himself gives primary emphasis to independence from every secular authority, and only then mentions dependence on Rome; but even this is carefully toned down in the ultimate clause.

In dealing with papal protection, it must be remembered that, as a legal institution, it was operative throughout the whole of central Europe. In drafting a privilege the papal chancery had necessarily to bear in mind the interests of the beneficiary—those of a German monastery, for example, differed considerably from those of an Italian house—while, on the other hand, it was inevitable that the suppositions on which the papacy acted in granting protection were far from identical with the motives and interests which led the beneficiaries to petition for a charter. It is fair, therefore, to say that in considering commendation solely from the point of view adopted in the papal charters, SCHREIBER has necessarily taken a one-sided view of the most important of the preliminaries which preceded a grant of papal protection. SCHREIBER distinguishes two types of " tradition "[29]—types which are, however, often found together in one charter. In the one the abbey and its properties are made over to St. Peter: in the other the Holy Roman Church itself is selected as proprietor. Such is the act of commendation as described in papal charters. But if we turn to the monastic authorities, deeds of renunciation issued by the proprietary lords and monastic chronicles, which SCHREIBER has mostly ignored, we find that they present a different picture. In these also a proprietor is named, who enters into the rights of the previous owner; but even those authorities which directly refer to papal protection designate for this function neither St. Peter nor the Roman church, but the patron saint of the monastery itself.

The first example is Hirsau itself. Here count Adalbert of Chalw conveys his proprietary monastery of Hirsau with full proprietary rights to the Blessed Virgin Mary, to St. Peter, St. Aurelius and St. Benedict;[30] the abbot receives the right of free disposition of monastic properties;[31] but a papal privilege is also obtained in order that the freedom

[29] *Kurie u. Kloster* I, 14 sqq.
[30] *Wirtemb. Urk.-Buch* I, 276: " in potestatem et proprietatem." The patron saints of Hirsau were Peter and Aurelius.
[31] *Ibid.*: " predicti monasterii abbati, nomine Willehelmo, eiusque successoribus in dispositionem liberam celleque necessariam."

conferred on the house may be maintained undisturbed and so that the abbey may participate in the protection accorded by the Roman Church.[32] The same expressions as are found in the Hirsau charter are used for all other houses whose charters were drafted after the Hirsau model.[33] Since it might, however, be maintained that the use of a fixed model and the consequent lack of freedom in formulation necessitates caution in accepting the charters dependent on the Hirsau model at their face value, it is of special importance to note that an identical conception of the effects of reform is put forward in the foundation charter of Alpirsbach, which is freely and independently drafted.[34] After the withdrawal of the founder the proprietors of Alpirsbach are God and St. Benedict; the pope is merely the guarantor of the liberty conferred on the house by the founder; and disposition of monastic property is in the hands of the abbot.[35]

The situation is more complicated when the monastic records simultaneously announce a renunciation in favour of the patron saint and an oblation to the Holy See. A number of such cases can be cited. Both the author of the " Acta Murensia " and the imperial charter issued for Muri in 1114 record count Werner of Habsburg's *traditio* to the Virgin, St. Peter and St. Martin, but speak also of commendation " in ius apostolice sedis ".[36] Similar are the records from St. Georgen in the Black Forest: here also the foundation is given over to God, the Virgin, St. Peter and St. George, but is simultaneously conveyed to the

---

[32] *Op. cit.*, 278: " ut libertatis istius et traditionis statuta tanto perennius inconvulsa amodo permaneant et ut predictum coenobium sub Romane ecclesie mundiburdio et maiestate securum semper stabiliatur et defendatur."

[33] It will be necessary to mention them by name in the course of what follows.

[34] Cf. *Wirt. Urk.-Buch* I, 315.

[35] " Deo et s. Benedicto omnino in proprietatem . . . Propter hoc autem ut eiusdem loci habitatores quieti semper manerent et ipse locus auctoritate Romani pontificis omnimodo liber constaret, decretum est pro obedientia subiectionis aureum nummum annue dari in palatio Lateranensi ad pedes apostolicos, et abbas ibi constituendus cum monachis fratribusque sibi obedientibus liberam semper haberent potestatem gubernandi et disponendi res illuc pertinentes."

[36] *Quellen z. Schweiz. Gesch.* III. iii, 33, 36 sq., 41 sq.

Holy See.[37]   At St. Paul in Carinthia the two apostle
princes are mentioned as owners: the monastic record
allots the place to St. Paul, but the papal charter of 1099
takes oblation to St. Peter for granted.[38]

These examples show clearly that the reformed monasteries and the Roman Curia were not of one mind in their
interpretation of the purpose of papal protection, or at
least that each was inclined to emphasize a different factor.
For the Curia the important point was that the renunciation of the lay proprietor or founder placed the house in
the ultimate ownership of the pope.   The belief that the
imperial churches were the property of the empire had
been the guiding idea behind the establishment and development of the German national church; and if the
Curia hoped to create a feudal and hierarchical bulwark
of defence against the powerful structure of the *Reichskirche*,[39] it was clear that it must be erected on a similar
foundation.   It was, without doubt, with this object in
mind that the papacy developed its policy of protection.
When it granted charters which brought monasteries under

[37] Cf. the *Notitiae fundationis et traditionis S. Georgii*, MG. *Script.*
XV. ii, 1008 sqq.
[38] *Ibid.*, 1058, and JL. 5784 (cf. *Germ. pontif.* I, 118 n. 1).   The
fundatio et notae monasterii Richenbacensis (MG. *Script.* XV. ii, 1079)
records the conveyance of the monastery to God and the Virgin, but notes,
a few lines later, that the foundation has been handed over " apostolicae
defensioni et potestati."
[39] That the tendency to claim not only churches but also territories
as the *proprietas S. Petri* was directed to this end, was perceived by Ficker,
Sitz.-Ber. d. Wiener Akademie LXXII, 442 sq., and papal protection was
the instrument used for furthering this policy, as far as monasteries were
concerned.   Blumenstock, *Der päpstl. Schutz*, 166, puts forward a different
point of view; but I have already disposed of it, MIÖG. *Erg.-Bd.* VII,
606 n. 1.   When Gregory VII received an abbey into the ownership of
the Holy See, he **was** proceeding on the same assumption as when he
claimed Gaul as a tributary land or Saxony as the property of the Roman
Church (cf. Scheffer-Boichorst, MIÖG. *Erg.-Bd.* IV, 77 sqq.).   The contrary is equally true.   The protection exercised by the Frankish-German
monarchy in its most powerful days over the Roman church was similarly
based on commendation—in other words, on the very legal transaction
which preluded the entrance of an abbey into royal protection (cf. Haller,
HZ. CVIII, 65 sqq.).   I am consequently unable to conclude (cf. Schreiber,
II, 272 n. 3) that " Ficker's opinion that the eleventh-century papacy
was trying to set up a clerical-feudal monarchy . . . seriously impairs his
conception of protection "—there is, after all, no need to take the words
" clerical-feudal monarchy " literally.   Cf. also Brackmann, *Studien* I,
16 sq.

the protection of the Holy See, its object was to raise up a force powerful enough to oppose the *Reichskirche*, and during the period at which papal power was at its height— between the pontificates of Pascal II and Innocent II—it was able to obtain increasing currency for its own conception of the object of protection. SCHREIBER has based his theories principally on the papal charters of this period, and his very precise formulation of the objects and effects of papal protection is therefore readily comprehensible.

To make this a basis for speaking of " papal proprietary monasteries " is nevertheless to adopt too exclusively the Roman point of view. It was certainly not the intention of the reformed monasteries of southern Germany to get rid of the proprietary rights of the laity in order to establish the proprietary rights of the papacy. For them independence was the main point, and this was to be guaranteed by papal protection. That is stated without ambiguity in the charters of Hirsau and Alpirsbach, and if the records of other monasteries place the proprietary lord's surrender in favour of the patron saint on an equal footing with commendation to the Holy See, it is evident that the conveyance to Rome—apart from the payment of tribute, which the records consistently note—was regarded sometimes at least as little more than a formality, or was at all events not considered to be the main effect of protection.[40] The pope was only the ultimate and indirect proprietor, and free disposal of monastic properties was placed in the hands of the abbot. It is very characteristic that at the beginning of the survey of the lands of Schaffhausen—a reformed monastery which for the most part adopted a thoroughly papalist conception of protection—it is stated that the monastic properties have been given over " quasi dotaliter " to the Saviour, the apostles Peter and Paul and the Roman church.[41] Thus, besides the Roman Church

[40] One consequence was that a special deed relating to the commendation was practically never drawn up. There is, in fact, a document for Lorch (*Wirt. Urk.-Buch* I, 334); but its contents prove how little the Curia cared about the conditions under which the founder completed the " tradition." Duke Frederick reserved the *Vogtei* over Lorch as an hereditament for his family: Innocent II's privilege (JL. 7771) simply ignores his act.
[41] *Quellen z. Schweiz. Gesch.* III. i, 125.

and its patron saints, mention is made of the Saviour, to whom Schaffhausen was consecrated, and the word " quasi " betrays the fact that a distinction was made between the legal relationship created by the papal charter and a real proprietary right. I can only find one case in the whole history of the south German reformed monasteries in which, at the time the house was placed under papal protection, the pope was also given absolute dispositive rights.[42]

This view of the purpose and significance of papal protection, which is far from identical with the object the Curia had in mind in issuing its privileges, did not originate in Hirsau. Once again the foundation charter of Cluny, the prototype of the Hirsau charter, was of influence. It was only as protector of Cluny that William of Aquitaine had called in the pope: he did not establish him as owner, and among those adjured to desist from meddling with the abbey's rights is found the " pontifex supradicte sedis Romanae ".[43] The charters obtained by Cluny from the French crown in the tenth century state explicitly that the foundation was delivered to the Holy See " ad tuendum, non ad dominandum ".[44] This older conception of monastic *libertas* was plainly operative in Hirsau. There also protective dependence on Rome did not alone typify the full content of the idea of the " abbatia libera." There were additional criteria, and among them we may single out as particularly important the existence of an " advocacy " or *Vogtei* in which powers of high criminal justice were vested, and the grant to the monastic dependents of the manorial customs and rights peculiar to an " ecclesia libera ".[45]

---

[42] Cf. my remarks about St. Georgen, MIÖG. *Erg.-Bd.* VII, 487. Schreiber, I, 20, brings forward other examples of the exercise of full dispositive powers by the pope; but they all refer to non-German territories.
[43] Bernard et Bruel, *Recueil des chartes de l'abbaye de Cluny* I, 126. On the position of Cluny as a protected house, cf. Sackur, *Cluniacenser* I, 41, 270 sq., and Schreiber, II, 316 n. 2. The clear definition of Cluny's position as a *proprietas* of the Roman church was only slowly achieved.
[44] Bernard et Bruel, *Recueil* I, 281, 484; cf. also Fabre, *Etude,* 57.
[45] The passage in the Hirsau charter and its derivatives which relates to manorial custom is as follows (*Wirt. Urk.-Buch* I, 278): " Ministris quoque et familie sanctuarie eandem concedit legem et servitutem, quam

It is, of course, possible to object that what matters in the criticism of the legal content of any particular charter is the intention of the grantor rather than that of the beneficiary. But it is with no desire to quibble that I have emphasized, in contrast to SCHREIBER, the somewhat independent attitude adopted by the reformed monasteries of southern Germany. It was an inevitable weakness in the development of papal protection that its operation extended to lands both nationally and culturally so different as Germany, France and Italy.[46] In these circumstances there could be no question of an identical application of protection in every country of Europe. The Cluniac movement had in the same way been forced to modify its aims when its victorious progress carried it across the boundary between the German and Romance languages. The subjection of a daughter-house to the mother-church could not be enforced so strictly in Germany as in France, and the consequent change of programme was far from adding to the force of the movement. It is equally certain that the reformed monasteries of southern Germany had a greater sense of independence in their relations with the papacy than similar houses in Romanized lands. For this reason papal protection as understood in the Curia could only be fully effective during the period when the fervour created by the contest between church and state united all factions within the reform party. Later, when the papacy had achieved emancipation from the secular power and had diverted its struggle with the latter into the field of politics, protection sank in importance and ultimately acquired a different significance.

With these last sentences, however, I have anticipated what has yet to follow. Even now we have not fully

cetere in regno nostro libere abbatie habent, ut tanto fideliores prelatis suis per omnia serviant."—For a discussion of this clause and its significance, which must be omitted here, cf. Hirsch, *Klosterimmunität*, App. II.

[46] It may be willingly admitted that the subordination of protected houses to the Holy See was stronger in the Romanized lands, and there, as a consequence, the conception of a system of papal proprietary churches is more strongly accentuated.—Brackmann, also, has drawn attention in his *Studien* to the dependence of the Curia, in drafting letters of protection, on the wishes and interests of the recipients.

exhausted the significance of papal protection at the time of the Investiture Contest. It was more, and was intended to be more, than a mere guarantee against the system of lay proprietorship over churches. The papal privilege conferring protection was the constitutional charter of the reformed monastery. It took the name *immunitas*, and its stipulations leave no doubt that it was intended, in certain of its sections, to usurp the place of the royal " immunity " of earlier times.[47] Already in Leo IX's charters of protection a special place was assigned to those regulations which governed and defined the institute of " advocacy ". The papacy was to provide for the immunity of the foundation on the strength of the proprietary rights which—according to curial ideas—the pope had obtained when the house was placed under his protection; for an application for royal protection and for a royal grant of immunity would, it was clear, have been dangerous to the connexion with Rome which papal protection had created.[48] This was realized and was made a principle of curial practice under Leo IX; but it was under Gregory VII that the principle was developed to the full. Under him opposition to the monarchy stands out undisguised.

Gregory VII only conferred two privileges on south German reformed monasteries. But small though this number is, it does nothing to diminish the importance which the privilege granted to Schaffhausen must assume in our judgement, when we turn to consider the effects of papal protection on the institution of advocacy; for Gregory VII's charter for Schaffhausen was the model, both in its negative clauses dealing with monastic independence and in its positive clauses concerning the *Vogtei*, for a series of similar grants by Urban II and his successors to other south German abbeys.[49] In the clauses dealing with the advocacy, Gregory VII rejects every possible

[47] This fact was emphasized simultaneously by myself (MIÖG. *Erg.-Bd.* VII, 605) and by Heilmann, *Klostervogtei*, 41.
[48] Cf. Hirsch, *Klosterimmunität*, 15 sqq.
[49] Cf. MIÖG. *Erg.-Bd.* VII, 498 sqq., and p. 545, where I have established a similar influence of the Hirsau formula (particularly of those clauses which relate to the advocacy) in privileges of Honorius II.

form of influence which might be claimed by a lay or clerical
person on grounds of proprietary rights, hereditary rights,
advocacy or investiture; and king, duke and count are
expressly named as typical representatives of the secular
power. The monastery has the right to elect its advocate
freely and to dismiss him if he misuses his office.[50] In these
stipulations we have the maximum which the Curia could
demand for the freedom of a protected house; and STENGEL
had therefore every reason to speak of such a development
of protection as " exclusive " in character.[51] Every power
which could exert any influence without the house's assent,
was excluded from the abbey over which the pope had
spread his wings. The pope is now conferring immunity
not, as previously, in agreement with the monarchy, but
directly to the exclusion of the supreme authority within
the state, and the most the latter can now do is to provide
confirmation of the pope's ordinances. If it is remembered
that the royal charter of immunity was, as late as the
middle of the eleventh century, accounted the *magna carta*
of a monastic constitution, Gregory VII's ordinances reveal
the extraordinary change which had taken place in the
development of immunity during the bitter struggle of
empire and papacy at the end of the eleventh century.

This fundamental principle of monastic freedom from
secular authority in all questions bound up with the advocacy was adopted and maintained by the popes who
succeeded Gregory VII. The most they admitted was a
limited hereditary right, confined to the founder's son[52].
But SCHREIBER has very cogently pointed out[53] that in

[50] *Quellen z. Schweiz. Gesch.* III. i, 21: " ut nullus sacerdotum regum
vel ducum aut comitum seu quelibet magna aut parva persona presumat
sibi in eo loco aliquas proprietatis conditiones non hereditarii iuris non advocatie non investiture non cuiuslibet potestatis, que libertati monasterii no-
ceat, vendicare, non ornamenta ecclesie sive possessiones invadere minuere
vel alienare. . . . Abbas autem advocatum, quem voluerit, eligat. Quod si
is postmodum non fuerit utilis monasterio, eo remoto, alium constituat."
[51] *Immunität* I, 386 sq.
[52] Cf. my remarks, MIÖG. XXV, 268, and *Jahrb. f. Schweiz. Gesch.*
XXXI, 104 sq.; also Schreiber, II, 257. This was not, however, a limitation imposed by the Curia alone: the reformed monasteries themselves
emphasized the limitation of heredity to the next generation; cf. for Muri,
Quellen z. Schweiz. Gesch. III. iii, 36, 42.
[53] *Op. cit.*, II, 254 sqq.

this regard the efforts of the Curia ended in complete
failure, while even before he wrote, other historians had
drawn attention to the existence of an hereditary advocacy
over a number of important reformed monasteries, thus
making it clear that the theoretical freedom of an abbey to
choose and remove its advocate cannot always have been
effective.[54] The reasons for this failure are not difficult
to discover. As protector the pope had, no doubt, taken
over the rights of the earlier proprietary lord. But the
advocacy itself had necessarily to remain in secular hands,
since it was, as SCHREIBER says, in its very nature " avow-
edly secular, and the *advocatus* was not a clerical official."
The advocate of the reformed monasteries was not an official
in charge of the immunity, but practically without exception the former proprietary lord, on whom the abbey—
however considerable the precautions and limitations
imposed—had conferred the authority of *Vogt*. Under
the title of advocate, therefore, the secular founder of the
monastery retained a share of the rights which had formerly
been comprised in his general proprietorship. He had
established the foundation in the very district in which
his power and interests were centred: the pope was distant,
he himself was near at hand. In such a situation, and in
view of the pressing needs of the reformed houses for protection, it is self-evident that the right of freely electing
the *Vogt* was almost always illusory.[55]

From this point of view, moreover, it is very noteworthy
that, long before Gregory VII formulated his radical statement of clerical demands, Leo IX had approached the
issue by way of compromise. Leo IX's privileges,[56] with

[54] The evidence for Schaffhausen and Alpirsbach will be found in
MIÖG. *Erg.-Bd.* VII, 528 sq., 531, 534 sq., and Heilmann, *Klostervogtei*, 42
sqq., 63 sq. For St. Peter in the Black Forest and St. Märgen, *ibid.*, 69, 73.
[55] All the cases, moreover, in which we hear of a change of advocate
at this period, are not to be considered as the result of a free expression
of monastic wishes (cf. Schrieber, II, 258). When St. Blasien, for example,
replaced its advocate, Adelgoz, by the duke of Zähringen in 1125, what
we know of the power of the ducal house makes it permissible to doubt
whether the monastery was absolutely free in its action. And similar
considerations must be entertained, if the statement that Zwiefalten chose
duke Welf IV as *Vogt* after the founder's death (Heilmann, 57) is to be
correctly interpreted.
[56] Cf. Hirsch, *Klosterimmunität*, 16 sqq.

their approbation of an advocacy permanently and hereditarily invested in the founder's family, were widely known in southern Germany, and were certainly one reason why the Hirsau foundations never strenuously opposed this exercise of secular power. The Hirsau charter of 1075 explicitly announces that the advocacy is to remain hereditary in the family of the count of Chalw and—a distinct reminiscence of the earlier proprietary relationship—goes so far as to grant the *Vogt* the right to participate in deposing an unworthy abbot.[57] The relations between monastery and advocate were, in fact, regarded as patriarchal in character. The advocate was to exercise his office, apart from a paltry indemnity, in the expectation of heavenly reward alone. And if he kept to this understanding, an hereditary advocacy was as little objectionable—from the point of view of the Hirsau foundations themselves—as was the advocate's interference if it became necessary to maintain against a refractory abbot the basic principles of the reform programme.

But such an understanding between monastery and advocate was, of course, only too frequently more honoured in the breach than in the observance. And when this occurred, papal protection had few tangible advantages to offer. Not that the papacy regarded its protective obligations lightly: there are numbers of mandates in which Rome urges both lay and clerical magnates to aid a monastery which has placed itself under papal protection.[58] But by the time these paper measures could take effect, the harm was ordinarily done, and the monasteries could not but realize that more efficacious help might be obtained from the neighbouring lord—a lord who was either advocate

[57] *Wirt. Urk.-Buch* I, 277: " Concedit etiam comes predictus prefate celle advocatum de posteris suis fieri." As regards the abbot: " Qui si forte preter necessitatem monasterii et communem fratrum utilitatem sacrilegus . . . abuti presumpserit instituta libertate . . . si forte libertatem monasterii pervertere sibique locum sanctum subicere attemptaverit . . . mox posteri comitis predicti cum suffragio fratrum . . . rite a fratribus hunc accusatum iusteque ab eis convictum dignitate sua abici perficiant aliumque . . . substituant."—It is characteristic that the passage concerning the advocate's participation in a deposition was not incorporated in all the charters which were copied at a later date from the Hirsau model.
[58] Cf. Schreiber, *op. cit.* I, 7, 21.

and former proprietor in any case, or who was finally able
to acquire the advocacy as a direct result of the protection
he, and he alone, could afford. The strength and weakness
of the reformed monasteries, in short, lay in their relations
with the advocate. If he accepted the limitations on his
rights which ecclesiastics proposed, the monastery was in
fact " free " in the sense of the reform programme: if, on
the other hand, he misused his powers, the abbey was
exposed to serious external threats and disturbances.[59]

It is from the point of view of the relationship between
monastery and advocate, moreover, that all the questions
connected with the " immunity " of the reformed foundations must be considered. In the older monasteries the
advocacy was the result of a royal grant of immunity, and
the advocate was the officer in charge of the immunity or
franchise. In the reformed monasteries, on the other hand,
the *Vogtei* had developed out of the secular proprietary
right which the founder exercised in his church, and not
out of the immunity. The reformed monasteries of the
Investiture Contest were for the most part founded at a
time when it was impossible to obtain a royal charter of
immunity. On the very eve of the outbreak of the struggle
between church and state, in 1075, Hirsau had obtained
a comprehensive confirmation of its rights and liberties from
Henry IV, which may, in view of its detailed regulation
of the position of the advocate, be called a charter of immunity. But thirty years were to pass from that date
before Henry V once again conceded immunities or franchises on the Hirsau model, and then only a fraction of the
monasteries in question took the opportunity to obtain
official sanction for the advocacy which had already been
in existence for many years: the others simply assumed
the same rights without the emperor's permission. Moreover, Henry V's charters were often no more than confirma-
tions of the privileges previously conferred by the papacy
—in other words, of the real constitutional charters on which
the Hirsau foundations depended.[60] But if the Curia

[59] Cf. MIÖG. *Erg.-Bd.* VII, 535.
[60] *Ibid.*, 605 sq.

thus assumed the power to define and delimit the advocate's rights, the co-operation of the former proprietary lord and subsequent *Vogt* was nevertheless the essential precondition, without which such rights could not be effectively exercised. In actual fact, therefore, the reformed monastery held its immunity by the grace neither of king nor of pope but of the *Vogt* himself. The consequence was that immunity definitely lost the character of a legal institution controlled by the state and used by the crown as a part of its governmental machinery, which it had possessed during the Ottonian and Salian period. Immunity and advocacy suddenly broke apart; and this separation was, without doubt, one of the major losses which the German crown suffered as a result of the struggle of Empire and Papacy.

How this transformation came about, and what were its early stages, are questions which cannot be considered in detail here.[61] Investigation has, in fact, revealed that even before the Investiture Contest there were a number of monasteries without immunity whose position was nevertheless similar to that of immune foundations, though it originated not in any formal charter of immunity, granted by the crown, but in the power of the founder and proprietary lord. The lawless times of the Investiture Contest resulted in a multiplication of such foundations, and the papal privileges which sanctioned these proceedings, signified the conclusion of a development which had occurred without the permission or participation of the crown.

The new type of immunity was the result of the alliance between papacy and princes. This fact is clear. But the very recognition of the fact forces us to seek a full answer to the further question: what were the vital forces, the motives, interests and aspirations, from which the south German monastic movement sprang? The most perfect programme of reform, all the fervour of abbots and monks, even papal privileges would have been of no use if the lay founders had not given their land for the endowment of

---

[61] The early stages of the development are traced in detail in Hirsch, *Klosterimmunität*, cap. I (" Das Stadium der Vorreform "), and this paragraph summarizes the results of the first chapter.

reformed monasteries or had not allowed reform to be introduced into their existing proprietary houses. What, then, led the secular lords to take this decisive step which, in view of the legal situation as a whole and of the political situation during the years of strife, must inevitably bring them into conflict with the monarchy ?

This question has already been raised by SCHREIBER, and he has rightly emphasized the fact that religious motives " alone were very rarely decisive."[62] No historian, it is true, will doubt that purely religious considerations were from time to time vitally effective. It is impossible, for example, to ignore the account, given first by Bernold and then by Ortlieb of Zwiefalten,[63] how high and low flocked to the reformed monasteries in order to realize the ideal of evangelic equality.[64] There is, further, no difficulty in agreeing with SCHREIBER that the proprietary lord only suffered a partial loss of rights through his surrender; that, in exchange for what he gave up, his most important prerogatives—those, namely, which centred in the advocacy— were securely guaranteed by papal authority; and that even after its transformation into a " free " house, a proprietary foundation remained a " profitable investment " for the former proprietor. Nevertheless, the foundation and reform of the Hirsau monasteries falls for the most part in the last decades of the eleventh century and must therefore be, in part at least, an expression of the dissension which the struggle between Empire and Papacy aroused throughout Germany and in Swabia in particular. Considerations of a political character must, in short, have figured among the reasons which led so many Swabian dynastic families to support the papacy and to found reformed monasteries.

It is the merit of recent investigations, for which we are

[62] *Kurie u. Kloster* I, 16 sqq.
[63] MG. *Script.* V, 439; *ibid.* X, 85.
[64] Notable also is the fact that founders withdrew as monks into their own monasteries; e.g. count Eberhard of Nellenburg, the founder of Schaffhausen, even before the reform of the abbey (*Quellen z. Schweiz. Gesch.* III. i, 15) and count Liutold of Achalm, the founder of Zwiefalten, immediately before his death, after six years' residence in the immediate neighbourhood (MG. *Script.* X, 100 sq.). Cf. further Schreiber, I, 16.

indebted to SCHULTE[65] and VON DUNGERN,[66] to have laid
due emphasis on the fact that Germany, in the tenth and
eleventh centuries, possessed an exclusive and privileged
nobility, which had a monopoly of all offices, lay and
clerical. It was, however, precisely from this overmighty
aristocracy that the founders of the Hirsau monasteries
were descended—from a class which, according to all our
information, the Salian emperors were far from favouring.[67]
In combining in their own hands both public and manorial
rights, in consolidating rights derived from government
with rights accruing to them as lords of their own immune
estates, these " dynasts " shewed themselves to be the true
precursors of the later territorial rulers of Germany. And
it was precisely in the eleventh century that they achieved

[65] *Der Adel u. die deutsche Kirche im Mittelalter* (1910).
[66] *Der Herrenstand im Mittelalter* (1908).
[67] Cf. Waitz, *Verf.-Gesch.* VI (2nd ed.), 375 n. 1, for evidence that
Henry IV gave his confidence to the *inferiores* and *vilissimi homines*, and
not to the *potentes, optimates, nobiles* and *maiores. Inferiores*, however,
cannot refer to " dynasts," i.e., persons of the rank of count. This is clear
from a passage in the *Annales Altahenses* (MG. *Script.* XX, 823 sq.), where
the chronicler contrasts *inferiores* and *optimates* and defines the latter
more precisely as " episcopi, duces aliique regni primores." *Optimates*
cannot, therefore, mean dukes and bishops alone, but must include people
of count's rank, who might, like the Egisheimer and Nellenburger, even
be related with the Salian dynasty, and who formed a supreme privileged
class, for which the term " minor nobility" is inadmissible. It is not
necessary to dispute the facts which Brackmann has brought forward
(*Hist. Vierteljahrschr.* XV, 182 sqq.) to prove that a number of south
German princes were among Henry's supporters in the decade 1070—1080.
But there is every reason to ask whether Henry sought the support of the
" high nobility " or " dynasts" because he considered them an essential
foundation for his power, or whether he merely compromised with them
because they were an important factor in the political balance of power.
In my view the second alternative is correct. Henry naturally sought
an alliance with a section of the powerful aristocracy as a counter-balance
against the rebellious dukes, though this support inevitably led to opposition from other sections of the secular aristocracy. In Bavaria, in particular, it is clear that there were supporters of the king among the lay nobility;
but in judging Henry IV's relations with the Bavarian dynastic families
as a whole, it is more important to note that it was a conspiracy of Bavarian
" dynasts " which brought about the ultimate collapse of the old king
and the rise of his son. Henry IV based his power on the *ministeriales,*
on the cities and in part on the peasantry. The interests of the " dynasts "
ran parallel with those of the dukes and against those of the monarchy.
Dukes and " dynasts " were faced at that moment by the transition
from the older forms of government of the Ottonian period to the principalities and territorial states of the future, and their efforts were concentrated on reaching their ends either in harmony with or in opposition
to the monarchy. The lay nobility was, therefore, not an element on which
Henry could rely in his struggle with the papacy.

their first substantial successes. This was the period at which they began to take their titles not from the counties which they held as offices from the crown, but from their castles, and since the old administrative division of the *Gau* (hundred) disappears completely from twelfth-century charters, it is easy to conclude that the development of a privileged " dynastic " class with hereditary rights, which is marked by the rapid progress of castle-building, was a main cause of the break-down of the old county organisation.[68] Such a development of the old Carolingian official nobility was not, however, in the interests of the monarchy, and was therefore hardly promoted by the crown. For this reason it is possible that certain south-German " dynasts " went over to the papal cause for the same reason which led the great princes to refuse service and fealty to their royal master—a strong sense of independence and a realization that the uncertain political situation created by the revolt against Henry IV might be used to promote their private interests. ·

Another factor to be considered is the rivalry and the struggles of the Swabian magnates among themselves, which naturally led to the rise of certain dynasties and the decline of others. The Investiture Contest falls in this period of dynastic change. If one count was loyal to the crown and consequently sure of abundant reward, a mass of family considerations and particularist plans inevitably drove his rivals over to the papacy and to the anti-king whom the pope recognized.[69] " Because of the menace of war and because no man knew when his own father or son

[68] The view that the construction of castles by the "dynasts" was the means by which " the imperial demesne was eaten away and the original official connotation of the dignity of count was destroyed," is found already in Stälin, *Wirtemb. Gesch.* II, 656, and it is a merit of Schrader, *Befestigungsrecht*, 31 sqq., to have pointed this out. On the revolutionary effects of castle-building on the county organisation of the Rhinelands, cf. J. Friedrichs, *Burg- u. territoriale Grafschaften*, 22 sqq.; and for other examples, Heusler, *Verf.-gesch.*, 175 sq.

[69] The discords of the age even drove members of one family into different camps. In the battle of the Unstrut, for example, two sons of count Eberhard of Nellenburg fell fighting for Henry IV, while the third (Burkhard) was one of the leading reformers in Swabia. Among the counts of Achalm, Egino was on the imperial side, but Cuno and Liutold were supporters of Rudolf of Rheinfelden.

or brother would bring death or ruin upon him, many gave
their property to God and built monasteries, while some
even left the world and consecrated themselves a sacrifice
to God." Such are the words with which Berthold of Zwiefalten, candid as ever, describes the connexion between the
foundation of monastic houses and the wild unrest which
the Investiture Contest called forth throughout the whole
land.

Party struggles among the Swabian magnates preceded
and to some degree accompanied their monastic zeal. In
this regard it is only necessary to recall the more important
of the well-known facts.[70] Count Ulrich of Lenzburg
proved his worth as an adherent of the imperial party in
1077, when he captured Bernard of Marseilles, the papal
legate, on his way back to Rome, and was rewarded by
Henry IV with a grant of fiefs.[71] The feud which existed
between the Lenzburger and their relatives and rivals, the
papalist Habsburgs, was an expression of political antagonism and the result of the marked divergence of interests
between the two houses. In eastern Switzerland the energetic abbot Ulrich III of St. Gallen maintained the imperialist cause against the monastery of Reichenau, which
Henry IV had placed in his hands, and against count
Hartmann of Kiburg, who fell into his power in 1080.
Count Burckhard of Nellenburg and duke Berthold of
Zähringen lost their counties in Breisgau, Zürichgau and
Neckargau because of their adherence to the papacy, while
the counts of Kiburg, on the contrary, owed possession
of the Thurgau to their support of the Zähringer.

All these are events which we should expect to effect
the position of the reformed monasteries, even if we had
no direct evidence of such consequences. But direct
evidence is not lacking. Hirsau, which is known to have
maintained close relations with the anti-king, Rudolf of
Rheinfelden, suffered in consequence from imperialist

[70] The situation in Swabia during the Investiture Contest has been
dealt with in detail by E. Heyck, *Gesch. d. Herzöge von Zähringen*, 119 sqq.;
cf. particularly the lists of imperial and papal adherents, pp. 78 sq. and
129 sq.
[71] Cf. Merz, *Die Lenzburg*, 12 sq.

attack.[72] The general excommunication promulgated by Gregory VII brought Schaffhausen to such a pass that, in 1093, abbot Siegfried considered transferring the whole convent to Marseilles.[73] For Muri the feud between Lenzburg and Habsburg, which we have mentioned, meant a change of advocate, since the freely elected protectors, Lütold of Regensberg and Richwin of Rüssegg, could not provide adequate protection. In 1086, therefore, count Werner reassumed, for himself and for his sons, the advocacy which he had voluntarily surrendered in 1082.[74] At Petershausen, finally, the success of the imperialist anti-bishop, Arnold of Constance, resulted in the ruin of all reform.[75].

To understand these facts correctly we must realize what was the foundation on which the immune position of the reformed monasteries was based during the thirty years which intervened between the beginning of the Investiture Contest and the death of Henry IV. This basis was the power which the founder and advocate could employ, the protection he was able to afford. There is no doubt that the advocate possessed powers of " high justice " or jurisdiction in life and limb over the monastic tenants. But these powers were based not on a charter of immunity, forbidding royal officials to enter the franchise, but on the personal position of the advocate himself. He exercised jurisdiction because he was already count in the district within which the major part of the monastery's possessions lay, or because he claimed this faculty in virtue of his status as a high-born " dynast ". For only the peer of a count could at that period be the advocate of a monastery,[76] and the advocate of a monastery therefore felt

[72] Cf. Heyck, op. cit., 83, 122.
[73] MG. Script. V, 455.
[74] Cf. Caro, Hist. Vierteljahrschr. IX, 172 sq. and Steinacker, Zeitschr. f. d. Gesch. d. Oberrheins, Neue Folge XXIII, 403 sqq. and XXIV, 161.
[75] MG. Script. XX, 657.
[76] Cf. v. Dungern, Herrenstand I, 304. This fact, which provides a very significant indication of the nature and extent of the advocate's rights, was also pointed out by Heilmann, Klostervogtei, 23, with reference to a passage in a forged Reichenau charter (" ex eis, qui inter potentes seculi noverint esse equitatis et modestie amantiores, eligant ... advocatos," where potentes seculi has the technical sense noted supra, n. 67).

justified in claiming as his birthright the prerogatives of a count. It is, of course, true that the essential precondition which alone made it possible to substantiate such a claim, was to desert the cause of Henry IV. Once that step had been taken, however, it could be claimed that there was no lawful and duly recognized German king; and in such a position the right to exercise high criminal justice over freemen could be quietly assumed, where in more normal times it could only be obtained by royal grant.

It was a weakness in the constitution of the Hirsau monasteries that they were limited in their choice of advocates to the narrow circle of dynastic families. In these circumstances the *Vogt* could never be a mere monastic official. In order to exercise his office he had to be strong; but his strength could, if necessary, be used against the monastery itself. The reformed monasteries of the eleventh century owed their foundation or at least their specific character to the " dynasts "; but the " dynasts " of the twelfth century, as we shall see, undermined their independent position.

The security of the reformed monasteries, therefore, was based solely on the protection afforded by the advocate when, with the accession of Henry V and the adoption of a more favourable attitude towards the church party, it once again became possible to obtain a royal privilege. The connexion between reformed house and dynast was, indeed, so close, that it is hard to say whether Henry made advances to the monasteries because he needed the " dynasts ", or whether he won over the latter[77] because he was seeking a compromise with the ecclesiastical reform party. No doubt both explanations are correct. In any case the relations of the last of the Salians with the dynastic houses demand full emphasis, because this was one of the points in which there was

[77] The margraves of Austria and Styria, the count palatine of Chalw, the counts of Habsburg, etc., are frequently found among the witnesses to Henry V's charters—there is, indeed, no doubt that Henry V's close relations with the dynasts were one of the reasons for the introduction of a " witness clause " in German royal charters. On the significance of the participation of dynasts belonging to the church party in Henry V's Hungarian expedition, cf. Brackmann, *Studien* I, 27.

a marked contrast between Henry V's policy and that of his father.[78]

It was clearly realized in the Hirsau abbeys that a permanent exercise of the rights to which they laid claim was in the last analysis impossible without the consent of the crown. Even before the outbreak of the Investiture Contest Henry IV had issued a comprehensive privilege confirming the changes which the reform movement had brought about in Hirsau itself. And it is very noteworthy that the author of the " Acta Murensia ", writing about the middle of the twelfth century and describing the reform of Muri, states that the regulations introduced at the time of the reform were such as count Werner would later have to get confirmed " coram rege et principibus ac populo."[79] This attitude was based, after all, on the simple considera- tion that the advocate needed a royal grant of jurisdiction, if he was going to exercise high criminal justice ; for it was only in the course of the twelfth century that the idea that all jurisdiction derived from the king, was under- mined. Thus Paschal II ordained in a charter for Alpirs- bach: " nec alius advocatie bannum a catholico rege suscipiat, nisi qui ab abbate et fratribus electus exstiterit."[80] Even the Curia, therefore, recognized that royal authorisa- tion was necessary before the advocate's powers could be properly exercised. The only condition was that the king must be a *rex catholicus*—in other words, a monarch recognized by the church—and Henry IV had not fulfilled this condition.

With the accession of Henry V, however, the situation was immediately changed. For almost every year of his reign, except those spent in Italy, there are privileges confirming the rights and liberties of the Hirsau founda- tions.[81] They are modelled in part on the Hirsau charter

[78] It was Henry V's participation in a conspiracy among the Bavarian dynastic nobility which irrevocably separated father and son; cf. *supra*, n. 67.
[79] Cf. *Quellen z. Schweiz. Gesch.* III. iii, 32. The obtaining of a royal charter in 1114 is noted, *ibid.*, 40.
[80] JL. 5866.
[81] The following is a list of the most important: Usenhoven-Scheiern (*St.* 3012, 3197), St. Georgen in the Black Forest (*St.* 3026, 3088), Gottesau

158 H. HIRSCH

of 1075, in part on papal privileges granted to single houses.[82] On the whole, therefore, it would appear that the beneficiaries were left to formulate their own wishes; and it was, no doubt, for this reason that the Hirsau formula was often taken over without even the elimination of the admonitary clauses directed against the crown.[83] Other passages in the charters, however, clearly indicate the interest which the monarchy had in these concessions. By taking over the clause: " a rege accipiat bannum legitimum," with or without verbal modification from the Hirsau model, royal intervention in the appointment of a new advocate was in almost every case safeguarded. The great importance which was attached to this factor is proved by the charter for St. Blasien, where the words: " volumus etiam, ut advocatus petitione abbatis legitimum bannum a nobis vel successoribus nostris accipiat ", were added at the end of the otherwise complete text.[84] And a similar importance attaches to the modifications of the " advocacy-clause ", noticeable when Henry V's charters for Schaffhausen, Muri, Alpirsbach and St. Blasien[85] are compared with their prototypes. Where the Hirsau formula had decreed the deposition of an unworthy advocate by the abbot " cum consilio fratrum ", the St. Blasien charter, which is based on the Hirsau text, adds " et nostro nostrorumque successorum patrocinio ", and thus creates a place in the proceedings for intervention by the king.[86] In the

(St. 3041), Schaffhausen (St. 3076, 3184), St. Lambrecht (St. 3100), Muri (St. 3106), Paulinzelle (St. 3116), Rüggisberg (St. 3121), St. Blasien (St. 3185, 3204), Alpirsbach (St. 3186), Odenheim (St. 3189), Engelberg (St. 3202).
   [82] Cf. my remarks, MIÖG. Erg.-Bd. VII, 598 sqq. and Schulte, Der Adel u. die deutsche Kirche, 158 sqq.
   [83] Wirtemb. Urk.-Buch I, 277: " si regibus ... consentaneus annuerit"; ibid., 278: " si forte quispiam regum . . . hoc ullo ingenio infirmare vel infringere presumpserit "; and cf. St. 3012, 3041, 3189. The clause has, on the other hand, disappeared from St. 3106 and 3116, and it is noteworthy that both these charters were products of the chancery, whereas those previously mentioned were drawn up outside the chancery.
   [84] St. 3185.
   [85] St. 3076, 3106, 3186, 3185.
   [86] There is a similar modification of the Hirsau text in the Muri charter (St. 3106): " omnino potestatem habeat abbas cum consilio fratrum hunc penitus reprobare et alterum [regia adiutus potestate, si aliter fieri non potest,] sibi utiliorem undecumque eligere." The words in square brackets are newly added, and were not found in the Hirsau text on which the Muri charter was modelled.

charter for Schaffhausen the text of the papal privilege, which was otherwise adopted without alteration, was amended so as to provide that the advocate could only be deprived after indictment before the king and royal sentence.[87] At Alpirsbach a limitation of the free choice of advocate was introduced: the royal ban was to be conferred at the abbot's and brothers' request on such a person as seemed worthy and suitable for the office.[88]

These emendations and additions to the text of the charters used as models[89] are a decisive proof that Henry V had other objects in mind, in issuing his privileges, than merely the reconciliation of the reform party. The monasteries founded during the Investiture Contest, which in theory at least had hitherto remained exclusively under the influence of the papacy, were now to be assigned a place within the structure of the German *Reichskirche*. But this connexion could obviously not be established on the old proprietary basis, which had governed the relations of church and state before the Investiture Contest; for it was precisely with the object of destroying the old proprietary nexus that the Curia had made a conveyance of proprietary rights the essential preliminary to a grant of papal protection. The only alternative, therefore, was to associate the interests of the state with that element in the monastic constitution which, on account of its essentially secular nature, must inevitably be the object of transactions between the crown and the monastic churches. This was the advocacy. The advocate needed royal licence for the exercise of high criminal justice; and under Henry V this fact proved a valuable safeguard for the maintenance

---

[87] Cf. my remarks, MIÖG. *Erg.-Bd.* VII, 524.

[88] *Wirt. Urk.-Buch* I, 355: " Nec alius advocacie bannum a rege sive imperatore suscipiat, nisi qui abbate eligente et fratribus petentibus ad tantum officium dignus et idoneus videatur." In the papal charter which was the basis for this privilege, the passage in question goes much further in the direction of monastic liberty: " Nec alius advocatie bannum a catholico rege suscipiat, nisi qui ab abbate et fratribus electus exstiterit " (JL. 5866).

[89] Cf. also *St.* 3012: " Rogant etiam predicti comites per nos concedi predicte celle advocatum unum ex ipsis," with the emphasis on the phrase *per nos concedi.*

of royal influence in the appointment and consequently in the deprival of the *Vogt*.[90]

There can be no doubt that, if privileges of the type we have considered had been granted in larger numbers to the newly founded houses, the result would have been a strengthening of the German *Reichskirche*. In this way Henry V would have found a solution for one of the major problems which the circumstances of the day thrust upon him. But his premature death and the subsequent change of dynasty interrupted the course of the new development, which might otherwise have proved a really important factor in the maintenance of imperial rights. The privileges which Lothar III conferred on reformed monasteries give no indication of a decided policy.[91] Under Conrad III, however, the need once again arose for the crown to define its attitude to the new religious foundations; but this time it was the new foundations of the twelfth century, and the cause was the rapid growth of the Cistercian order. The settlement of the Cistercian question was one of the most important features of Frederick I's ecclesiastical policy. But the measures taken by the Hohenstaufen emperor were not new: the path he followed was that which had already been marked out by the last of the Salians.[92]

[90] There is an actual example of dismissal by the king at St. Blasien; cf. *St.* 3204.

[91] *St.* 3258 (Beuron), 3318 (Formbach), 3319 (Bürgel). It is characteristic that in the first two of these charters the monastery's position as a house protected by the papacy is more emphatically enunciated than in Henry V's charters for Hirsau houses.

[92] On Barbarossa's policy in regard to the Cistercians, cf. Hirsch, *Klosterimmunität*, cap. IV ("Die Verfassung der Zisterzienserklöster"). "The restoration of the German *Reichskirche*," it is there stated, "was not completely assured when the ancient rights of the empire were once more strictly enforced in regard to bishoprics and imperial abbeys. It was necessary also for the crown to define its position in regard to the new forces which the Investiture Contest had created within the ecclesiastical organisation. Henry V, as we know, had patronized the Hirsau foundations because he wished to bring them within the imperial sphere of interests, and Frederick I was faced by a similar task with regard to the Cistercians . . ." (pp. 111—112). "A monastery was brought into immediate connexion with the central authority if its *Vogtei* was in the ruler's own hands or at least under his direct influence. It was this fact on which Henry V relied in his efforts to make the reformed houses dependent on the crown. With greater emphasis and—favoured by the general situation —with greater success, Frederick I pursued the same object. It was the

With this glimpse into the future we can turn from the legal position of the Hirsau foundations to the more general question of the importance and significance of the innovations which they introduced into the constitution of the German church in the twelfth century. A consideration of the subsequent fate of the reformed monasteries will show, also, how far the Hirsau movement achieved its objects and how far its success or failure led to further legal development.

The constitution of the Augustinian canons was not substantially different from that of the Hirsau monasteries.[93] In this case, also, a papal charter of protection was frequently the foundation of the monastic constitution, and the relations between monastery and advocate were similar to those in Hirsau houses, but imperial confirmation of the papal charter was less frequent. Hirsau influences therefore dominated in the constitutional development of the Augustinian order. But Hirsau influence was not confined to the Canons Regular. It is also a recognized fact that it was due to the Hirsau movement that the charter dealing with the advocacy became one of the commonest types of twelfth-century document. Genuine and forged imperial charters, episcopal charters, charters issued by princes and even mere *notitiae* dealt with the advocate's duties and substantially limited his rights. For this reason both LAMPRECHT[94] and DOPSCH[95] have regarded the regulation of advocate's rights as the main feature of what is known as the later type of " immunity ". And these charters dealing with the advocacy prove beyond doubt that immunity and advocacy are separating in the twelfth

result of his ecclesiastical policy that his successors, particularly Frederick II and Conrad IV, could insist that the houses of the Cistercian order had, and could have, none but the emperor as advocate " (pp. 114—115).

[93] In Bavaria and Austria the Augustinians were very important as champions of the reform movement; cf. Brackmann, *Studien* I, 14 sqq. The *notitia* recording the foundation of Formbach proves that the idea of the *abbatia libera* was well known in Bavaria: " Ipsa abbatia ad Formbach est libera et monachi illi post mortem abbatis liberam potestatem habent ad eligendum sibi abbatem " (*Urkundenbuch d. Landes ob d. Enns* I, 779); " ut ea ipsa abbatia ad Formbach sit libera " (MG. *Script.* XV. ii, 1128).

[94] *Deutsches Wirtschaftsleben* I, 1021 sqq.

[95] MIÖG. XVII, 27 sqq.

century.   If the existence of the advocacy was previously
a consequence of immunity, it had acquired from the
twelfth century onwards a separate existence of its own.[96]

The regulation of advocate's rights which now took
place, should not, however, be regarded simply as a measure
directed against the advocates themselves or as a result
of the oppression which the monasteries suffered at the
hands of secular lords.[97]   To free the spiritual from the
secular authority, to limit to the utmost the question
over which the two must perforce come into contact, had
long been one of the foremost postulates of the church
party; and now, when the struggle was finished, the church
was strong enough to make its demands generally effective.
But however much the charters, which were mostly drafted
by the monasteries themselves, emphasized what was advantageous to the convent, it was impossible to avoid
mention, side by side with prohibitions and duties, of
the rights which really made the possession of an advocacy
a profitable investment in the twelfth and thirteenth
centuries.   One-third of the profits of jurisdiction is usually
fixed as the advocate's income.   But the Hirsau charter
also assigns criminal jurisdiction in life and limb to the
Vogt, and if it speaks of the heavenly reward, in expectation
of which his duties should be carried out, it also grants on
the occasion of each of the three annual *placita* a measure
of corn and wine, a wild boar, " et cetera ad hec pertinen-
tia ".[98]   For the development of financial and judicial
organisation, therefore—the mainstays of the sovereignty
of the princes which was soon to develop—advocacy over
a reformed monastery offered scarcely less opportunities
than the possession of a county or of the advocacy over a
monastery of more ancient origin.

From this point of view, it is very notable that the fate
of the reformed monasteries of south-west Germany
differs in no important respect from that of the ancient
imperial monasteries of the region.   It is therefore com-

[96] For preliminary developments in the tenth and eleventh centuries,
cf. Hirsch, *Klosterimmunität*, cap. I.
[97] Schreiber, *op. cit.* II, 280 sq. has also briefly emphasized this fact.
[98] Cf. *Wirt. Urk.-Buch* I, 278.

prehensible that both groups sought, in their charters, to accomplish the same ends. But each took a different path. The charters of the Hirsau foundations are all genuine: those of the imperial abbeys are all false, and all fabricated in the Swabian centre of Reichenau. LECHNER, to whom the discovery of this unique group of forgeries is due,[99] correctly surmised that the charters forged for Reichenau itself, for Kempten, Lindau, Buchau, Rheinau and Stein am Rhein, were intended one and all to establish the same rights—above all, free election of the abbot and safeguards against the advocate—for the houses in question, as the Hirsau abbeys had already obtained in their genuine privileges. This conclusion was supported by SCHULTE,[100] who emphasized the similarity of the constitutional objects of the two groups on the one hand, while on the other hand his important conclusions regarding the class composition of the houses—the imperial abbeys only accepted monks of noble birth, but the Hirsau foundations recognized no class distinction—clearly shewed the difference between the legal position of the two groups.

SCHULTE is correct, also, in maintaining that the emphasis on the free election of the abbot in the Swabian forgeries is intended to provide a means of resisting the proprietary rights of the German king; for it was on the basis of his proprietary rights, and within the framework of the *Eigenkirchenwesen*, that the king exercised the right of appointing the abbot without regard to the convent's right of free election. But it was not against the king alone that the forgeries were directed. Discoveries made after the appearance of the works of LECHNER and SCHULTE have shewn that the Reichenau forgeries had an even wider circulation than they supposed. To the monasteries which LECHNER named as possessing forged charters, Einsiedeln, Schuttern and Ebersheim must now be added.[101] Besides

---

[99] MIÖG. XXI, 28 sqq.

[100] *Der Adel u. d. deutsche Kirche*, 214 sqq.

[101] Cf. for Einsiedeln and Schuttern, my article in the *Neues Archiv* XXXVI, 395 sqq. The attribution of the forged Ebersheim charter to the Reichenau workshop was made simultaneously by myself (*ibid.*, 285) and by Stengel, *op. cit.* I, 702.

the imperial abbeys of the old type, the list thus includes three foundations (Schuttern, Stein am Rhein and Ebersheim) which at the time in question were episcopal proprietary monasteries. Thus the proprietary rights of the bishops were also attacked. The main object of the forged charter of Henry II for Stein was to define the relations between the abbey and the bishopric of Bamberg, in which proprietary rights were vested, and the forged charter of Arnulf for Ebersheim was probably only fabricated as a means of resisting the proprietary rights of the bishopric of Strassburg. If, therefore, the Hirsau monasteries regarded the destruction of the proprietary régime as the most important point in their programme of reform, the other Swabian foundations followed their lead with hardly less ardour.

In the second question, the regulation of relations with the advocate, the Reichenau group even outdid the Hirsau houses. If the latter had been content to regulate rights and establish prohibitions, the former proceeded to direct complaints.[102] But we have few facts which would enable us to test these accusations, and since there is no evidence to prove that the possession of advocacies over imperial monasteries was a major factor in the rise of the Swabian dynastic families before the forgeries were issued, it is necessary to beware of accepting at face value the Reichenau outbursts against the advocates. There is no doubt, on the other hand, that the first quarter of the twelfth century saw a very marked growth of the territorial ambitions of the secular nobility; and these ambitions were so serious a menace to all categories of monastic foundation that they may well have been the reason for the fabrication both of genuine and of false charters. A charter, in short, was a last, desperate attempt to escape the control and domination of the growing territorial princes. But, as HEILMANN has pointed out,[103] most advocacies in Swabia fell into the

---

[102] Cf. for example Mühlbacher, *Reg. imperii* I (2nd ed.), no. 1402: " satis audivimus et veraciter scivimus, scilicet plerosque eorum, qui ecclesiarum vocantur advocati debita potestate in tantum abuti, ut qui deberent esse modesti defensores, inpudenter effecti sint rapaces et iniuriosi exactores."

[103] *Op. cit.*, 132.

hands either of Hohenstaufen, Welfs or Zähringer. Of the advocacies in the possession of the Zähringer, only those at St. Georgen and St. Peter were accounted for by the circumstances in which the monastery had been founded. The advocacy over St. Blasien only passed into Zähringer hands in 1125 after Henry V had deposed the *Vogt* Adelgoz —a neat commentary on the freedom of election enunciated in both papal and imperial privileges! At the same period (1120) abbot Adalbert of Schaffhausen was complaining of oppression by Conrad of Zähringen.[104] Was the intention to bring Schaffhausen into dependence on the house of Zähringen in the same way as the adjoining abbey at Stein am Rhein, where the advocacy passed into Zähringer hands about the middle of the twelfth century?[105] In 1127 the dukes of Zähringen were made rectors of Burgundy, and soon afterwards they must have laid hands on the most important priory of the Bernese Oberland, for an authentic charter issued by Conrad III in 1146[106] speaks of the advocacy at Interlaken as " a duce Conrado iniuste retenta ". These facts speak for themselves. As advocacy was piled on advocacy, the sphere of influence of their possessor grew;[107] and so the advocacies in the new monastic foundations of the twelfth century provided a solid basis for the secular magnates' endeavours to consolidate their lands and build up their territorial power.

If the Black Forest was the centre of Zähringer power, the Lake of Constance was the sphere of influence of the Welf dukes. During the course of the twelfth century the advocacies over Reichenau, Kempten, Weingarten, Ochsenhausen and Zwiefalten are all found in their possession.[108]

[104] *Quellen z. Schweiz. Gesch.* III. i, 93.
[105] Cf. Heilmann, *op. cit.*, 36.
[106] *St.* 3521; as to its authenticity, cf. my remarks in the *Jahrb. f. Schweiz. Gesch.* XXXV, 6 sqq.
[107] The immediate and—for the monasteries—very undesirable result of the union of a number of advocacies in one hand was that the actual exercise of the office passed to an " assistant advocate " or " sub-advocate." The twelfth century sees the appearance of the distinction between *advocatus principalis* and *Untervogt*. Ordinances of Eugenius III and Frederick I prove how great a burden the latter were for the monasteries and how general must have been the abuses which arose from their appointment.
[108] Cf. Heilmann, *op. cit.*, 24, 30, 48, 56, 57.

Some of these were reformed houses, others were older imperial monasteries; but it is clear that the claim of the former to " liberty " made little difference to their actual constitutional position. The Welfs were able to control all equally; and the same is true of their successors. The heirs of the Welfs were the Hohenstaufen, while in the thirteenth century the Habsburgs replaced the Zähringer. Each of these dynasties in succession was to obtain the leading place in south-west Germany, and in both cases the possession of a large number of ecclesiastical advocacies was without doubt one of the main foundations of the family's power.

These facts alone are sufficient to indicate how unsuccessful the reformed monasteries were in their attempts to free themselves from secular control, and particularly from the control of the territorial princes. Engelberg alone, so far as I can see, achieved real liberty, as understood in the period of the Investiture Contest; but here it was a peculiarly favourable geographical position which permitted the formation of a miniature ecclesiastical state[109]—a state which kept its independence until the French invasions at the end of the eightenth century. With this exception, the monasteries which arose under the banner of *libertas* during the Investiture Contest, all fell, as a result of the advocacy, into one degree or another of dependence on the secular power.

These facts shew that the question of the advocacy was inevitably the most important issue in the whole Hirsau reform programme; but it was precisely at its most vital point that the programme of the reformers was unattainable, and for that very reason the whole movement was destined to end in failure. The advocacy was neither more nor less than a continuation of the proprietary church régime, and the advocate was consequently hardly less insufferable than the earlier proprietary lord. The reformed houses were almost exclusively founded by " dynasts ", and the support of the founders alone made the introduction of reform a feasible proposition. But monastic liberty

[109] Cf. Oechsli, *Die Anfänge der schweiz. Eidgenossenschaft*, 82 sqq.

was never more seriously threatened than at the moment when the secular founders began their rise to the position of territorial princes.[110] In examining the constitution of the Hirsau foundations we are therefore dealing simultaneously with a decisive phase in the history of the German nobility; for an inspection of the relations between the reformed monasteries and their dynastic founders and advocates enables us to define the special constitutional position of that privileged section of the nobility for which the investigations of VON DUNGERN[111] and SCHULTE have given us the technical name " dynasts ". The reformed monasteries hoped to shake off the proprietary lord and replace him by an innocuous " dynast "; but when the dynasts became territorial princes the monasteries once again found themselves dependent on a secular magnate.

Papal protection was unable to stave off this development. Transference of ownership to the Holy See was regarded by the monasteries as nothing more than the necessary preliminary to acquiring independence, and the papacy was consequently never able to lay claim to full proprietary rights over the protected abbeys.[112] Since the advocacy was really only a modified form of the older proprietary right which the lord had exercised in his churches, the heritage of the proprietary lord inevitably passed to the advocate and not to the pope. For this reason I have avoided speaking of the reformed monasteries as papal proprietary monasteries. However strong the pretensions of the Curia may have been, the importance of the reformed houses diminished abruptly, once the Investiture Contest was over. Even in the legal position a change is noticeable; and it is no accident that the first signs of this change occur under Innocent II, at the very moment when papal influence in Germany was at its height. Nothing is more

[110] Cf. also Schreiber's remarks, *Kurie u. Kloster* II, 257.
[111] Cf. his remarks in the *Deutsche Literaturzeitung* (1912), 1164.
[112] Heilmann, *Klostervogtei*, 109, similarly sets none too high a value on papal privileges, while Schulte, *Der Adel u. d. deutsche Kirche*, 156 sq., regards independence of the secular power as the main object of the Hirsau movement. As always, he finds the appropriate expression for the connexion between monasteries and papacy, when he says (p. 215): " papal influence only faintly affected secular transactions."

typical of the failure of the papacy's monastic policy than
the new interpretation which was then placed on the
conception of *libertas*. If liberty had originally signified
freedom from the secular proprietary régime, it gradually
came to mean freedom in the purely ecclesiastical sphere
—in other words, exemption from the authority of the
diocesan bishop.[113] It was in this connexion that the clause
in charters of protection which stated that tribute was paid
" ad indicium libertatis," was so valuable to the monasteries. For the same reason Alexander III decreed that
only those tributary houses whose privileges contained the
clause in question, and not thé formula: " ad indicium
protectionis ", were to be regarded as exempt from episcopal authority.[114] The emergence of this changed conception is discernible under Innocent II. At that date
for the first time the Curia issued a series of privileges
which instituted no direct protective connexion between
the monasteries and the Holy See and established no
tributary payment. But at the same time Innocent II's
chancery revised the " ad indicium " formula, introducing
the more precise expression: " ad indicium, quod idem
cenobium iuris beati Petri existat ", and thus accentuating
the significance of the clause. Under Innocent II, therefore, a beginning was made of the distinction between
German monasteries which were under the immediate
protection of the Holy See, and those for which a papal
charter constituted no such privilege. The latter type of
charter has no significance for our purpose; but the other
category, also, gradually changed its content, for its purpose, as we have said, was soon confined to granting exemption from episcopal authority. There could be no surer
sign that, from the time of Innocent II, the development
of papal protection was leading away from politics and back
to the narrower but more appropriate field of canon law:[115]

[113] Cf. Schreiber's admirable observations, *op. cit.* I, 24 sq., 46.
[114] Cf. Schreiber, *op. cit.* I, 38 sqq. But he treats all types of the
" ad indicium " formula together, although the variant: " ad indicium
quod idem cenobium iuris beati Petri existat," only appears under
Innocent II.
[115] Cf. Fabre, *Etude*, 98 sqq.; Schreiber, I, 42 sqq.

the main purpose of papal protection, in short, was again confined to the sphere of internal ecclesiastical organisation.

The union of papacy and " dynasts " had given the reformed monasteries of Swabia their constitution. But the changes in the seignorial rights of the dynasts, the growth of their political powers, which occurred in the course of the tenth and eleventh centuries, are evidence of a tendency which, if logically pursued, would inevitably lead, a century or more later, to territorial sovereignty. In their efforts to make the most of this tendency in constitutional development, it could only be advantageous to the lay aristocracy if the proprietary church régime and the rights they derived from it—rights which at bottom were essentially seignorial in character—were transformed into a right of a public nature: the advocacy. The dynasts therefore surrendered their monasteries to the papacy, and the result was to bring about a constitutional situation which established the independence of their foundations from the organisation of the *Reichskirche* and seriously impaired the rights of the crown, but which left the dynasts themselves—in fact, if not in theory—with the exercise of the substantial rights vested in the advocacy. At the moment when this development in monastic constitutional history had almost been brought to fulfilment, Henry V sought to save for the monarchy what little remained to be saved. If in the end success fell not to the crown but to the dynasts, we must attribute the failure to the course along which the relations of church and state as a whole had developed. The sovereigns in the territorial principalities of the later middle ages, the natural successors of the older dynastic aristocracy, once again transformed the *libertas* of the reformed monasteries into dependence on secular authority. After the middle of the twelfth century the Hirsau monasteries rapidly declined in importance. Those alone remained prominent whose dynastic advocates were most successful in the struggle to acquire territorial sovereignty. Among them St. Blasien must be given pride of place, and its subsequent prosperity was due above all else to the fact that its advocacy was vested in the powerful dynasties of Zähringen and Habsburg.

The process which we have followed,[116] is a process of disorganisation and dislocation, in which the "dynasts" were closely implicated: it is the process by which the old "immunity" or franchise, which had attained real constitutional importance in the Ottonian period, was transformed, or rather was destroyed. At first glance, it might appear that this destruction should be attributed to the papacy, which at the time of the Investiture Contest opposed the old organisation of the German national church by a new organisation of papal churches, and claimed the right to grant charters of immunity to the monasteries which belonged to the new organisation. But if we look more closely, we can see that the revolution in the constitution of the German church was really the result of a coincidence of external and internal forces. Long before the outbreak of the struggle between Empire and Papacy, the more powerful members of the privileged dynastic class, which as late as the eleventh century still claimed a monopoly of all secular and ecclesiastical offices, had emphasized the proprietary rights which they exercised in the monasteries of their own foundation in a way which was as unfavourable to the healthy development of the German national church as it was favourable to the plans of the reforming party. Common opposition to the king's proprietary rights—rights which were the essential and irreplaceable foundation of the German *Reichskirche*—subsequently brought the dynasts and the reform party into close association, and it was Leo IX who, in his double capacity as pope and scion of a German dynastic family, contrived to unite the two factions, widely differing though they were in their ultimate objects. His successors during the period of the Investiture Contest, from Gregory VII and Urban II onwards, bluntly asserted both their own proprietary rights over the Hirsau reformed foundations,

[116] The foll..wing paragraphs are taken from Prof. Hirsch's conclusions, *Klosterimmunität*, 214—219.

REFORMED MONASTERIES

and the exclusion from them of every species of secular power. Free choice of the advocate and the right to depose an unworthy advocate were the essential elements in the immunity which the popes, and not, as previously, the German kings, now granted in their charters of protection. As a consequence of the pope's intervention, the immunity definitely lost its peculiar constitutional importance—an importance it had retained until the closing years of the eleventh century—as a privilege conferred exclusively by the German king, and a bond which united the churches of the realm to the monarchy.

And yet the failure of the pope's monastic policy is evident in at least two directions. In the first place, Henry V was far-seeing enough, even before the conclusion of the Concordat of Worms, to resume relations with the reformed monasteries and to fashion them in such a way that the most important of the remaining sovereign rights of the German king, his judicial supremacy, was preserved and royal control over the appointment of advocates was maintained, while the monasteries themselves were brought directly under the crown and so saved, temporarily if not permanently, from the danger of subjection to the local princes. In the second place, the provision for free election and for the eventual dismissal of a troublesome advocate could not be made effective in practice. The proprietary rights of the dynasts were only theoretically replaced by papal proprietorship; in reality, the old *Eigenkirchenrecht* was transformed into the advocacy, and the seignorial rights of the founders thus became truly public-or governmental rights. In this way new perspectives opened out before those privileged dynastic families which began, already in the twelfth century, to mount the path which eventually led to territorial sovereignty.

From the point of view of the " dynasts ", the most important feature of the new situation lay, without doubt, in the fact that the advocate of a Hirsau monastery exercised criminal jurisdiction in life and limb over the monastic dependants. Even if we had no charters dealing with *furtum* and *effusio sanguinis*, the typical cases of major

crime,[117] there would be no doubt about this; for control
of high criminal justice was not only the almost unfailing
attribute of the dynastic and comital families, but was also
the one factor above all others which really made the possession of an advocacy desirable. Above all else, it furthered
the aristocracy's territorial ambitions. Through the exercise of justice in life and limb, which accrued to them as
advocates, the dynasts of comital rank got the opportunity
to extend their sphere of power beyond the confines of the
counties in their possession and beyond the boundaries of
their own allodial estates. To all appearances the Zähringer
were the first dynasty which succeeded in extending the
territories under their control on a grand scale by uniting
a number of advocacies in their own hands; but the
Babenberger and the Hohenstaufen soon followed their
example, and the Habsburger later pursued the same
policy.

The successors in the legal position won by the dynastic
advocates, however, were the territorial princes; and what
the " dynasts " won by a skilful exploitation of the situation resulting from the Investiture Contest thus provided
an essential element for the construction of the later
principalities. It is for this reason that an analysis of the
constitutional position of the reformed monasteries which
were founded at the time of the Investiture Contest helps
us to understand more fully one of the decisive phases of
German history; for the power of the dynasts was built
up during the conflict of church and state, and in the
closest connexion with the demands of the clerical reform
party, and the monarchy was never able to break the power
thus obtained. On the contrary, Henry V realized to the
full that the only chance of restoring the German constitution to its old state of poise and balance was to come to
terms both with the new monastic foundations and with
the dynastic aristocracy. But Henry's attempt to create
a new foundation for government was too closely bound up
with his person to succeed. When he was succeeded by the
Saxon, Lothar, his policy was dropped, and the local

[117] Cf. Hirsch, *Klosterimmunität*, cap. III.

" dynasts " were left to exploit the situation. The Hohenstaufen tried once more to pick up the threads of Henry V's
policy, but by then the decisive moment was past. It is
impossible, in surveying the whole process of development,
to ignore the parallel developments in France, where the
Investiture Contest and the questions of church and state
it raised had presented a similar problem to the statesmen
of the twelfth century. In France, the problem was decided
in favour of the crown by a process of centralisation: in
Germany, on the contrary, it ended in the first great victory
of the princes over the monarchy and thus strengthened
and furthered the growing independence of the sovereign
principalities.

VI

THE STATE OF THE DUKES OF ZÄHRINGEN[1]

By THEODOR MAYER

IN speaking to-day in this place of the state which was welded together by the dukes of Zähringen, and more generally of the rise of the mediaeval state, I am following the lines drawn by the man whose long years of outstanding achievement gave a permanent purpose and direction to the chair which it is my privilege to hold as his successor. GEORG VON BELOW gave his energies in the most comprehensive way to legal, economic and social history; but all these subjects were for him merely subsidiary parts of the greater topic, the history of the German state, the investigation of which was his ultimate purpose. He not only carried historical studies into new fields, but put the finishing touches to the work of a whole generation and built a solid foundation for a new generation of historians. On the other hand, every generation places its own problems before the historian, gives him specific tasks which keep his work in direct contact with contemporary life; and the present-day belief that state and people are one entity, that the state is the organisation in and through which the people acquires a capacity for political action, means that for us the history of the state is essentially the history of the people, and that no division can be made between the two.

And there is another factor. Since the external form and organisation of a state and the political life of a people are conditioned and determined by the soil and by the land

[1] " Der Staat der Herzoge von Zähringen," *Freiburger Universitäts-reden*, No. 20 (Freiburg im Breisgau: Fr. Wagnersche Universitätsbuch-handlung, 1935).—Thanks are due to the University Library, Freiburg, and to the publisher for permission to translate this inaugural lecture, which was delivered on 23 May, 1935, and to reproduce the map on p. 187.

175

they occupy, it is essential also to consider the geographical
situation when investigating any question connected with
the state and constitutional development.	State and land
are inseparably connected.	For that very reason, however,
we no longer consider the history of one German state or
region as a separate topic, but rather as a section cut from
the totality of German history.	The long-observed con-
trast between the general history of Germany and the history of any particular German principality is no longer
accepted in its old uncompromising form, for it was in
the principalities that the destiny of the German people
was decided over a period which lasted for many centuries.
The principalities shaped the structure of the German state
and of the German nation, and the development of particular territories—those, in particular, which lay along the
frontiers—constitutes an important chapter in the history
of the German people as a whole.	This, therefore, is the
spirit in which we shall approach German history and
German constitutional development in the south-western
parts of the German lands: it will be, for us, a section from
and a reflection of the development of the whole German
people.	If, in performing this task, we limit our attention
to the central period of the middle ages, it is because the
Zähringer state, which is our topic, failed to outlive the
era in question; but we hope nevertheless to be able to
make some contribution to the understanding of the
decisive period in German history, for, as HERMANN
HEIMPEL has said, it was the middle ages which determined
the destiny of Germany and produced the forms of government and political organization on which German public
life was to be based through centuries of change down into
our own day.

The Germanic state was originally the state of a united
folk, in which people and government were one body.
But the growing strength of the monarchy destroyed this
early unity, and both Germanic and German constitutional
life were thenceforward characterized by a dualism which
found expression in a variety of ways and even developed,
in many fundamental constitutional questions, into a

direct antithesis. This antithesis between two self-competent elements is particularly clear in the relations of the German empire and the German principalities. The very fact of their coexistence is characteristic of the German state, in which we find a complex interlocking and intermingling of independent rights and duties which is altogether inconceivable in the modern world. The Germanic state was characterized also by the fact that it was a community of persons, held together by personal bonds, notably by the bond of fealty. Corresponding to this conception of the state as an association of persons, we find that constitutional rights and functions were organized and distributed on the basis of the relations of lord and man—a relationship characteristic of the early Germanic *comitatus*, or sworn following, and later of the feudal system. This form of state—in essence a graded hierarchy—was found in Germany in the earlier period of its history. It is certainly true that the central government sought to use its administrative powers to break through the rigid hierarchy and make direct contact with the people; but all such attempts ended in failure. The Carolingian organization of countships was ultimately unsuccessful because it ceased to be a sure instrument in the hands of the king. Later Henry IV attempted to create a new basis for royal power by making the exercise of criminal justice strictly dependent on royal authorization; but his action was not thorough enough to meet the situation. Finally a third method of constitutional reform was attempted by Barbarossa, who gave recognition to the territorial states which were in process of formation, but at the same time tried to bind them directly to the central authority by feudal ties. But even if the immediate failure of Barbarossa's plans was due to the particular political circumstances of his day, it still remains doubtful whether feudal bonds were in the long run a really adequate means of confining the ever more vigorous life of the principalities and their independent constitutional development within fixed boundaries. Above all, it is clear that the type of political organisation we are considering depended much too closely on the personality of the ruler. A state which was held together by personal bonds could rise to great heights under a ruler of exceptional powers, who knew how to create a following and build up a sense of solidarity; but the very fact that it depended on the ruler's energy meant that its stability was doubtful, its existence conditioned by the continued activity of its statesmen. Such states were the work of men of genius, whose abilities were sometimes so immense that they were able to create not only a community which could outlive them but also a durable tradition.

If this type of constitutional organization depended ultimately on a strong personal following and the personality of the ruler, there was a second type of state which stands out in marked contrast. Here the starting point was the exercise of administrative functions. States of this class grew from small beginnings within narrow boundaries, developed slowly, were based on institutions and on the machinery of government, and the machinery of government was their very essence. We may well call them institutional "states"; and they were more durable in character than the state which was an association of persons and which could not exist without great rulers. The institutional state was governed by solid, acquired capacity rather than by genius; and the specific danger which it faced was therefore the risk of petrification, of transformation through excessive bureaucracy into an autocratic state, existing solely for itself. The association of persons was the older form of the German state: the uniform institutional state developed in the course of the middle ages side by side with, and subsequently in opposition to, the principle of personality on which the older state was based. This process is generally referred to as the "rise of the sovereign principalities"; but actually the main change which this process brought about was the transition from the state which was an association of persons, not merely with far-reaching distinctions of rank and class, but with rank and class used as the vital element of government, to the administrative state where all subjects were placed on an equality before the law and government was uniform —the transition, in short, from the mediaeval to the modern state. There is, indeed, a fundamental contrast between the German realm as a whole and the German principalities; but the transition which began in the principalities at the turn of the eleventh and twelfth centuries took place not so much in opposition to the Empire and the central government as in competition with it. Between the imperial government and the government of the principalities the question was not whether the one should defeat the other, but which should play the larger part in developing still further the functions and competence of government; which was going to assume and discharge the new duties which new social movements were creating; and which finally would be able to develop the governmental machinery which alone could give the state the means to cope with the new problems of a new age.

Our purpose here is to illustrate this critical phase of German constitutional development from the history of the state of the dukes of Zähringen, a state which arose in the course of the eleventh century and perished in 1218 when the Zähringer dynasty died out.

The region in which the Zähringer were active was the Swabian or Alemannian land in the south-west of Germany, a region which could only with great difficulty be moulded into political and geographical unity since it was cut in two by the Black Forest. It is true that the Black Forest was no longer altogether uncolonized when the eleventh century began, nor was it an absolute check on communications, since it was already traversed by roads which could be used for military purposes; but the fact that— south of the road which led from Offenburg through the valley of the Kinzig to Villingen, and thence to the valleys of Neckar and Danube and to Schaffhausen—no major road crossed the Black Forest before the bend of the Rhine at Basel meant clearly enough that for all practical purposes the Rhine valley was abruptly separated from the region east of the Black Forest. The upper Rhine valley itself,

on the other hand, was so closely knit together on both
banks of the river that it formed one undivided geo-political
unit. It was therefore no accident, but rather the natural
result of the geographical situation, that the colonization
of the valleys which ran westwards out of the Black Forest
was carried out by monasteries like Gengenbach, Schuttern,
Ettenheimmünster and St. Trudpert, which had been
founded by monastic settlers from the west, although the
region of the Black Forest belonged as a whole to the
diocese of Constance in the south. And to the houses
mentioned we must add also the Cluniac abbeys of St.
Ulrich and Sölden, although these were in fact founded by
monks from Basel. It is at any rate notable that monasteries which, like those we have enumerated, were directly
under French influence, were only to be found on the
western slopes of the Forest and specifically in the district
influenced by Basel. East of the Black Forest there is not
one single house. A few monasteries like St. Gallen and
Einsiedeln, which lay within the boundaries of modern
Switzerland, had properties in the Breisgau; but since they
were merely remote outposts of the monasteries in question,
they exercised no influence as far as the cohesion of the
lands east and west of the Black Forest was concerned.

There were also only two great lay families with possessions on both sides of the Black Forest: the house of
Bertold, the forbears of the Zähringer and of the later
margraves of Baden, and the counts of Hohenberg. The
Hohenberg dynasty originated in Swabia and had properties
in the Dreisamtal with the castle of Wiesneck as their
centre. They were nevertheless considerably less powerful
than the Bertold-Zähringer dynasty, which held the
countships in the Thurgau, the Albgau, the Ortenau and
the Breisgau, together with a number of ecclesiastical advocacies, and also doubtless possessed allodial properties,
the extent of which remains uncertain. Thus the Zähringer
belonged, together with the Hohenstaufen and the Welfs,
to the small and select group of great Swabian families who
were destined to play a decisive part in German history.

In the eleventh century the Bertold family split into two

branches: the margraves who took over the countships in the Breisgau and the Ortenau, and the ducal line which acquired the family's Swabian possessions and began, about 1100, to call itself "von Zähringen", a title which it derived from one of the fiefs it held in chief from the crown. Only an imperial fief, it would seem, and not an allodial lordship, was considered a suitable basis for a ducal position. Bertold I had been made duke of Carinthia as early as 1061, but had never obtained actual possession of the duchy. During the Investiture Contest he is found with his sons, Bertold II and Gebhard, bishop of Constance, on the anti-imperial side. Bertold II was son-in-law of the anti-king, Rudolf of Rheinfelden, and from Rudolf he received the duchy of Swabia. But here again it was impossible to obtain effective control, and in 1098 Bertold renounced Swabia, though retaining both the *Reichsvogtei* in Zürich and the title of duke. He had succeeded in 1090 to the heritage of the extinct house of Rheinfelden, and with it obtained a firm foothold in Switzerland. His son, Conrad, became rector of Burgundy in 1127, and so acquired a position on the left bank of the Rhine which was approximately the equivalent of that of a duke, though its substance could hardly be exactly defined. The dynasty had thus risen high without holding a duchy in the ancient sense of that term, and Otto of Freising explicitly refers to the dignity of the dukes of Zähringen as an empty title. But such a title, if recognized by the imperial government, expressed a definite claim; and the only question was whether this claim would be substantiated, how it might be given content and reality.

The geographical and economic situation in south-west Germany created two main problems, the answer to which would affect the whole political situation. Who, in the first place, was going to obtain economic control of the Black Forest ? And who, secondly, would be capable of consolidating and organizing it as a coherent political unit ? Whoever succeeded in these tasks was assured of predominance along the upper reaches of the Rhine and in Swabia.

One attempt to solve the problem was made by the Hohenstaufen, who had already extended their power from Swabia into Alsace. There can be no doubt that Henry VI's acquisition of Breisach in 1185 and Frederick II's subsequent efforts to obtain a share in the Zähringer inheritance were intended to fit in with this ambitious Hohenstaufen territorial policy. But it was impossible to make a complete success of this programme for the very reason that the vital connecting-link between Swabia and Alsace was not in Hohenstaufen hands—because the Hohenstaufen, in other words, were not in control of the Black Forest—and because with the extinction of the dynasty its territorial policy perished and the duchy of Swabia ceased to exist.

The most efficient means of getting economic control of an unpopulated or only thinly settled land was colonization and cultivation; and this was left for the most part to monastic foundations. In the Black Forest, as we have seen, colonization had already begun and was proceeding eastwards from the western boundaries of the district; but it had as yet scarcely reached the more elevated and mountainous parts. The eastern side of the forest was still practically unsettled, and as colonization had also not yet reached the heads of those valleys which ran westwards, there was still plenty of room for new monastic foundations. The abbeys of Reichenbach and Alpirsbach were founded in the upper parts of valleys running westward, but the foundation was carried out by monks coming from the east, and the upper valley of the Simonswald, although it actually fell within the zone of settlement to which Waldkirch laid claim, passed under the control of St. Peter because it was from there—that is to say, from higher up the valley—that colonization took place. The monastery of Peterzell, which was a cell of Reichenau, lay at the very peak of the Black Forest; but it was so distant from the mother-house that its colonizing activities were inevitably checked; and in the same way neither St. Gallen nor Einsiedeln played a leading part in the Black Forest, while St. Blasien only acquired importance as a centre of agrarian development after its separation from the mother-house at Rheinau.

It was in the second half of the eleventh century, and in the closest connexion with the widespread foundation of reformed monasteries which then took place, that the work of colonization made greatest progress. The outstanding personality in this movement was abbot William of Hirsau. There is no doubt that he owed much to the inspiration of abbot Bernard of St. Victor of Marseilles, who was taken prisoner by the count of Lenzburg when discharging the functions of papal legate in Germany, and as a result stayed in Hirsau between October 1077 and September 1078. It is well-known that the abbey of St. Victor of Marseilles had brought so large a number of monasteries under its own immediate control that a huge ecclesiastical organiza-tion had been built up—an organization which has been called " the ecclesiastical state of Marseilles." BRACKMANN has observed that William of Hirsau pursued a policy similar to that of the abbot of St. Victor. He also was going to have his " ecclesiastical state "; and William's success stands out very clearly if Hirsau is compared with the second great reformed monastery of the district, St. Blasien, which failed to achieve prominence by the founda-tion of dependent houses in the Black Forest, except within its own immediate neighbourhood. The same is true of Cluniac houses like St. Ulrich, the activities of which were confined within narrow limits. Abbot William, on the other hand, succeeded in getting the abbey of Schaffhausen, which the count of Nellenburg had founded in 1050, both reformed and, in 1080, placed under the control of Hirsau. Among the monastic foundations in the region of the Black Forest which were directly due to abbot William and to Hirsau, we may mention that of Reichenbach in 1082 and that of St. Georgen in 1083–1085, while the Zähringer family monastery of Weilheim was transferred in 1093 to St. Peter, and Alpirsbach was established in 1095. In general, therefore, it is possible to recognize a systematic policy of obtaining control in the central and eastern parts of the Black Forest by the establishment of new monastic foundations.

This fact is illustrated by an interesting account of the foundation of St. Georgen, which the monastic chronicler has handed down to us. This monastery had originally been established in Königseckwald in the Saulgau, and given to the papacy by the founder. Shortly afterwards the abbot of Hirsau was called in to organize the new establishment. But he declared the site to be unsuitable, and declined the task, demanding instead that the house should be transferred to the Black Forest. The founders, however disagreed with his proposal, and, explaining that they had already handed the monastery over to the pope, declared that it was no longer in their power to dispose of it. Abbot William therefore sent a monk without delay to the Holy See and got papal sanction for the proposed removal. As a result the monastery was transferred to the Black Forest and set up on a site near the source of the Brigach and the crossing to the valleys of the Kinzig and the Elz—a site which, though wild and desolate, was extremely important from the point of view of communications. From this point of view, indeed, the position, a few miles north, of Peterzell was perhaps a little more favourable; but the properties of St. Georgen extended north of Peterzell, and this gave it control of the road to Hornberg. The whole incident therefore provides undeniable evidence that abbot William had a thorough understanding both of political geography and of the significance of communications, and that such considerations guided his policy of monastic foundation. He reminds us on a smaller scale of St. Boniface who first obtained control of the region between the Main and the lands inhabited by the Saxons and then established Fulda, an abbey exempt from episcopal authority, in the very centre.

But HANS HIRSCH has shown that a plan so majestically conceived was more than a monastery even as important as Hirsau could put into execution. Opposition to abbot William's schemes quickly came to a head, especially in ecclesiastical circles. Bishop Gebhard of Constance, a pupil of William, deserted his master when he proposed to place St. Georgen under the permanent control of Hirsau, and

Urban II finally brought the various monasteries of the district under the immediate protection of the Holy See. And abbot William was as unsuccessful against the secular powers as he had been with the ecclesiastical opposition. His struggle against the ancient proprietary régime was completely successful; but he could do nothing to prevent the transformation of the more expressly political elements in the proprietary system into the hereditary advocacy which was monopolized by the dynastic lords. He failed, in other words, to bring the advocacy under monastic control. Where a monastery had hitherto belonged as a whole to the proprietary lord, a division of powers was now introduced: the ecclesiastical body obtained freedom to direct its own spiritual life and to administer its economic resources, but secular matters—in other words, the exercise of governmental authority over the monastery's lands and subjects—remained in the hands of the proprietary lord in his capacity as hereditary advocate of the monastery. But if the advocate, whose task it was to protect and represent the house before the secular authorities, was himself the possessor of secular authority, his tenure of the advocacy meant neither more nor less than the incorporation of the monastic territories in the advocate's own lordship. The unity of the monastic lordships was thus split up: on the one hand, there were the ecclesiastical and economic elements which remained under monastic control, on the other, the political element which was brought into direct contact with the general currents of political and constitutional life by the advocacy and through the advocate. The monasteries tried to stave off this process, which took different forms in different cases, by the wholesale use of forged privileges; but nothing could hold it in check.

It was at this stage in the process of historical development that the Zähringer intervened. They had already formed connexions with the reformed monasteries, and particularly with William of Hirsau, through bishop Gebhard of Constance, a brother of duke Bertold II; and this circle of men was responsible for the foundation and

development of the Zähringer family monastery at St.
Peter. They had long been advocates of those properties
of the bishopric of Bamberg which lay in south-west Germany, and they therefore held the advocacies in the
monasteries which belonged to Bamberg—Gengenbach,
Schuttern and Stein am Rhein—while the advocacy of
St. Trudpert was exercised by one of their ministerial
dependents. They were, moreover, hereditary advocates
in their own family foundation of St. Peter; they acquired
the advocacy over St. Georgen in 1114, if not before, and
that over St. Blasien in 1125; and finally they made
repeated attempts—which, though unsuccessful, are an
interesting revelation of their objects—to get possession
of the advocacy of St. Gallen. A glance at the map shows
that these advocacies gave the Zähringer control of the
whole Black Forest from the Kinzigtal southwards: there
was, in fact, no crossing through the forest which did not
pass through Zähringer lands. Particularly important in
this regard was the acquisition of the advocacy of St.
Georgen; for this brought the whole of the valley of the
Kinzig into the hands of the Zähringer and closed a possible
route from the Elztal through St. Georgen to the east.
With this acquisition the possessions of the dynasty were
rounded off and their position in the Black Forest set on
a firm foundation. It seems that duke Conrad—associated
in the first place with his brother, Bertold III—was the
driving force in the realization of this policy, for immediately
he took control on the death of his father Zähringer policy
was vitalized by an accession of energy which can be traced,
in particular, in the advancement and development of
St. Peter.

Between the Kinzig valley and the upper Rhine there
were, in addition to the Zähringer, two independent baronial
families: the margraves of the Breisgau, who were related
to the ducal dynasty, and the lords of Schwarzenberg, who
were the advocates of Waldkirch. Both these families,
however, were obviously completely under the dominance
of the Zähringer, in whose charters they constantly figure
as witnesses. But there was still another enclave within

Hirsau

STRASSBURG

Reichenbach

OFFENBURG

Schuttern
Gengenbach

Schutter

Kinzig Alpirsbach

Ettenheimmünster
Tennenbach

BREISACH
Waldkirch St.Georgen Peterzell ROTTWEIL
St.Peter
St.Märgen VILLINGEN
FREIBURG
Sölden
St.Ulrich
St.Trudpert Friedenweiler
NEUENBURG
Sulzburg

St.Blasien

Schaffhausen
Allerheiligen Stein a.Rh. Reichenau

Wiese Wutach Rheinau
Säckingen Constance
BASEL Lake of Constance
RHEINFELDEN

Aare

Lake of Zürich

Reuss

BURGDORF

Lake of Neuchâtel
OLTIGEN
Gümmenen BERN
MURTEN LAUPEN
FREIBURG i.Ü.
Lake of
Lucerne
HOUDON THUN

● *Zähringer towns*

+ *Monasteries*

⊕ *Monasteries reformed by Hirsau*

✤ *Other reformed monasteries*

= *Roads* ⚬ *Castles*

the Zähringer sphere of power and influence. This was the demesne of the counts of Hohenberg in the Dreisamtal which, although not large, was of particular importance because of its position dominating the best line of communication between the Breisgau and Swabia. The foundation and endowment of St. Peter clearly indicates that the Zähringer intended to give the monastery control of as long a stretch as possible of the route which led from the Glotter valley through Rohr to St. Peter and thence over the Hohle Graben to the east. In particular, no doubt, the idea was that it should control those parts of the Black Forest which were still uncolonized, and where questions of ownership consequently still remained unsettled. This intention, however, was thwarted by the foundation of St. Märgen in 1118. An Augustinian house, it was established a few miles east of the monastery of St. Peter by Bruno, a prebendary of Strassburg, who filled it with French canons regular. And Bruno, later bishop of Strassburg, was a member of the Hohenberg family. A sharp struggle between St. Peter and St. Märgen immediately ensued, on the grounds that the tenants of St. Märgen had carried their work of reclamation into the territory of St. Peter. The contest was brought to an end in 1121 by arbitration. St. Märgen had to surrender two manors, but was allowed to extend its demesnes northwards as far as the boundaries of Waldkirch. The result, therefore, was that the lands of St. Märgen advanced like a wedge from the Wagensteig valley into the otherwise well-rounded territory of St. Peter, and that some two miles of the road from St. Peter to the Hohle Graben passed under the control of St. Märgen.

It is very striking that the Zähringer gave way on a question of such importance; for there was no issue more critical in the whole of their territorial policy than the question whether or not the road from the Breisgau to Swabia should traverse their lands alone and those of their family monastery, since the whole significance of this route for them lay in the fact that it provided a way from Breisgau to Swabia which avoided the Hohenberg estates in the

Dreisamtal. Unfortunately we have no direct information to explain why they accepted the arbitration of 1121; but an indication may perhaps be obtained from other sources. The place of Wiesneck, which was, as we have seen, the centre of the Hohenberg estates, is mentioned in the *Rotulus Sanpetrinus* under the year 1112 without any qualification. In 1121, on the other hand, and again in 1136, there is mention of a " castrum dirutum." A survey of the boundaries of St. Peter, moreover, which is found in the *Rotulus* and which is based on the survey of 1112, substitutes for the simple entry: " Wiesneck," which had been used in 1112, the phrase: " castrum dirutum Wiesneck "; and this later survey was inserted in the *Rotulus* by a scribe writing towards the close of the thirteenth century. The conclusion we must draw, therefore, is that the castle at Wiesneck was still standing in 1112, that it was destroyed between 1112 and 1121, and that its destruction was so thorough that it had not been rebuilt by 1136 or even by the thirteenth century. We know further that political power in the Dreisamtal subsequently passed to the Zähringer and their successors—in other words, that the Hohenberg dynasty was not able to create a territorial principality for itself. The lordship of Wiesneck was in fact finally sold to a citizen of Freiburg, Burkart Turner, in 1293, and had therefore obviously lost the last semblance of baronial character. In this connexion, therefore, there can be no doubt that the Zähringer won a complete victory over the Hohenberger; and it is a fair assumption not only that it was they who destroyed the castle of Wiesneck— we know of no other dynasty which could have done so— but also that the occasion for this action was the foundation of St. Märgen. We can also conclude that, having acquired control over the road through the Dreisamtal by this victory over the Hohenberger, the Zähringer had no further interest in the secondary route from the Glottertal through St. Peter, St. Märgen and the Hohle Graben to Swabia, and were therefore willing to accept the results of the arbitration between St. Märgen and St. Peter in 1121.

At first sight this conclusion may appear hazardous, but it is confirmed by still another circumstance Shortly after the Zähringer acquired full control of the road from the Breisgau through the Black Forest, they founded the towns of Freiburg and Villingen.   They thus created an urban centre at each end of the route, and so put the final touch to the system of communications they had built up. This fact shows how closely inter-related were all the incidents and aspects of Zähringer policy which we have enumerated.   But they still constitute but one side of that policy: for there is small reason to doubt that the foundation of the town of Offenburg was contemporaneous with that of Freiburg.   Our information here is incomplete, but the similarity of idea in the planning of Offenburg and Freiburg is very striking.   It is evident, above all, in the way in which the junction with the long-distance roads is effected and the market-place is laid out.   The market-place is in reality no thoroughfare; for there was originally only an entry at one end, and the other was made later. This peculiarity is even more characteristic than the rib-like planning of the side-streets which branch out from each side of the market.   Above all, there is no central crossing of two mainroads, such as is found in Villingen. Similarity in all these features, which are otherwise unparalleled in the whole district, is so conspicuous that there is every reason to suppose that Freiburg and Offenburg were constructed at the same time and by the same lord. Such being the case, there can be little doubt that the foundation of Offenburg was an immediate result of the acquisition of the advocacy over the monastery of St. Georgen, which gave the Zähringer control of all the ways of communication through the Kinzig valley.   Thus the road and land policy of the Zähringer was completed by the creation of the urban triangle: Offenburg, Villingen, Freiburg.   Further development of the system occurred subsequently with the acquisition of Breisach in 1198; but the main exponent of this energetic policy seems nevertheless to have been duke Conrad, the founder of Freiburg, under whom a new, more vigorous current can be perceived

in Zähringer policy. It is usual to consider urban development and the foundation of towns as a separate chapter
in history, and particularly as a part of economic history.
The abundant literature about Freiburg itself is an example
of this; for it is repeatedly emphasized that Freiburg was
a centre of local trade, the market for the surrounding
villages, and if it has sometimes been regarded as a town
with distant trade, there is small foundation for this view.
But the fact is that the foundation of Freiburg can only be
properly understood as an element in the general political
programme of the Zähringer; and it will probably be found
that this applies to most towns, and that their origins and
functions cannot be comprehended except in relation to
the greater movements of economic life, and above all, of
politics.

The political activities of the house of Zähringen, the
establishment of their lordship and the formation of their
state, are a striking testimony to the significance of the
occupation of a land by reclamation and colonization, an
outstanding example of the process by which the results
of such a policy were made to bear political fruits in the
organization and development of the state. Exactly the
same process can be seen at work on a similar scale in the
case of the lords of Schwarzenberg, who used their position
as advocates of Waldkirch to found a lordship which
comprehended the whole of the Elztal and only failed to
become a true principality because the Schwarzenberger,
hemmed in by more powerful neighbours, lacked the essential political power. Land which was acquired by reclamation was regarded and treated as allodial in character.
This fact alone enables us to explain how duke Conrad
could call his own the land, surrounded and shut in by the
demesne lands of the crown, on which Freiburg was built;
for there is no reason to suppose that the few acres enclosed
within the new walls were given by the crown to the
Zähringer—indeed, it may be doubted whether this was
really a case of colonization at all, and whether colonization
was not perhaps simply made an excuse to claim allodial
rights. In the same way the district occupied by St. Peter

was called private property and then given to the papacy;
and it was the same at St. Märgen. Another example is
the district round Rohr, which was stated to be the allodial
property of Arnold of Kenzingen. In none of these cases,
however, is there any evidence to indicate that the property
in question was either an ancient family holding or an allodial land bought or exchanged by Zähringer, Hohenberger
or Kenzinger. Reclamation and colonization therefore
not only meant the economic advantage of a more extensive
demesne, but it also allowed whoever carried out the
colonization to claim the land as his allodial property and
therefore to exercise supreme political rights within the area
of settlement—or so, at least, if the occupant was already
otherwise in possession of such rights as was the case both
with the dynastic families of the high aristocracy and with
those persons who held counties or duchies. Anyone who
acquired new land in this way by reclamation also acquired
increased political power: he rose above his fellows, who
more or less balanced each other out politically, and so
got the opportunity of building up a lordship on a larger
scale, of organizing a veritable state. It is a well-known
feature of German constitutional development that the
colonial lands of the east witnessed the rise of political
organizations constructed on a broader basis than anything
which was known in old west Germany—principalities
which were not burdened with the historical traditions of
the older regions and which consequently developed more
uniformly. These new states in eastern Germany, it is
well known, rapidly outstripped the politically disjointed
west in political development, and therefore played a decisive part in the formation of a united German state.
But this process was no innovation confined to the east
colonial lands. It can be observed equally clearly in old
west Germany, where the distinction between the regions
of ancient settlement and the newly colonized areas is no
less evident, both from an economic and from a political
point of view. But the opening up of new land and its
political organization paved the way also for still another
conception: the conception of government based on the

land itself, on the territorial unit, instead of on persons and on an association of persons. The advocacy played its part in the exploitation of this idea as the means by which ecclesiastical lands were brought within the orbit of secular politics. In the newly colonized regions, finally, conditions were not so circumscribed, there were not so many competing authorities, each standing in the way of the other's rise and progress. And instead of being scattered and parcelled out, as in the older regions, landed property in the newly-settled areas was practically without exception formed into great consolidated demesnes, uniformly administered as part of a coherent manorial organization. All these factors played the · part in development throughout mediaeval German; · but there is hardly another German principality in which the construction of a " state " in the modern sense of the term was carried out at so early a date and with such systematic consistency as in the lands ruled by the Zähringer.

It is only possible to speak of a state in the true sense of the term when internal administrative autonomy, at the very least, has been obtained. Such autonomy, according to German conceptions, was the prerogative of the duke, but not of the count. It was only obtained by counts where they were politically independent of ducal authority, where there either was no duchy or where a pre-existing duchy had for one reason or another been destroyed; where, in short, the counts had themselves stepped into the duke's place. For the most part, however, the rise of comital houses in this way did not occur until a somewhat later period: in the eleventh century a legal title of one sort or another was still regarded as essential. Such being the case, the value of the ducal title borne by the Zähringer is evident enough. Since it was recognized by the imperial chancery, there was no doubt that it entitled them to the high rank of duke, and—placed in this way on an equality with other dukes—they could automatically claim independence from any other ducal authority. When Otto of Freising said that the ducal title to which the Zähringer laid claim was an empty formality, he was doubtless thinking in terms of the older type of " stem " duchy; and in this sense he was unmistakably right. The Zähringer had no such duchy and could not think of founding one anew. But the charters relating to the foundation of the Austrian duchy in 1156 and of the duchy of the bishops of Würzburg in 1168 prove that one of the essential features of ducal authority in the twelfth century was the dependence of every exercise of governmental authority, of the maintenance of public peace, and of every form of jurisdiction, on the duke himself: he alone had the right to set up courts of justice. It is clear, however, that such rights could easily be exercised by the Zähringer, since in the district which concerned them, the Black Forest, they had absolutely no rivals to face. Their rights were consequently never disputed. And the guarantee of free conduct to merchants, which duke Conrad included in the foundation-charter of Freiburg, is proof of their determination to exercise all governmental rights and to fulfill all governmental duties. On the other hand, their ducal title safeguarded them from the dominance of the duke of Swabia. The Zähringer duchy was therefore a duchy like any other, so far as its constitutional and legal capacities were concerned; but its internal structure was different, for it was a territorial state and not the continuation of an ancient tribal duchy, from which it had only taken over certain external characteristics and the claim to independence in the exercise of administration.

The new territorial state also developed a new relationship with its subjects. The state which was an association of persons was based, as we have seen, on the linking together of the population by such bonds as vassalage and villeinage. The state based on territorial unity, on the other hand, had no use for the bonds of personal dependence. Governing a wide territory by uniform methods, and claiming equal obedience from all inhabitants, so that the dependence of the subject on the state and that of the villein on his lord were gradually assimilated, its rulers had no reason to continue to emphasize servile bonds, which consequently fell into oblivion in the older states and in the newer ones were never established. The duty of allegiance which was imposed on all subjects by public law—whether its source was the exercise of governmental rights which was the essence of the advocacy, or whether it resulted simply from direct control over a certain territory, is a question which hardly matters—was considered to be sufficient for all purposes. And this new outlook was necessarily most effective of all in the newly settled lands, where it was the policy to attract colonists by granting more favourable rights and where government was not hampered by old-fashioned conditions. But it was not these external circumstances alone so much as the changed attitude of the new authorities to the whole problem of government, which really set the new constitutional movement going. The new situation is, of course, very conspicuous in the colonial lands of east Germany, where ideas which gave rise to many a struggle in the motherland were introduced in their purest, most uncompromising form. In the east, the governments of the new states and not merely local manorial lords were the pioneers in the work of colonization, and this difference was reflected in the wide liberties which were there conferred on the new settlers. Yet this was not a measure confined to the east; for the same policy which we can observe in east colonial Germany can be seen at work also in the Zähringer state.

The first example which meets us is the freedom granted to the citizens of Freiburg—a freedom which is generally regarded as the pattern of civic liberties. The inhabitants of the towns, it is well known, were rarely, if indeed ever, of free origin; but the new form of political organization, the new relationship of subject and state, which was in process of formation, destroyed the motives for conserving the old personal bonds, which consequently died out, with the result not only that we always speak of free townspeople but also that the word " citizen " itself has ultimately become the established term by which we denote free subjects. There is, however, another perhaps even more striking example of the same change in the growth of the " free peasantry ", which is found not only in the

east but also in old west Germany. It is true that there
had always been a free element in the rural population;
but its significance was small, for the freemen were scattered over the countryside and lacked constitutional organization. With the arrival of the twelfth and thirteenth
centuries, however, when our information begins to be
fuller, we once again find free peasants in far from incon-
siderable numbers. But these free peasants were not the
descendants of the old free element; for they are consistently
found on newly cultivated land, and above all in districts
where the state itself had been directly concerned with the
work of colonization. In the eleventh century the manorial
lords had still been settling their lands with servile bonds-
men. But with the split, which then ensued, between
manorial lordship and governmental rights, a corresponding
change took place in the position of the peasant colonists.
The *Freiamt* north of Emmendingen, a few miles from
Freiburg—the administration established for the freeman
of the district—is a striking proof of this transformation
and of the fact, not only that the colonists were now being
granted freedom, but also that the new state authority
was interesting itself in the free peasants and organizing
them into administrative units. But the *Freiamt* at
Emmendingen was only one example of a new development
which, as WELLER has proved, was found throughout
Swabia, and there is evidence of a similar innovation in
Upper and Lower Austria, in the Tyrol and in the territory
of the archbishops of Salzburg. The new administrative
unit may have had a different name in different places;
but the fact remained the same everywhere. The " modern'
state of the later middle ages deliberately refrained from
setting up the old social order in the newly colonized lands;
it neither needed nor desired the organization of the population by bonds of status and personal dependence; it got
rid of them in the colonial lands and broke through them,
if it was strong enough, in the older regions. These facts
indicate how immensely important reclamation and colonization were as factors in the political and social development
of Germany. And no princes played a more outstanding

part in this process than the Zähringer. They introduced free peasants on their Swiss estates as well as in the Black Forest; and it was in Switzerland, where they made a name for themselves as founders of towns, that they applied their constitutional policy in its purest form. For their activities extended to the free townsfolk as well as the free peasantry, and Burgdorf, Oltigen, Bern, Thun, Gümmenen, Laupen, Freiburg, Murten and Moudon are all examples of their energy in stimulating civic life on the left bank of the Rhine. The rectorship of Burgundy meant as much for the Zähringer in this region as the ducal title on the right bank of the Rhine. It gave them, above all else, the opportunity to act and govern in those parts of Burgundy east of the Jura which alone belonged to them—that is to say, in central Switzerland—with the same freedom from superior authority which they possessed in the Black Forest. The Burgundian rectorship, in short, took the place of the titular duchy.

As compared with these facts about the actual historical process by which the state of the dukes of Zähringen was formed, the legal problems with which the question of the rise of the sovereign principalities bristles—what was their legal root, whether it is to be sought in manorial lordship, in the exercise of high criminal justice, in the county organization, and so forth—are in my view relatively unimportant. Indeed, I should go so far as to say that, by adopting a legal and analytical method of approach, we make it difficult to escape the danger of passing over the real problem, which is simply the problem of the origin and rise of the modern state in the middle ages. Apart from the fact that neither manorial rights nor count's rights nor jurisdiction in life and limb are sufficient in themselves to explain the sovereign dominion of the princes, and that even taken together they would not give us the essentially new constitutional structure which is found in the uniform territorial state, it must be emphasized that what we may call the legal and analytical method of approach to the problem of the rise of the German principalities implies that the new form of political organization which they represent was simply a continuation and development of the state which was based on an association of persons. It ignores the fact that the two constitutional forms, the old and the new, stand each on an utterly different plane. The new state naturally took over both the functions and the administrative machinery of the old state, so far as it could put them to its own uses. In this way it absorbed the duties of the count, assumed jurisdiction either by direct exercise in its own courts or through the claim to subject the old courts to its judicial supremacy, took over the guardianship of public peace, developed and appropriated regalian rights wherever possible, and made full use of manorial rights, where it possessed them, both because they were useful instruments in the tasks which faced it and because manorial rights at that time included a large measure of public authority. But all these rights and functions were no more than a reflection of the will or purpose which the new state expressed, and the fact that they were being exercised merely proved that it had now become a constitutional and political reality. Taxation, jurisdiction, the maintenance of public peace, regalian rights and the rest, were the outward forms, the fulfilment or the emanation of the conception of state sovereignty which was making itself increasingly felt by all the inhabitants of any politically organized region; they were not themselves component parts of the new state. In relation to these subordinate functions the new sovereign will—and with it the new state itself—was the primary phenomenon: it was the essential precondition without which any of its particular functions would have meant nothing, and not merely a structure in which they were combined and compounded. Above all else, power to enact and ordain was indispensable. For this reason it was essential for the new territorial prince to be absolutely or substantially independent or autonomous, at least so far as internal administration was concerned. Such autonomy was the right of the duke, and the duke was consequently the prototype of the territorial prince; but the new duke, as is shown by the Austrian *privilegium minus* or the charter which established the duchy of Würzburg, was fundamentally different from the old racial duke, the *Stammesherzog*. The duke had the opportunity to build up his sovereignty over his lands, to make it a political reality. For the Zähringer, therefore, the ducal title was of fundamental importance because it afforded them a legal title to the exercise of sovereign rights. What they had lacked in the first place was a territory in which to exercise their ducal authority; but they created such a territory for themselves, transformed the possibilities inherent in their situation into realities, and so established a state of their own. The land on which they built their state was colonized and reclaimed land— land which, because hitherto unoccupied economically and free politically, was neither burdened with pre-existing constitutional rights nor bound by tradition. Here, therefore, the plans of the dynasty could easily be put into effect: here also it was possible to win the constitutional powers, hitherto latent, which were essential for the realization of the new policy of constitutional reconstruction. State sovereignty, constitutional powers and the exercise of governmental functions cannot be separated, for these are the forms in which the state emerges as a living organism. The state is first and foremost an entity, a unity of functions performed, and not a system of rights: it is a living reality and not a legal abstraction. The state which was an association of persons had also, in the last analysis, possessed much the same abstract rights as the territorial state; but it neither developed them nor exercised them itself, and so it was incapable of developing into the new state which was distinguished by an unparalleled concentration and strengthening of governmental powers.

The region inhabited by the Alemannian people, which was originally intended to be one territory under the sway of the Swabian dukes, was too large and geographically too disjointed to be organized as a single political unit. The dukes themselves took no steps to make this possible. But the consolidation and organization which were necessary, were taken in hand by a number of aristocratic families, of which, however, many died out at an early date and others were only partially successful. Only three, the Welfs, the Zähringer and the Hohenstaufen, rose to such eminence that they could really conceive of political reconstruction on a large scale within the Swabian region. All three achieved much, and it was a serious blow to the progress of political organization in south-west Germany that all three died out prematurely, the Welfs in 1190, the Zähringer in 1218 and the Hohenstaufen in the middle of the thirteenth century. Whereas the Welf heritage passed directly to the Hohenstaufen, and their work was thus salved, the extinction of the other two dynasties resulted in the destruction of their political and constitutional achievements. After the death of the last duke of Zähringen his state passed in part to the Urach dynasty; but it was seriously weakened and the Urach-Fürstenberger were unable to obtain a position in any way comparable to that of the Zähringer. This is most evident in regard to the lands on the left bank of the Rhine, which the Zähringer had brought within their duchy and united with their territories on the other side of the river. Their Burgundian or Swiss possessions now fell to the Kyburger, and so the Rhine became a frontier: had the connexion forged by the Zähringer dynasty been maintained, it is probable that northern Switzerland would have remained a part of the German realm. The extinction of the Hohenstaufen dynasty, on the other hand, resulted in the destruction of the Swabian duchy and with it of all hopes of a Frankish-Alemannian state in south-west Germany. The Hohenstaufen territorial organisation had forged a link which united Swabia and Alsace; but this also was destroyed. Henceforward, in both Swabia and Alsace, petty principalities took the place of one strong, united authority. Finally, the Kyburg house also died out in 1263. Their heirs, and consequently the leading family in the upper Rhine zone, were the Habsburger. But although the Habsburg dynasty made some attempt to erect a south German state, in which German Switzerland, Alsace and the Swabian lands on the right bank of the Rhine were to be united, these efforts were brought to nothing, first by the growing concentration of Habsburg power in the east, and then by the fluctuations and misfortunes of imperial policy, the election of Adolf of Nassau, the premature death of Albrecht I, the election of Henry of Luxemburg, and finally the double election of 1314. In this way all those factors were eliminated which might have produced a political organization worthy of the name. In its place there flourished the smaller baronage, which rose in rank because its real lords had disappeared from the scene, but which was as incapable of really constructive work as the democratic associations and organisations which also came into existence. The result was a dismemberment and disorganisation of government which went further in this region than anywhere else in the empire—a disorganisation due not to any hypothetical inability of the Swabian people to carry out constructive work, but to the definite, concrete historical and political causes which we have reviewed.

We have thus discovered the real significance of the Zähringer state in the general development of mediaeval Germany; but our task cannot be considered finished until we have attempted to explain more generally the significance of the new form of political organization, of which that state was one of the earliest examples, in the history of the German people. We may, in this connexion, disregard the political disruption which the new state either generated or at any rate contributed to keep alive. From the point of view of German history as a whole, it can only be deplored that there was no more direct path towards the creation of one united state than the formation of a number of small states which can fairly claim to represent the most, politically and administratively, which could be achieved at the period in which they originated, but which later lost their early vigour, hardened into inflexible autocracies, and so held up the future development of the German people. On the other hand, it is important to perceive that the new form of political organisation which the later middle ages produced, really did build up the

institutional side of the state, and thus provided the essential
foundations for the fuller conception of the state which
was to come. It would be hard to exaggerate the significance of this achievement. Nevertheless the state whose
growth we have followed in one particular case, only offered
a partial solution of the problem of political organization,
for it neglected the basis of the older mediaeval form of
government, the association of the people and the popular
foundation of political organization, and so finally suc-
cumbed to the dangers of bureaucratic routine and petrified
into a system of princely autocracy. For this reason it
ultimately collapsed, after centuries of valuable work. It
is right to emphasize these limitations and to realize that the
territorial principality was no perfect form of political
organization. But it is equally necessary to realize how
much it achieved, and how radically it transformed the
basis of mediaeval government. What was necessary was
a synthesis of the institutional state which came into existence in the later centuries of the middle ages with the
old Germanic state, the ancient folk-community; and this
the modern German state has achieved. Personal loyalty
and the will to serve have again become vital elements in
the life of the community, and have given both state and
folk that moral foundation without which they cannot
exist. As at the beginning, so at the end of fifteen centuries
of political development, state and folk are one.

VII

CONSTITUTIONAL REORGANISATION AND REFORM UNDER THE HOHENSTAUFEN[1]

By OTTO FREIHERR VON DUNGERN

THE whole period of three hundred years between the death of the last East Frankish Carolingian and the age of the Hohenstaufen was for Germany a period of constant cultural progress. But progress in culture, the growth of civilisation, necessarily means progressive complication of social relationships, and the growing complication of social life demands continuous reorganisation of the political system. Throughout the whole period, therefore, the relations of crown and people must have been undergoing constant change. One phase alone in this process of social and constitutional change is dealt with in the pages which follow: the phase which follows the upheavals of the Investiture Contest and culminates in the period between 1180 and the death of Henry VI, though it extends more widely still over the whole period of Hohenstaufen rule from Conrad III to Frederick II. There is no difficulty in recognising in twelfth-century Germany a series of far-reaching changes in the relations of the various classes of the population not only to each other but also to the imperial government. All recent studies of such questions as the rise of the principalities, manorialism, the development of the German cities, advocacy, the *ministeriales*, and even the transformations effected in the procedure of royal election, presuppose almost revolutionary changes of this category; but it is only rarely that the problems at issue have been approached from the point of view of the relationships between the various classes of German

---

[1] " Die Staatsreform der Hohenstaufen " (§§ III—VIII), *Festschrift für Ernst Zitelmann* (München and Leipzig: Duncker & Humblot, 1913).— Thanks are due to the publishers for permission to translate.

society. Legal and constitutional historians are naturally concerned in the first place with institutions, not with political or social transformations; and so they have rarely given sufficient consideration to the fact that the genesis of every legal institution is conditioned by the social environment in which it is born.

The changes in the organisation of social groups with which we are here concerned began in Germany shortly before the Hohenstaufen period. Somewhere about the middle of the eleventh century the old social formations began to dissolve and new groups and classes were formed out of new elements in the population. In order to understand the new grouping of society, however, we must cast our eye much further back, for even in regard to the Carolingian period, when the mechanism of political organisation was to all appearance clearly defined, a proper insight into the social structure of the state is still lacking.

The early Germanic monarchies ruled over a people which consisted partly of freemen and partly of bondmen who had no direct connexion with government but were completely in the hands of their lords. In the struggles during the period of tribal migration the free population, which was synonymous with the " folk ", had not infrequently—to a particularly large degree, for example, in the case of the Ostrogoths—been supplemented by freedmen. Franks, Swabians and Bavarians must also, as a result of constant warfare, have lost more of the free population than was replaced by births. In Gaul, moreover, and in the Alpine districts there were native landed proprietors who, in spite of a rigorous policy of conquest and spoliation, could not be robbed of all their wealth and influence. How far, during the four centuries of migration, conquest and unrest, such elements were incorporated into the free " folk " still remains a matter of speculation. During the Carolingian period, however, the position seems to have been that every individual who owned tax-free property was regarded as a free citizen with all the rights which accrued to a citizen, and that there was no inclination to ask too minutely how he had obtained such property, which, in the Germanic past, had been the monopoly of the free element in the population.

The freemen of the Carolingian period were nevertheless no longer the socially co-ordinated class which they had been in the earlier Germanic states. From out of their midst there had arisen a small but exceedingly powerful aristocracy which based its position—wherever we have sufficient information to form a judgement—on the possession of immense landed properties. It is only in recent times that these two categories of the free population, the dynastic aristocracy which was probably a closed caste by the ninth century, and the class of small free proprietors whose possessions only amounted to a few hides of land, have been sharply differentiated. Many earlier scholars, it is true, were aware of a contrast between the two social groups; but it was held that, as far as its constitutional position and rights were concerned, the free class was one and undivided, such differences as existed being regarded merely as the difference between rich and poor, while it was supposed that intermediate groups connected the two extremes.[2] But the most striking feature of the situation is precisely the fact that transitional or intermediate groups were completely lacking before the Hohenstaufen period. There are no connecting links between the two branches of the free population, just as there is no known case of inter-marriage between the two divisions. We nowhere see a member of the inferior class raised to the position of count. When the lesser men perform military service in wartime, the scions of the aristocracy are always their leaders. And on the other side we cannot name one single aristocrat who allowed himself to become the tributary of a church or of a prince: when, at a later date, we find " dynasts " holding tributary lands, the legal position has been altered so that they can do so without lowering their aristocratic position.

There are good reasons why historians have failed to distinguish clearly between the two divisions of the free

---

[2] Cf. my book, *Der Herrenstand im Mittelalter*, 451 n. 440, and *ibid.*, 386, on the " Herren genoz ".

population. Both, in the first place, appear in contemporary
records with the same predicates: *liber, nobilis, ingenuus*.
And if, from time to time, the authorities contrast one
predicate with another, the terminology employed is not
constant: *nobilis*, for example, sometimes means more and
sometimes less than *liber*. It is, in fact, only by adopting
a new method of approach and reconstructing the social
position of each single family that the two classes can be
properly distinguished. I myself have attempted this task
for the families settled in the Austrian lands in a study of
the evidence provided by the lists of witnesses in mediaeval
charters;[3] BODE[4] and STRNADT[5], working within narrower
limits, based their investigations on a survey of the landed
property of each single family; and CARO, in his works
on St. Gallen, found evidence in the literary authorities
which proved the existence of a class of free *milites* in
pre-Hohenstaufen times. Unlike BODE and STRNADT,
however, he made no explicit distinction between these
milites and the greater " dynasts ", and although there are
a few further studies in which the existence of a class of
free knights of moderate means has been more or less clearly
demonstrated, these works also accept the institutional
equalization of the two groups of freemen, which is the
basis of the orthodox theory still held by most legal
historians. Within the last few years attempts have been
made, both in England and in France, to obtain more
accurate knowledge of the aristocratic class and particularly
of the number of families which it comprised; but in
Germany, if we consider the country as a whole, little has
been done to obtain similar results. Two facts are nevertheless already clear: on the one hand, the aristocracy's
landed property was scattered property, stretching often
into the most widely divided parts of Germany and even
across the frontier into France or Italy, and on the other
hand, the amount of property controlled by the dynastic
aristocracy was so much greater than that in the hands of

[3] O. von Dungern, *Entstehung der Landeshoheit in Österreich* (1910).
[4] G. Bode, *Der Uradel in Ostfalen* (1911).
[5] *Arch. f. österr. Gesch.* XCIX (1912), 700 sqq.

the small peasant proprietors that the aristocracy alone was qualified to exercise public offices. Countships, advocacies, and normally bishoprics and abbeys, were in its hands; and naturally also the leadership in war.

This dynastic aristocracy, with its landed wealth and its privileged position in the state, remained intact until about the end of the eleventh century. The small freemen, on the other hand, were faced—so far as the records allow us to judge—by attacks which threatened their very existence. It is easy to exaggerate the effectiveness of Carolingian legislation against the depression of the small freeholders; but it is only necessary to consider the immense area of land which was settled and colonized after Frankish times to realize that there could be no question, as late as the eleventh century, of the existence of a compact and unmixed population directly descended from the small freemen of an earlier age. In certain districts it appears that the freemen were completely merged into the villein and *ministerialis* classes. Where they persisted in considerable numbers—the districts where such is known to have been the case are Frisia, certain parts of Saxony, Bavaria and the Alpine lands as a whole[6]—their composition was radically altered by the inclusion of freedmen. It is true that emancipation did not necessarily imply inclusion in the free class; but if the freedman managed by one means or another to get possession of free or allodial property, if he became the owner of a *praedium libertatis*—and there was no enactment or rule of customary law to prevent him— he then became socially a member of the class of freemen.

For both classes of freemen a ruinous crisis began at the time of the Investiture Contest. The development of military organisation meant that the individual knight

[6] Recent investigations, it must now be added, have modified if not undermined the theory of the persistence of a free element, even in the few regions specified. It is now clear that the " free peasantry " was intrudoced into waste and forest in the twelfth century, and that the " freedom " they enjoyed was a special privilege conferred on them as colonizers, an advantage conceded in order to stimulate colonization. Nor is it accidental that the development of this new class seems to have been an integral part of Hohenstaufen policy. Cf. particularly Th. Mayer, " Die Entstehung des " modernen " Staates im Mittelalter und die freien Bauern," ZRG. *Germ. Abt.* LVII (1937), 210—288.

was met by ever increasing demands in the way of equipment and training. The small free landowner, with but few hides and few servile dependents, was no longer able to bear the expense of military service which was demanded of him and his class. For people in this position entrance into the tributary or *ministerialis* class—an expedient to which, as we know, they had frequently enough been driven in Carolingian times by the oppression of the counts—had hitherto resulted in loss of caste. In the second half of the eleventh century all this was changed. The *ministeriales* were being increasingly employed by their lords as knights, and a pressing need arose for knightly *ministeriales*. Every means, therefore, was used by the magnates to make entrance into the *ministerialis* class attractive. The result was a rapid break-up of the old class of small freemen, who had hitherto lived as large farmers with serfs and bondmen of their own, but who were now not rich enough to become knights. Anyone of this class who, by about 1200, had not become a *ministerialis* was already a mere peasant, freed of the duty—but also deprived of the right—to perform military service as a knight. The state, in short, had no further use for him.

The second half of the eleventh century saw also the disintegration of the dynastic class of large landed proprietors, but a disintegration of a very different kind. It is hard for us to realize how small and narrow a class this still remained even as late as the tenth century. An absolutely exclusive caste, it comprised only a few hundred richly endowed families. In these circumstances a knowledge of genealogy and family history or a comparison with the results which have been obtained by study of the contemporary aristocracy of France and England immediately suggests the likelihood that the German " dynasts " of that period were welded closely together, by ties of blood and marriage, into a close and united corporation.

Within this German aristocracy of the pre-Hohenstaufen period there began in the eleventh century a process of disintegration. The families divided into distinct branches, and the branches distributed themselves over the scattered possessions of their house. Where there was a number of sons, each built himself a castle, as far as possible in a different district from his brothers, named himself after his stronghold and founded a new family. Provided that each name which meets us is not, as still too frequently occurs, uncritically supposed to denote an independent dynasty, the sudden appearance from about the end of the eleventh century of different family names for branches of one family provides us with evidence of this historical process. The family names of the German " dynasts " about 1180 run into thousands; but if we follow them back for only two or three generations, the fusion of aristocratic houses is astounding. The growing intensity of economic life and the striking growth in internal and external coloniza-tion, which becomes so marked at the end of the eleventh century, doubtless increased the resources of the aristocracy; but the expansion and division of the aristocratic families themselves was out of all proportion to the growth of their resources, and as they simultaneously weakened their family unity, it was inevitable that the unity of the whole dynastic caste should suffer also. The division of families into a series of independent branches resulted, furthermore, in differentiation or discrimination between individual " dynasts " according to their material means. One family divided continuously, another gathered its properties together, and the result was that soon there were rich " dynasts " and poor " dynasts ".

At the moment when government passed into the hands of the Hohenstaufen still another section of the population had reached a turning-point in its history: the class of *ministeriales*. But here, whatever point of view we adopt, development had been in a forward direction. The *ministeriales*—this fact, at any rate, has been clearly brought out by recent controversy regarding their origin and posi-tion—possessed considerable holdings which yielded them the means of existence and which they cultivated, like free proprietors, as separate estates with serfs and dependants of their own. Whether they were stewards in the manorial centre of their lord's honour, revenue officials in charge of customs and traffic duties, castellans, or the simple knights whom monasteries, bishops and " dynasts " needed to fight for their interests—in every case they held a property, the income from which afforded them a livelihood suitable to their rank. It was consonant with the legal ideas of the age and also with the needs both of lord and man, if this property remained hereditarily in the hands of one family, and was not granted to the individual as a temporary holding in return for services actually performed. Already in the eleventh century, therefore, we find that the benefices held by *ministeriales* had become hereditary. At the same time there was a marked change in their personal position. Originally the *ministerialis*, like other bondmen, had been personally subject to his lord's will. But this disability gradually weakened. The more useful the ministerial class became, as an instrument for furthering not only the political aspirations of the magnates but also their colonizing activities, the more the tendency grew to confine the dependent or servile element in the relationship of lord and man to the properties held by a *ministerialis*, where previously it had extended to his person as well. Already by the eleventh century, therefore, the *ministerialis* was free to leave his lord, provided that he left his tenement at the lord's disposal. And the lord had no difficulty in finding others, serfs or preferably small freemen, whom he could endow with the *ius servientium* and settle on the vacant estate. Towards the end of the eleventh century interchange between various bodies of *ministeriales* and the movement of ministerial tenants from one estate to another was so common that the *ministeriales* attached to certain manorial centres drew up special statutes, in conjunction with their lords, in which the conditions of entrance into and exit from their ranks were systematically regulated. In part at least these codes of ministerial law, or *Dienstrechte*, seem very rigorous, and appear to leave small freedom to the individual. But if we bear in mind the contemporary charters which attest the frequent entry of small freemen into the ministerial ranks, and remember the accounts in many a contemporary chronicle of the part played by individual *ministeriales* in the counsels of their lords, if we note also the attitude of independence and even of opposition frequently adopted by the *ministeriales* as a body, it is clear, in spite of the *Dienstrechte*, that the movement which resulted in the formation of the ministerial class of the twelfth century meant nothing less than the emancipation of peasants, serfs and bondmen from personal dependence, and their elevation to a position of almost unqualified liberty. Already at the beginning of the twelfth century, therefore, the new ministerial class—a class of knights who were lords of estates and yet accustomed to service and obedience—constituted an important and rapidly growing section of the population; and it was inevitable that the *ministeriales* as a body should sooner or later attract the interest of the state and of government.

No less dynamic was the development through which the German towns were passing at the very moment when the Hohenstaufen began to rule. But here the Swabian emperors seem to have missed their opportunity. Instead of continuing Henry IV's attempts to link up the cities and the central government, they seem, so far as we can judge,[7] to have misunderstood the special character and independent spirit of the urban movement or—for example in Flanders—to have ignored it. The towns, therefore, remained on one side and played no part in the introduction of the new and vital constitutional principles which the Hohenstaufen formulated on the solid basis of the social changes of their age.

[7] Recent investigations seem to indicate that the Hohenstaufen pursued a more active urban policy than was supposed at the time this essay was written: cf. K. Weller, " Die staufische Städtegründung in Schwaben," *Württembergische Vierteljahrshefte f. Landesgesch.* XXXVI (1930). This policy is seen in the foundation of " free " royal cities; cf. Mayer, *op. cit.*, 245, 286. But it is not clear that this policy, suggestive as it is of royal interest in urban development, extended beyond the bounds of the imperial demesne in Swabia and Alsace; cf. Knöpp, *Die Stellung Friedrichs II. u. seiner beiden Söhne zu den deutschen Städten* (1928), 83. It must therefore be considered rather as a part of demesne policy than as a distinct urban policy extending over the whole kingdom; and it is clear that a sharp line has to be drawn between the attitude of the Hohenstaufen to royal cities, on the one hand, and to seignorial (particularly episcopal) cities, on the other; cf. Rörig, HZ. CXLI (1929), 568.

When, in our survey of the elements on which Hohenstaufen constitutional policy was based, we come to the church, we must adopt a very different point of view. In this regard it will be well to begin with some general considerations.

For the early mediaeval state the various classes of the population, each leading a separate life of its own, provided the foundation for social organisation of every kind. The question was not—as it is to-day, when in principle every man is equal in the eyes of government—the personal qualification of the individual, but whether the individual was born to any particular position. Feudal law was a law of equals, but only a law of equals for members of one particular class; and the same is true of the law which governed the position of the *ministeriales*, of property law, the law of succession, criminal law, and even of the law governing succession to the throne or the right to elect the king. The dynast who had lost everything in a feud and sought refuge in a foreign land was there a born candidate for the hand of a rich aristocrat: it was never supposed, because he was poor, that he should marry a farmer's daughter. The knightly *ministerialis*, on the other hand, who may have been a person of outstanding importance while on crusade, returned home to his servile position: if his daughter—" bond woman " is the term by which the daughters of even the most powerful *ministeriales* were known as late as the fourteenth century—married a " dynast ", the union was regarded as a misalliance. Facts such as these illustrate the strength of class consciousness, and enable us to understand the influence which class considerations exerted over political organization. In face of powerful class distinctions it was inevitable that political organization took a form which, from a modern point of view, appears illogical and inefficient.

But this class organisation had soon to meet, on three sides, the attack of novel principles.

Since, in the first place, the whole economic and social position of a man was dependent in the last analysis on his landed property, it was a natural consequence that the property which he held came to be regarded as belonging to a particular category which varied according to the rank of its holder. The honour or lordship held by a " dynast ", for example, was the basis of its lord's immediate relationship with the crown, of his tenancy-in-chief; and as time passed, it became the rule that even a part of such an honour would raise anyone who acquired it, whatever his earlier rank, to the position of a " dynast ". In the same way any freehold property ultimately came to confer the rights and duties of a freeholder[8] on anyone who got possession of it. But this rule was only formulated in the later middle ages, and even then it was only partially effective; for if it had been uniformly applied, acquisition of villein land would have deprived the possessor of his freedom, and we find on the contrary that even at a relatively early date a " dynast " could acquire villein land, and later ministerial fiefs, without losing caste. This principle, therefore, though marking a breach with the old order, was only of limited importance.

Many generations earlier, however, the personal organisation of the mediaeval state, the conception of a state organized as an association of classes, had to face the attacks of the church and clerical attempts to introduce a less personal scheme of political organisation. To understand the innovations which the church sought to introduce, we need only go back to the idea, rife in Carolingian times, that public officials might not exercise their powers within the boundaries of ecclesiastical estates. This conception, it is clear, differed fundamentally from the older view that birth alone placed one individual either in dependence on or—in other circumstances—on an equality with any other individual. Church lands were not, indeed, pronounced " immune " as a whole: single exemptions were the rule. But in each exemption from public authority a principle was recognized which was foreign to and incompatible with the ancient principles of government and which finally

[8] I.e., suit of court and payment of taxes—for no property was entirely free from services. In North Germany the small freeholders seem originally to have been free from service in the local courts, but not so in the Alpine lands: further investigation of these problems is necessary.

created so wide a network of exceptions that the ordinary administration was dislocated. On the other hand, it is clear that this ecclesiastical conception and the principles of political organization which it comprised, could never have become prevalent unless it had found support in the actual political situation. In other words, the immunity from the ordinary administration which ecclesiastical establishments were claiming must have been a development of an " immunity " which the dynastic owners of great allodial properties already possessed. This question, admittedly difficult and controversial, cannot be discussed in detail here. It is sufficient for our purposes to insist that the immunity which secular estates are known to have enjoyed cannot be explained—as is still usual—as a franchise conferred in a series of personal exemptions, for which, however, a curious chance has deprived us of all documentary evidence. At a later date a " dynast " was occasionally granted a privilege similar in appearance to the " immunity " of a church; but what he received was merely a confirmation of his pre-existing rights. The exemption which the " dynasts " enjoyed—in the first place for themselves and their families, and only later for their lands—was rather the natural result of their rank and condition, and far from being copied from the immunity conferred on churches, it was really the earliest form of exemption from the control of the king's local officers. For the " dynasts ", moreover, no privilege was necessary in order to claim exemption; for it never entered anyone's head that a dynastic, aristocratic proprietor, who belonged to exactly the same class as any count, could ever be subject to a count, except in the single case when both parties were present at a meeting of the county court or any other royal tribunal. If that is true of the count, however, it is equally true that the authority which a duke or margrave possessed over the dynastic aristocracy was merely a consequence of his exceptional military powers, and therefore only of secondary and occasional importance. Except during the sessions of the royal court or while serving in the army, therefore, the high-born aristocracy was outside the control of royal officials and their lands were exempt from the operation of the ordinary routine of government.

The church, on the other hand, had no such privilege of class; but the king, by a special act of grace, could raise any particular church to the position of the dynastic aristocracy. To obtain that independence from the control of public officials which was the dynast's birthright, abbots and bishops needed a royal enactment in the form of a charter of " immunity ". But the church which was privileged in this way was originally a democratic institution. It is, indeed, well known that many German monasteries only opened their doors to members of the high-born aristocracy;[9] but abbeys of this class were relatively late in origin, and stood in marked contrast with the oldest democratic foundations. In the same way, the success of the aristocracy in obtaining a monopoly of bishoprics merely marked the recovery of lost ground by the " dynasts". It seems probable, moreover—in this respect SCHULTE'S investigations are not final—that non-aristocratic bishoprics existed throughout the middle ages, just as at all times there were certainly monasteries which opened their doors to all classes of the people. Such democratic foundations, however, were as much in a position to obtain " immunity " or franchises from the crown as were the aristocratic houses; and so the principle of organisation by classes was undermined. The significance of this fact, it seems to me, must not be underrated; for nothing was more likely to awaken a spirit of legal reflection and meditation than the interaction of a number of radically different principles of social order, and legal awareness was precisely what German statesmen lacked before Hohenstaufen times. For that reason they failed to co-ordinate the important legal elements in public life, and as long as they were unable to do this, there was naturally no question of a uniform, systematic organisation of government.

During the Investiture Contest the German church fell into dependence on the papacy, and from the papal stand-

9 Cf. A. Schulte, *Der Adel u. die deutsche Kirche* (1910).

point co-operation between the German government and the various ecclesiastical establishments in such matters as collection of taxes and military service conflicted with its own demands, and was therefore regarded as an abuse which must be swept away. In this way, therefore, the new dependence of the German church on Rome rapidly undermined the opportunist and unsystematic connexion of church and state which had existed before the Investiture Contest. Even more destructive, however, was the democratic reform movement, which spread rapidly after the middle of the eleventh century. Its result, as described in the works of ALOYS SCHULTE, was that the aristocratic bishoprics and the convents and monasteries which only opened their doors to the nobility, suddenly found themselves in a very insecure position. Such was the situation at the beginning of the twelfth century. In regard to the church, therefore, and in regard to the principles of organisation which it sponsored, the Hohenstaufen found themselves faced by disintegration and by the necessity for reconstruction.

So we come to the third of the factors which led to a dissolution of the old social and political organisation. The administrative mechanism which necessarily came into existence as a means of governing a unified state extending over wide territories was itself foreign to the Germanic conception of political organisation. A government ruling a vast territory could not be purely democratic. Technical difficulties, questions of distance alone, made it impossible to obtain immediate unanimity of purpose between the head of the state and each single member of the " folk " in every act of government, even when the " folk " was represented by no more than a couple of hundred aristocrats. Between king and people, therefore, a bureaucracy was necessarily introduced.

Such a bureaucracy existed already under the Carolingians; but it would certainly be mistaken to suppose that the bureaucratic state of Charles the Great, with its county organisation, was so harmoniously contrived as would appear from the capitularies. We have already briefly indicated that the picture presented by Frankish legislation was more consonant with Carolingian ideals than with Carolingian realities. Nevertheless the three-fold hierarchy: king, bureaucracy, people, once it had been introduced by the Franks into the legal conceptions of the middle ages, remained an active force, and from Carolingian times onwards the bureaucratic principle stood opposed to the older principle expressed in the co-ordination or equality of all " dynasts " below the king. But the hierarchical principle implicit in the institution of counts and *missi* was never completely assimilated in Germany, and even Charlemagne himself was forced to tolerate a number of highly significant exceptions. The Carolingian reform, in other words, was only a partial success, and the inevitable result was the growth of a series of mixed political and constitutional forms. In the first place a distinction was made between fee and allod—which from the point of view of the Carolingian state had merely been two different forms of dependent tenure—and again between county and advocacy. But an assimilation of legal forms soon began. The dynastic advocate of the latter part of the eleventh century, even if he was not count in one of the old county divisions, normally possessed the essential attributes of the count's office: above all, he had acquired jurisdiction in life and limb over persons dependent on other lords. In this way an assimilation and a uniformity of the two institutions was achieved, though at the cost of a dismemberment of the old administrative districts which finally resulted in complete confusion. But the extension to the advocate of the attributes of count produced also a change in the character of the count's office. The break-up of the old administrative districts necessitated the systematic construction of a new administrative organisation, in which the principle of the equality of all " dynasts " was implicitly denied. Already in Carolingian times, in spite of the unity of the dynastic caste and apart from the superior powers of the *missi*, a few great men had exercised an authority over the smaller counts and lords which was based not on legally constituted powers but on *de facto* predominance. Influenced by the idea of the feudal hierarchy—an idea which had been theoretically formulated in Italy and rapidly put into practice in France—the notion then arose in Germany that subordination did not alter the class or rank of a " dynast ", did not force him out of his caste or destroy his direct relationship with the crown, provided that this subordination was the result of a feudal contract and sprang from feudal obligations. There thus developed the intermediate ranks of duke, count palatine, margrave, landgrave, and all the other grades of the feudal hierarchy, exactly as in France, except that the feudal tenants of the first, second or third degree were not divided into separate categories. In other words, an impossible attempt was made to combine the dynast's claim to equality with his fellows with the fact of feudal differentiation. But an illogical and unsatisfactory compromise of this sort between incompatible forms of organisation inevitably called for intervention. Once again, in short, circumstances were ready for a strong government, willing to intervene in order to disentangle the complications, compromises and ambiguities which could no longer be allowed to burden the political system.

There was, we have seen, an inherent contradiction between the various institutions on which the German state of the ninth, tenth and eleventh centuries was built; and this contradiction makes it difficult to discover in the constitution of that period the specific elements which, systematically co-ordinated, provide a framework for every type of modern political organisation. Administration, legislation, judicature; popular assemblies, monarchical powers, rights of succession, duties of office, taxation, military service—all these are conceptions with which the mediaeval state was familiar, but which it had failed to weld together into a coherent system. Because this lack of order seems to defy survey, it has often been said that the mediaeval empire lacked a truly constitutional outlook, that constitutional issues were regarded from the point of view of private law. But this is a mistaken conception.

The lack of order which is evident enough to modern eyes was due rather to the fact which we have already observed, that every element both of public and of private law was dominated, in constantly changing intensity, by widely different and even contradictory principles of political organisation. If we try to arrange all the phenomena of the constitutional life of that period within the framework of a modern constitutional code, the exceptions to every rule are so numerous and so important that clarity is completely lacking. We can find every institution known to modern constitutional law by an analysis of the German state of the early middle ages; but the mediaeval conception of the state and of its constitutional structure can never be brought to life in such a way. Yet the German state under the Saxon and Salian dynasties had its fundamental principles of government, and they were perfectly lucid. The legal situation of that day can be reduced to a few cardinal elements, provided that a specifically mediaeval point of view is adopted. Legal security lay not in general rules of law, as is now the case, but in the special legal standing not only of every individual but also of every piece of land. Instead of a systematic legal order, to which all were equally subjected, there was a series of personal relationships, and each person and thing had an individual place in the legal order. The guiding principle, in short, was concrete personality and not abstract system.

This unsystematically constructed state nevertheless functioned badly. Each individual thought only of his own particular legal standing, fought to maintain it, and attacked his neighbour whenever the latter was momentarily the weaker. Interest in political calm was suspended. No class of society or individual any longer wanted the state to maintain order for their benefit; and the inevitable result among those who were powerful enough to fight for political interests, was sooner or later a struggle of all against all. Such approximately was the position in Germany about the year 1100.

Such a period of social unrest and political disorganisation was virgin soil on which to build a new and stronger system of government. All that was necessary to guide constitutional life into a new legal orbit was governmental initiative and systematic intervention. In this way the general disorder could be turned to advantage. It was necessary to set aside the various incompatible principles of government and to replace them by others. The old constitution must make way for a new constitution, and so it would be possible to build up again the authority of the central government which during the internecine struggles of the Investiture Contest had lost its power to direct and lead.

Such a policy, it seems to me, was systematically pursued by the Hohenstaufen.

To prove this statement in full it would be necessary not only to enumerate all the relevant legal acts of the Hohenstaufen rulers but also to consider in equal detail the evidence in the narrative authorities of the period. Even so, inference and deduction would still play a major part; for little legislation remains, and probably little more than remains was ever promulgated,[10] while we possess few contemporary narratives in which the constitutional policy of the Hohenstaufen is directly discussed. For this reason alone, therefore, it is necessary to reserve a comprehensive survey for another occasion. Such a survey would have to be executed on the broadest possible basis—best of all as a sequel to WAITZ's " Constitutional History," beginning where WAITZ broke off with a fine and clearly expressed perception that thenceforward utterly novel principles and methods of government were in the ascendant. Nevertheless it seems to me that it is not only possible but also useful to set down the conclusions to which, in my view, such a work would lead. The Hohenstaufen rulers intervened so

[10] The question whether, as Ficker believed, the transformation of the class of imperial princes (*Reichsfürstenstand*) in or about 1180 was effected by an imperial decree, since lost, still remains undecided in spite of Güterbock's recent investigations. It seems to me that, wherever a process of legal regulation can be perceived in the middle ages, it is safest to suppose customary development, so long as nothing is known of actual legislation.

skilfully in the confused public life of their day, they pursued their work of regulation and construction with so little respect for persons and with such quiet logic, their measures are, on the one hand, so radical and, on the other hand, so skilfully adapted to the tendencies of contemporary constitutional development, that—considering all we know of their personalities—it is hard to escape the conclusion that they were consciously guided by truly statesmanlike principles and pursued a definite programme of constitutional reform. Mere opportunist reaction to circumstance could never have proceeded along so direct and logical a course as the policy which the Hohenstaufen put into effect. Everything which they did to reform the machinery and organisation of government can be reduced so easily to two main conceptions that it is hardly too audacious to consider these conceptions as their guiding principles.

Conrad III made a start by utilising the most modern methods which his age knew to strengthen the position of his house. Barbarossa continued this policy with such success that the idea of developing the king's private powers and estates was transformed under him into a system of government. Henry VI continued on the same path. Frederick II was guided by the same ideas. In the meantime, however—and I consider this the most significant confirmation of my thesis—the same principles of organisation which the crown employed were adopted by the princes in their territories. Here they were systematically applied, whereas imperial policy, in this particular respect, had already come to a dead end during the reign of Frederick II. In the various principalities, on the other hand, the principles developed by the Hohenstaufen became the basis of princely sovereignty, and thus contributed to the development of the modern state.

The first thing to be noted in the activity of Conrad III, if we look at it from this point of view, is not merely that he ceased to grant away imperial demesne—even before his time emperors had become chary of making grants— but that he gathered properties together, and gave particular

attention to accumulating the " immune " or " exempt "
lordships of the dynastic aristocracy. Barbarossa carried
on this process with all his energy. Both the emperor
himself and other members of his house inherited, bought,
exchanged and even usurped as many immune lordships
as they could lay hands on. In addition there were the advocacies which they had no compunction about receiving
as fiefs from churches. Here the Hohenstaufen showed no
hesitation: feudal law had to accommodate itself to the
position as best it could, theory had to be made to fit the
facts in such a way that the dignity of the crown was not
prejudiced if the emperor had a bishop or abbot as feudal
lord.

   If a county of the old type were acquired, and with it
the advocacy over all the estates and lordships which at
one time or another had been exempted from the count's
jurisdiction, it was only necessary to assume the rights of
count in the districts under the advocate's authority and
there resulted—by whatever title governmental rights
were exercised in the various subdivisions of the new lordship—a compact, unified territory. This was simplification
and consolidation in the modern sense. And this was
precisely what was done. We have no direct statement
that there was a definite programme of consolidation
behind the king's actions; but the very fact that we can
watch the Hohenstaufen proceeding logically in this direction forces us to believe in the systematic nature of their
policy. And there is no doubt that royal policy was
furthered by the disorganisation of the dynastic class,
which we have already described. If the king's efforts at
expansion turned against a particular family, one small
family alone, cut off on a small estate from its fellows, was
involved in the conflict, and not a whole association of
families, bound together by ties of blood and kin, with
far-reaching connexions and resources, as would have been
the case only a few generations earlier.

   The lordships thus acquired had, however, to be administered. If earlier practice had been followed, they would
have been handed out to vassals as fiefs. But the vassals

of the crown were precisely the aristocratic families who were the object of attack. The old methods were therefore useless, if what had been won was both to be held together and kept under governmental control. A change in the constitution was necessary, and a change occurred. A bureaucracy in the modern sense was created, and henceforward the functions formerly exercised by the count were committed to a dependent person, not as a fief, but as an office.

The method by which this result was achieved was not that which Charles the Great had already unsuccessfully employed. His policy had been to place a county in the hands of an unfree and therefore completely dependent man; but such a course was unfeasible, even in the twelfth century, for the reason that it was still contrary to general sentiment. An unfree man could not preside over the ancient county court, in which high-born " dynasts " were suitors. The desired result was therefore obtained indirectly. The estates of any *ministerialis* on whom it was desired to confer so outstanding a position, were exempted from the county jurisdiction, exactly as if they were a dynastic lordship. Supreme judicial authority, jurisdiction in life and limb, was conferred on the *ministerialis* for the lands over which he was lord, no matter by what title—freehold, fee, advocacy or ministerial service—he held his lordship. He was thus made the immediate representative of the king in the exercise of sovereign rights, and in this way he was qualified for positions from which he had previously been inexorably excluded. The result is that, from the middle of the twelfth century onwards, we find *ministeriales* marrying the daughters of " dynasts ", inheriting immune dynastic lordships, and ruling within their lordships in a way which had previously only been possible for a nobleman; we find them exercising the rights of " dynasts " as castellans, advocates, and soon even as mortgagees of noble properties; we find them in possession of jurisdiction over life and limb on their own estates;[11] and finally we

[11] Cf. Voltelini, " Die Entstehung der Landgerichte," *Arch. f. österr. Gesch.* XCIV (1907), 382; also Strnadt, *loc. cit.*

find them as bishops in sees which had previously been reserved for the high nobility.[12] This sudden change in the position of the *ministeriales* has long been a well-recognized fact, though it has rarely received the emphasis it deserves; but its revolutionary bearing can only be properly appreciated when it is realized that it was a small and narrow aristocratic caste, and not the whole " free " population, which for centuries had maintained an exclusive monopoly of the positions out of which it was now being systematically driven by the rise of a new element in society.

I am convinced that Barbarossa and Henry VI had the intention of destroying, by an uninterrupted development of this new principle of government, the special privileged position of the " dynasts ". Frederick II went so far as to confer on a *ministerialis* the office of *Landgraf*—an office which Barbarossa had patently made it his policy to develop out of the earlier, less significant position of reeve or bailiff on the crown demesne, and which quickly assumed a first place in local administration.[13]   In this way the idea of administration through a dependent bureaucracy was introduced into the constitutional organisation, and no sooner was it conceived than, in the minds of the rulers, it governed the whole state.

This fact is nowhere more evident than in Frederick II's policy towards the church. There can, I believe, be no doubt that Frederick II's whole struggle with the Curia was dominated by the idea of making the pope the chief metropolitan within the state. The precise way in which this problem was to be solved seems to have been a matter of indifference, provided that Frederick could succeed in making the whole ecclesiastical organisation, which threatened to become an *imperium in imperio*, an integral part of the imperial machine.   Unlike the secular "dynasts ", the ecclesiastical magnates in Germany could not be eliminated, their franchises could not be undermined, because

[12] Cf. the evidence in Schreibmüller, *Die Pfälzer Reichsministerialen* (1911).
 [13] Philip of Falkenstein appears as *procurator* of the Wetterau.

they had the power of the Curia behind them as a mainstay
against the attacks of the royal bureaucracy. Frederick II
therefore directed his attack against Rome, boldly attempted
to lay hold of the hierarchical organisation of the church
at its very centre, and sought to bring it as a whole within
the constitutional structure of the state. It was, in short,
to be made a part of the machinery of government. But
such a policy was only conceivable because Frederick had
already a modern conception of the state, because he regarded the state as an organism based not on the personal
feudal obligations of thousands of vassals but on the
vigorously enforced rights of government.

This modern conception of the state can be perceived
also in other activities of government. Certain sources of
revenue, for example, were exploited directly instead of
being farmed out to vassals. The conception of *regalia*,
it can safely be said, was a creation of Barbarossa, for the
evidence which earlier scholars brought forward to prove
the existence of *regalia* in an earlier period has proved
untrustworthy. The same is true of the idea of a standing
army; for—compared with the military organisation of
earlier emperors—the formation of a knightly army,
composed of *ministeriales*, from Barbarossa's time onwards
is nothing else than the introduction of a standing army.[14]

It was precisely this concentration of authority in the
hands of government, with its bold disregard for all earlier
constitutional principles, which proved fruitful in the future
political development of Germany. In the empire itself
it could not be brought to completion: the plan was too
prodigious and it miscarried. But the new system was
immediately taken up by the territorial princes. In both
lay and clerical principalities, from the middle of the
twelfth century onwards, the *ministeriales* were employed
in exactly the same way as they were used on the imperial
demesne, and, like the Hohenstaufen, the various princes
attacked and drove back the old dynastic aristocracy with

---

[14] Cf. v. Dungern, *Herrenstand*, 339 sqq., and " Die Sklavenheere der
Hohenstaufen," *Monatsblatt der Zeitschrift Adler* (1912), 164 sqq.; also
Bode, *op. cit.*, 77.

its scattered and immune estates.[15]   On this basis small
counts and even ministerial lords were ultimately able to
achieve territorial sovereignty.

If the very instrument which the Hohenstaufen created
to strengthen the authority of government and obtain
immediate control over their subjects, finally led, in the
hands of the princes, to a new phase of disorganisation and
the dislocation of the German kingdom, this very fact is
not only evidence of the serviceability of the new methods
of government, but at the same time a sign that the emperors themselves were not in a position to employ the new
administrative machinery for the benefit of the empire
as a whole.   Where the responsibility for this failure lay—
on individuals or on circumstances beyond the control of
individuals—is a question which hardly concerns the constitutional lawyer; but there is no difficulty in recognizing
the obstructive blocks of insuperable opposition which
barred the path leading from the mediaeval to the modern
state.

The main factor, without doubt, was the ecclesiastical
principalities.   However successful the Hohenstaufen may
have been in attacking the franchises of secular lords, they
could not get rid of the ecclesiastical lordships.   They
sought, in the first place, to undermine the powers exercised
by prelates over both men and lands by bringing advocacies
into their own hands, for the advocate exercised governmental powers in ecclesiastical territories, and so every
advocacy brought into the hands of the ruler meant an
extension of the demesne under the direct control of the
crown.   But this policy was not successful in every case;
and so Frederick II changed his tactics and tried, as we
have seen, to force the supreme head of the church to support
his attempts to bring the ecclesiastical organisation as a
whole within the orbit of the State.   But this policy was
not confined to the church.   Certain powerful members of
the secular aristocracy had maintained their position in

---

[15] This process is followed, as far as Austria is concerned, in my work:
Die Entstehung der Landeshoheit in Oesterreich.   Cf. also Strnadt, *op. cit.,*
and Grund, " Beiträge z. Geschichte d. hohen Gerichtsbarkeit in Nieder-
österreich," *Arch. f. österr. Gesch.* XCIX (1912).

spite of the rapid " mediatization " of the dynastic class; and in their case it was equally necessary to adopt new and less direct methods, for they could not all be removed from their preponderant position. The solution of this problem brings us to the second of the striking innovations brought about by Hohenstaufen constitutional policy.

After the fall of Henry the Lion in 1180 it seems, for a considerable period, as if the Hohenstaufen emperors are going to be able to drive the entire lay aristocracy out of their position of privilege. Even within the principalities we nowhere find the imperial government intervening to protect and save the weaker members of the aristocratic class, against whom the local princes are acting as energetically as the king himself. Henry VI's Italian wars, however, and above all the weakness of the monarchy under Philip of Swabia gave the remnant of less powerful nobles a chance to gather their strength. But even before this reaction occurred, Barbarossa had realized that there were a number of particularly powerful lords whom he could not hope to subdue like the rest, and with whom it was therefore necessary to deal separately. Because they could not be set aside, the only course was to neutralise them by bringing them—as Frederick II sought to bring the church—into a fixed and organic relationship with the central government; and the creation of this new relationship was the second phase in the Hohenstaufen programme of constitutional reform.

Before the Hohenstaufen took the situation in hand, the crown—as we have seen—had to reckon with a dynastic aristocracy exempt in fact if not in theory from every sort of official authority. Only those members of this caste who had been called to exercise the office of count, had entered into a position of dependence on the crown; but the bond created in this way had been irreparably slackened by the transformation of countships into hereditary fiefs.

In dealing with this situation, Barbarossa seems, in the first place, to have sought to reorganize German feudalism on the model of France or the Byzantine empire. We find,

228 FREIHERR v. DUNGERN

in the second half of the twelfth century, that " dynasts "
are feudally dependent on counts, counts on other counts,
the latter on princes: we find, in short, a feudal hierarchy
in existence, such as is found contemporaneousiy in other
countries. In these circumstances it was easy to form a link
with the higher ranks of the governmental machine—ranks
which had long existed in Germany, though certainly
without any very systematic organisation, in the person
of dukes and margraves. About the middle of the twelfth
century the position of dukes and margraves changed and
acquired new substance. The paramount authority exercised, for example, by the duke of Austria or Henry the
Lion and even by those counts who held the rank of *rectores
provinciae* over the petty counts and " dynasts " within
their territories, was decidedly more recognisable and
definite after 1156 than that exercised by dukes and margraves in former centuries. In other words, the duke was
becoming a feudal overlord, controlling by feudal ties the
nobility within the boundaries of his duchy; and so a clear-
cut feudal hierarchy leading through the dukes to the crown
was gradually being formed. But this movement gave way
after a short time to a more novel method of reorganizing
the feudal system; and in this new method it is possible,
I believe, to discern the second vital principle in the
Hohenstaufen programme of reform.

Enfeoffment, until the Hohenstaufen reforms were introduced, implied the conferment on one man of sovereign
rights over the inhabitants of a district. The persons
enfeoffed were the aristocrats, the "dynasts" whose privileged position we have portrayed, and among this small
but powerful aristocracy sovereign rights were distributed
by means of enfeoffment. If, in speaking of the period
before 1180, we talk—as is still usual—of " official princes "
or of an " official aristocracy ", of princes who were princes
because of their office, it must never be forgotten that the
offices which brought with them the right to exercise the
supreme powers of government were confined exclusively
to members of this aristocracy. The successors in office
of the old Frankish counts could claim as officials no

materially privileged position within the state. Henry " with the golden chariot ", the rich Welf of the tenth century, although he held no countship, was not for that reason any less a prince of the realm than one of the petty counts, and if the subsequent usage of the imperial chancery was to refer to counts alone as *principes*, this was merely a formal distinction, marking out the counts from their associates in the aristocracy.

Definitely turning his back on the French system of feudal organisation, Barbarossa sought to alter this situation. Once again he placed all the emphasis on the office. Anyone exercising count's rights—no matter how obtained —was, as a count, to be an officer of the crown. As far as possible the count's jurisdiction, his *Bann*, was to be obtained directly from the central authority. There was, however, no question of reviving or reconstructing the old Carolingian counties and administrative districts, which were by this time completely broken up. On the contrary, wherever a " dynast " held a position equivalent to that of count within a complex of territories—it did not matter how it had been formed—he was nominated count; or at all events all such lords were held to stand in an exactly similar position of feudal dependence on the monarchy by reason of the territories which they possessed. But as these territories varied considerably in importance and extent, and as all the " dynasts " within the larger territories had not yet been " mediatized " or forced out of their privileged positions, it was necessary to create one intermediate class between the new dynastic counts and the crown. This was the newly organized estate of princes, the *Reichsfürstenstand* which came into existence on the fall of Henry the Lion in 1180. The organisation necessitated by this innovation was based on feudal principles. The smaller " dynast " could accept a territory as a fief from one of the greater princes, but he nevertheless remained the king's representative in the exercise of sovereign rights within his own small district. On the other hand, the king alone decided who was to be a member of the new estate of princes, and who therefore was empowered to confer administrative rights on the dynastic baronage. In this way the king himself hoped to be able to maintain a more intensive control of the division of the land into administrative districts than was possible either in Western Europe or in the Byzantine state.

Such, in my view, was the plan behind the suppression of the so-called " official " estate of princes and the introduction of a feudal princely class, which Barbarossa undertook.

But the reform had other, equally significant results. Above all else, it made it possible to bring the *ministeriales* within the scheme of government as representatives of the king. Hitherto, though individual *ministeriales* had been endowed with aristocratic powers, the *ministeriales* as a body had been regarded as upstarts and had consequently been categorically distinguished from the dynastic class. Under the new organisation, however, emphasis no longer lay on the personal rank of the office- or fiefholder, but simply on the fact that he was actually exercising count's rights within a specific territory, even if it were only a petty franchise. Thus the purely systematic elements in feudalism triumphed over the individual and casual forms which had hitherto dominated German feudal relationships: the individual, personal element gave way before the concrete facts. It is true that an unsystematic distinction was made between ecclesiastical and secular princes; but this concession to the ecclesiastical magnates and other exceptions which were introduced subsequently, were an indication that feudalism was already undergoing that process of internal dislocation by which it was rapidly undermined, and cannot hide the fact that the innovations introduced about the year 1180 placed German feudalism for the first time on a truly systematic basis. This is particularly obvious in regard to the *ministeriales*. The basis of the new system, we have seen, was not as previously the appropriate person, but rather the appropriate territorial district; and if this principle applied in the first place to the territories in the hands of counts and " dynasts ", it is obvious enough that it was only necessary to go one step further in order to extend it to ministerial lands. In this way the landed property on which the economic position of the great ministerial class of knights and officials was based, was brought within the framework of the new system. Their estates were made the basis for granting them a fixed position in the feudal hierarchy; and once they had been granted a fixed position in the state, the knights themselves came as a body into contact, if only into indirect contact, with government, and were to some degree detached from dependence on their personal lords. Economically and socially they already formed a distinct body; but the changes introduced by Barbarossa established them also in a fixed legal position, gave them an independent place in the constitutional organisation, and banded them together as a separate category in the feudal hierarchy. The advantages of this change for the central government are obvious. When circumstances dictated, it could now hold out its hand, over the heads of the territorial princes, to the *ministeriales* within the various principalities.

Everywhere, in fact, the ministerial class at this period was in possession of landed property: everywhere the knights had built up their social position on the basis of considerable estates. The estates in question might be allodial lands, ministerial fiefs or even mortgaged property; but whatever the title by which they were held, they provided the material foundation which enabled it to be said that their holder was a feudatory. The *ministeriales* were not incorporated in the feudal system of the realm because fiefs were conferred on them, but because the estates which they already possessed were qualified as fiefs. And this principle naturally applied the other way round: anyone who acquired lands which were already regarded as a feudal tenement, or which were as large and self-sufficient as the average knight's fee, could take the title of knight and act as a knight. This development is very clear in the thirteenth century: the knightly class stood together as a class of landholders and landholding was the qualification for entry into its ranks, whereas the squire or bachelor— the *Knecht* whose only qualifications were knightly weapons

and a personal capacity to undertake military service—
was definitely excluded from the knightly class.

Here again, however, one feudal category was not enough.
During the thirteenth century two classes were formed, the
higher of which was privileged with the right to enfeoff
other knights as its vassals, while the lower class had only
a passive place in the feudal system, could be enfeoffed
but could not itself enfeoff others.   But this was a very
superficial distinction which was never legally perfected
and never put into full practical effect.   One authority,
it is true, speaks of inequality of birth between the two
classes; but it is clear that such a social distinction never
existed in fact, and we can therefore ignore this later
refinement, which did not affect the essential character of
the system.   The essential feature of the new order, apart
from the creation of the new estate of princes, was without
doubt the position assigned to the " dynasts ", on the one
hand, and to the *ministeriales*, on the other.   Each class
took its place within the feudal system: the former by a
process of subordination, the latter as a result of rapid
social advancement.   Taken as a whole, it is not too much
to say that this new feudal system, common both to
" dynasts " and to unfree knights, was an extraordinarily
revolutionary innovation, which might easily have led to
constitutional developments similar to those which transformed the French state into a strong feudal monarchy.

Ultimately, however, the Hohenstaufen system of feudal
reorganisation miscarried.   Why it failed, and how the
new constitutional order fell to pieces, to give rise to an
unparalleled variety of political structures, built up out
of its fragments—to describe and explain all this is the
business of the political historian.   But the sketch which
I have attempted to draw is only a beginning of the task
which awaits the legal historian.   Administration, jurisdiction, legislation, the law governing the crown, the development of the new feudal society on a basis of complementary
rights and duties, military law and the military system, and
all the other elements in constitutional life must be studied

as a part of the constitutional reform inaugurated by the Hohenstaufen. The task which I have set myself in this preliminary survey is accomplished, if it stimulates historians to compare the constitutional structure of Hohenstaufen Germany in its entirety either with that of the earlier centuries of German history, during which the state still retained the form of a loosely constructed association of persons and classes, or with the contemporary organisation of France or England or the well-defined feudalism of the Latin Kingdom of Jerusalem. If this is done, the originality and breadth of the programme behind the Hohenstaufen constitutional reforms will at once become obvious, and it will gradually be recognized that Germany was never ruled by more gifted statesmen than the emperors of the Hohenstaufen dynasty.

VIII

FEUDALISM AND THE GERMAN CONSTITUTION[1]

By HEINRICH MITTEIS

THE origins of feudalism in Western Europe take us back
to the Frankish period, and the incorporation of the growing
feudalism into the organization of the state was the work
of the Carolingian monarchs and especially of Charles the
Great himself. With the decline and ultimate break-up
of the Carolingian Empire the feudal system, exposed to
a variety of influences, ethnological, geographical and
political, lost the uniform character imposed on it by
Carolingian authority, and a period of regional or even
national development began, which led to very different
results in the different states of feudal Europe. Our concern
here is with the development of feudalism and of feudal
law in Germany—not, however, with its influence over
and place in private law, but with its effects in the constitutional domain, its influence over public law, and the
relationship between feudal law and state authority, between feudalism and the state. A knowledge of constitutional development in England, in France and elsewhere
is the best means of grasping the special features of the
German situation: it also helps us to understand the difficulty of providing a sure sketch of feudal development in
Germany. When we turn to German history we find that
the fixed points provided, in England and in Italy, by legislative enactments are lacking, and that it is impossible to
trace, as in France, a single current, the effects of which
can be followed through all the deviations and fluctuations

[1] *Lehnrecht und Staatsgewalt. Untersuchungen zur mittelalterlichen
Verfassungsgeschichte* (Weimar: Herman Böhlaus Nachfolger, 1933), pp.
415—463. The pages here translated comprise the fifth section of the
chapter entitled " Feudal law and the formation of the Carolingian suc-
cession-states," which is preceded by similar sections on France, Normandy,
England and Italy.—Thanks are due to the publisher for permission to
translate.

of history. All we can attempt in the first place, therefore, is to describe the more important stages in the history of German feudalism, covering in this way the period from the end of the Carolingian age to the moment at which feudal law begins to receive more definite shape in imperial charters and, finally, full definition in the German law-books of the thirteenth century.

We begin with the established fact[2] that the collapse of the Carolingian Empire brought about a series of feudal relationships, which could be used to maintain the idea of hegemony within, as well as outside Germany. It may be surmised that the relations between the Saxon royal house and the " stem "-duchies were constructed on this basis. And this surmise can, in fact, be made to-day with more certainty than ever. It is only a few years since the richest and most dependable narrative authority[3] for the beginnings of the German kingdom, the so-called *Annales Juvavienses maximi*, was discovered.[4] In this work the federal character of the kingdom, disputed by earlier historians,[5] is very clearly portrayed. We now know the significant fact that the election of Arnulf of Bavaria was intended to be the setting-up of an anti-king for the whole of Germany—this is, indeed, the first known use of the term *regnum Teutonicorum*.[6] We have a completely new perception of the independence both of Arnulf's Italian policy[7] and of his relations with the Bavarian church,[8] and also of his sovereign control over the succession, which he

[2] *Lr. u. Sg.*, 207 sqq.
[3] As to its value, cf. Bresslau, " Die ältere Salzburger Annalistik," *Abhandl. d. preussischen Akademie*, 1932, No. 2.
[4] Discovered and published in the *Mitteil. d. Gesellsch. f. Salzburg. Landeskunde* LXI (1921), 33 sqq., by E. Klebel; republished by Bresslau, MG. *Script.* XXX. ii, 727—744.
[5] E.g., Ranke, *Weltgeschichte* VIII, 636 sq., Dümmler, *Otto d. Gr.* 19 sq., Waitz, *Verf.-gesch.* V, 72, and *Jahrbücher Heinrichs I* (3rd ed.), 44.
[6] *Ann. Juv. max.* for the year 920: " Bawarii sponte se reddiderunt Arnolfo duci et regnare eum fecerunt in regno Teutonicorum." Previously the expression was attributed to the eleventh century; cf. Vigener, *Bezeichnungen für Volk u. Land der Deutschen* (1901), 198.
[7] He had his son Arnulf set up in Italy as anti-king in opposition to Hugh of Vienne; cf. Bresslau, 60.
[8] Bresslau, 26 sqq., followed by Riezler, *Gesch. Bayerns* I. i (2nd ed.), 518 sqq. Arnulf, moreover, dated his charters from the beginning of his own, and not the king's, regnal year; Riezler, 522.

GERMAN FEUDALISM 237

secured for his son by extorting an oath of fealty from all
Bavarians.⁹ We are thus compelled to regard the feudal
relationship as the sole connecting bond between Bavaria
and Henry I's monarchy, and this realization forces us to
recognize how great a service was performed by federalism
in feudal guise at the formative moment in German history.
There is no longer any reason to cast doubt on the statements of Widukind and Liutprand regarding Bavaria,¹⁰
particularly as they are applied with equal precision to
Swabia, and undoubtedly apply in fact to Lotharingia as
well.¹¹ The functions which the dukes perform in the
state—Arnulf's appearance, for example, at the now fully
attested¹² Ingelheim council of 929 or the earlier participation of Burkhard of Swabia in the meeting at Seelheim¹³—
are a result of their feudal obligations, just as Henry's
occasional grant of charters to Bavarian monasteries¹⁴ may
be a consequence of his feudal supremacy. There is, therefore, a core of truth in the view put forward long ago by
SAMUEL VON PUFENDORF,¹⁵ according to whom the German
kingdom, at the beginning of its history, was based on the
surrender of their lands by the dukes and their restoration
as fiefs from the hand of the Saxon king. This conception
of *feuda oblata* is a sounder proof of the insight of its author
than the censure with which it has been received by modern
critics.¹⁶

A high point in Otto I's reign is marked by the homage

⁹ Riezler, 526.
¹⁰ Widukind I, c. 27: Arnulf " tradidit semet ipsum cum omni regno
suo "; Burkhard of Swabia " tradidit semet ipsum cum omnibus urbibus
et populo suo." Liutprand, *Antapodosis* II, c. 23 (ed. Becker, MG. *in us.
schol.*, 37): " Heinrici regis miles efficitur, et ab eo . . . concessis totius
Bagoariae pontificibus honoratur."
¹¹ For Lotharingia, cf. *Lr. u. Sg.*, 217 sqq.
¹² Bresslau, 59.
¹³ Lintzel, " Heinrich I. u. das Herzogtum Schwaben," *Hist. Vierteljahrschr.* XXIV (1929), 7 sqq., with a discussion of the Swabian duke's
attempt to copy Bavarian ecclesiastical policy.
¹⁴ Riezler, 527.
¹⁵ *Severinus de Monzambano de Statu Imperii Germanici*, ed. F. Salo-
mon, c. III (p. 67 sqq.).
¹⁶ Particularly Landsberg in Stintzing's *Gesch. d. deutschen Rechtswissenschaft* III, 20, following Jastrow, " Pufendorfs Lehre über Mon-
strosität der Reichsverfassung," *Zeitschr. f. Preuss. Gesch. u. Landeskunde*
(1882), No. 7. For a correct judgement, cf. Bresslau in the introduction
to his German edition of Severinus, *Klassiker der Politik* III, 34 sqq.

238   H. MITTEIS

done by the dukes at the Coronation[17]—an act which is
evidence that Otto's first intention was to carry on the
work of construction on the lines prepared by his father.
As the reign proceeds, however, a change of outlook
becomes evident. What we know[18] of the attitude of the
Saxon people to feudalism may perhaps enable us to understand that the Saxon rulers could only regard the employment of feudal principles as a temporary expedient in
the building of the state. Their endeavours were necessarily concentrated on minimizing the contractual element
and on reviving the Carolingian conceptions of bureaucratic
organization. Otto's policy therefore leads—as is well
known—to a centralization of government in the hands of
the royal house and of the national church which itself
stands in close dependence on the monarchy.[19] Thus began
the period of relative freedom in dealing with the duchies,
which was to continue with few interruptions into the
twelfth century.[20] The development of the higher offices
of state runs exactly parallel, in this period, with that of
ecclesiastical offices. In both cases feudal elements fall
into the background and the conferment of office once
again takes the form of an act of administration, though
it may well have been more frequently clothed in the
external forms of feudal law than the rare and indefinite
statements of the chroniclers disclose.[21] Recognition of an

        [17] Widukind II, c. 1: " manus ei dantes ac fidem pollicentes operamque
suam contra omnes inimicos spondentes ". Cf. Lindner, Die deutschen
Königswahlen, 75, Köpke-Dümmler, Jahrbücher Ottos I, 34. There is,
on the contrary, no such homage at the election of Otto II in 961 (Waitz,.
Verf.-gesch. V, 73)—is this a conscious elimination of feudal custom ?
        [18] Lr. u. Sg., 238.
        [19] Cf. Hauck, Kirchengesch. Deutschlands III (ed. 1920), 28 sqq.;
Hampe, Herrschergestalten des Mittelalters, 77 sq.
        [20] Waitz, Verf.-gesch. VII, 109 sqq.; Varges, " Das Herzogtum ",
Aus Politik u. Geschichte. Gedächtnisschrift für G. von Below, 28 sqq.
        [21] For a survey of the authorities, cf. Schlotterose, Besetzung der
deutschen Herzogtümer bis z. Jahre 1125 (1912), 60 sqq. As compared with
well over a hundred passages which simply employ such terms as dare,
tradere, committere, accipere, obtinere, there are only sparse references to
enfeoffment, notably Thietmar V, c. 22 (p. 120) ad annum 1002: " Heri-
mannus dux eius gratiam impetravit et in beneficio . . . miles et amicus
eius fidus efficitur," and VI, c. 3 (p. 135) ad a. 1004: " militi suimet genero-
que Heinrico . . . cumque hasta signifera ducatum dedit ". Cf. further
Gesta epp. Cameracen. (MG. Script. VII, 487) ad a. 1039: " pontifex
manibus se illius [sc. regis] commisit, pariterque dux Gothilo "; Ann.

established right of royal vassals and their heirs or of the body of vassals as such to re-enfeoffment with a confiscated administrative unit is more distant than ever. Confiscation itself, moreover, takes the form of dismissal, of an autocratic act of government without judicial examination.[22] In this way duchies remained many years in the immediate administration of the crown, and if the ruler subsequently alienated them, it was not through any consciousness of legal necessity.[23] The situation regarding the counties under royal control was parallel, though in this case the principle of heredity, even of the hereditary rights of females, appears to have been more potent.[24]

A revival of feudal law did not occur until the struggles which filled the reign of Conrad II. He is the first and for long the only German king to whom we can attribute a conscious feudal policy. It would, indeed, be incorrect to regard the feudal legislation promulgated for Italy in 1037 as automatically binding in Germany. But the well known events during the rising of Ernst of Swabia shew that a similar political situation north of the Alps might lead the king to apply in Germany the policy he had adopted in Italy of seeking contact with the rear-vassals.[25] There is, however, even more specific evidence, in a passage inserted in a charter of Frederick I, from which we can learn the conditions on which Conrad II was prepared to make grants. This " insertion " records the grant to a certain

---

Quedl. (MG. *Script.* III, 67) *ad a.* 985: " ambabus in unum complicatis manibus militem se et vera ulterius fide militaturum tradere non erubuit."

[22] It seems nevertheless to have been a recognized rule that dismissal should take place within the " stem " or tribal boundaries.. For the whole question, cf. Lintzel, *Beschlüsse d. deutschen Hoftage,* 47 sqq.

[23] Stälin, *Würt. Gesch.* I, 486, seems to suppose the contrary.

[24] Waitz, *Verf.-gesch.* VII, 10 sqq. On vassals as counts, cf. Curs, *Deutschlands Gaue* (1908), 82 sqq. It is necessary to distinguish the office of count from the fief (often taken from church lands) with which it was endowed; cf. for example DH. III, No. 100, from the year 1042. Pöschl, *Archiv f. kath. Kirchenrecht* CVI, 339 sqq.

[25] Cf. Bresslau, *Jahrbücher Kenrads II.* I, 218. In a famous passage the chronicler Wipo allows two counts to express the views of the rest: " Nunc vero cum liberi simus et libertatis nostre summum defensorem in terra regem et imperatorem nostrum habeamus, ubi illum deserimus, libertatem amittimus. . . . Quod cum ita sit, quicquid honesti et iusti a nobis exquiritis, in hoc parere volumus vobis. Si autem contra hoc vultis, illic revertemur liberaliter, unde ad vos venimus conditionaliter."

Uto and his wife of a county and other tenements with
the same wide rights of hereditary succession as governed
the transmission of allodial lands,[26] and this invaluable
document therefore shows how far the king was prepared
to go—in one single case, if not necessarily as a rule—in
recognizing the hereditary rights of collaterals.[27] Wipo's
declaration that Conrad gave particular attention to the
position of rear-vassals[28] seems therefore to be correct.
On the other hand, he had apparently no intention of granting far-reaching guarantees to tenants-in-chief. The proceedings against count Welf, against duke Ernst of Swabia
and against Adalbero of Kärnten—unintelligible from the
point of view of non-feudal " folk-law "—were without
doubt directed against them in their capacity of vassals;[29]
but even as feudal proceedings they remain very rudimen-
tary in comparison with later developments. The rights
of the accused were so narrowly limited that even contemporaries were impressed by the disregard for formalities.
Conrad was, in fact, guided by the old Carolingian conception of disciplinary law: he believed in absolute, personal
subjection of the vassal to the arbitrary discipline of his lord,
and this disciplinary power had not, as yet, been limited
by any corresponding development of vassals' rights.

It is nevertheless very noteworthy that Conrad, like his
successor, Henry III, proceeded in general according to
the principles of feudal law, for Henry IV took up an
exactly contrary attitude and relied implicitly on administrative law in the dispossession of great vassals such as

[26] The significance of the document was perceived by Bresslau, *Jahrb.
Konr. II*. II, 371 sqq., who printed it *ibid.*, 510 sq. Its authenticity was
recognized by Simonsfeld, *Jahrb. Friedrichs I.*, 597, and by Ficker-Puntschart, *Reichsfürstenstand* II. iii, 450.—Through this privilege the county
later passed to Henry the Lion; cf. L. Hüttebräuker, *Das Erbe Heinrichs
des Löwen* (1927), 44.

[27] The crucial passage reads: " ut, quicumque suorum utriusque
sexus haeredum praedium illorum in loco, qui Einbike vocatur obtineret "
—i.e., according to the rules of succession to allodial property—" is quoque
praedicta duo beneficia, forestum videlicet et comitatum praedicti comitis
Utonis in Lisga . . . iure beneficiali possidere deberet."

[28] Wipo, c. 6: " militum vero animos in hoc multum attraxit, quod
antiqua beneficia parentum nemini posteriorum aufferri sustinuit." Cf.
Below, *Deutscher Staat*, 301 sq., and DH. III, No. 80. There is, incidentally
already mention of an hereditary fief in DH. II, Nos. 271, 1013.

[29] Cf. Mitteis, *Politische Prozesse*, 31 sqq.

Otto of Nordheim and Eckbert of Meissen. This attitude corresponds exactly with his policy of a return to the old popular basis of criminal procedure and the introduction of a true conception of crime into the ancient system of purely " compensatory " justice.[30] In these circumstances we cannot wonder that there is no sign, during his reign and that of his successor, of a conscious development of feudal law and feudal principles of government. It would indeed, rather appear that a harsh employment of administrative measures against the Saxon baronage, the use of the inquest and the royal policy of castle-building during the Saxon wars,[31] awoke in the baronage the first consciousness of a community of interests, and so prepared the way for the later formation of an association or estate of vassals. The struggle against the Salian monarchy strengthened the feeling of solidarity among the vassalage. So was engendered a situation into which the engagements obtained by the baronage on the election of the anti-king, Rudolf of Rheinfelden, naturally fit;[32] for these promises clearly reveal the intention to accord Rudolf the position not of sovereign but of suzerain.

From this point development proceeds with remarkable logic. The next king from whom feudalism received new energy was Lothar of Saxony, and he was only raised to the throne as an anti-king, opposed to the Salian line.[33] His feudal practice was guided by a conscious antipathy to the arbitrary proceedings with which Henry V had disregarded the strengthened legal conceptions of the baronage and above all of the Saxon nobility.[34] Particularly instructive are his recognition of hereditary right both in his conferments of the Saxon Nordmark,[35] and in his

---

[30] Cf. Hirsch, *Hohe Gerichtsbarkeit*, 221 sqq.
[31] Cf. Ulman, " Zum Verständnis des sächsischen Aufstands," *Hist. Aufsätze f. Waitz* (1886).
[32] Meyer v. Knonau, *Jahrb. Heinr. IV*. III, vi, 627 sqq.
[33] On his election Lothar received homage from the secular magnates. The technical phraseology in Ordericus Vitalis, *Hist. eccl.* XII. 43 (ed. Leprévost, IV, 470) proves beyond doubt that this was a real feudal *homagium* and not merely a general oath of fealty.
[34] Heinemann, *Albrecht der Bär*, 55 sq., cites examples; cf. also Giesebrecht, *Gesch. d. deutschen Kaiserzeit* III, 840.
[35] Bernhardi, *Jahrb. Lothars*, 221, 260; Heinemann, 82.

242   H. MITTEIS

proceedings against Hermann of Winzenburg,[36] which already follow the true form of feudal litigation. Incomparably more important, in reality, is the extension of the sphere in which feudal law was effective, by the introduction of the church into the feudal hierarchy of the realm— an event the effects of which began to be perceptible under Lothar, although they only reached maturity later in the century. On the basis of the Concordat of Worms[37] the direct administration of the imperial church by the crown was transformed into a control regulated by feudal relationships. This view, which represents accepted opinion,[38] has indeed been attacked. BOERGER[39], for example, proposes to place the change in the period after 1200; but his error is easy to detect. It lies, in the first place, in undue emphasis on phraseology, on the first appearance of the word *feudum* or of the phrase *regalia feuda*; but it is due also to a misplaced belief in the later theory according to which a fief held without homage was not a genuine fief. Here however, it must be observed not only that the prelates' oath of fealty could, as in England, take the place of homage, but also that the imperial government never surrendered its claim to homage and, as will be seen later,[40] was partly successful in its demands.

The crucial point in the situation engendered by the Concordat of Worms was not that investiture alone had now to be regarded as a full conferment of seisin,[41] or that the prelates now regularly undertook personal feudal obligations—this had already occurred earlier in individual cases[42]—but that it was now possible to perceive in rela-

[36] Bernhardi, 262.
[37] For the older literature cf. Stutz, *Kirchenrecht*, 314; Hofmeister, " Das Wormser Konkordat," *Festschr. f. Dietrich Schäfer* (1915). Cf. also Hirsch, " Reichskanzlei u. Reichspolitik im Zeitalter d. salischen Kaiser," MIÖG. LXII (1927), and Pivec, *ibid.* XLVI (1931).
[38] Cf. Werminghoff, *Gesch. d. Kirchenverf. Deutschlands* (1905), 197 sqq., and *Verfassungsgesch. d. deutschen Kirche* (2nd ed., 1913), 61 sqq.; Hauck, *Kirchengesch.* III, 921 sqq., IV, 118 sqq.; Brunner-v. Schwerin, *Grundzüge d. deutschen Rechtsgesch.* (8th ed.), 145 sqq.
[39] *Die Belehnungen d. deutschen geistlichen Fürsten* (1901), 38 sqq.
[40] Cf. *Lr. u. Sg.*, cap. VI. ii, where the whole question of episcopal homage is examined.
[41] Cf. Scharnagl, *Begriff d. Investitur* (1908), 80 sqq.; Wirtz, " Donum, investitura, conductus ecclesiae," ZRG. *Kanon Abt.* XXXV, 134.
[42] Cf. Hauck, *Kirchengesch.* III, 54, with references to Thietmar.

tions with the *Reichskirchen* a logical, causal connexion between the personal bond, on the one hand, and, on the other, the concrete rights conceded by way of compensation for service.[43] To this degree it is possible to speak of a return to the Carolingian conception of feudal relationships. The concrete compensatory rights acquired in this way were the *regalia*—for the most part sovereign rights conceded to the churches by the king, as formerly, to be administered in the interests of the state.[44] The conferment of *regalia* was, therefore, a conferment of rights and not of properties.[45] Properties and lands might also, of course, be held as a tangible substratum;[46] but where this occurred, they were regarded simply as appurtenant to the regalian rights and were consequently comprehended in the original enfeoffment *per sceptrum*. It is conceivable, furthermore, that in this way the whole property of any particular church might be subjected to or included in the grant of *regalia*; but the innumerable grants of ecclesiastical fiefs both to emperors and to lay princes, which can be traced during the period, are a sure indication that considerable allodial properties still remained in ecclesiastical hands.[47] The widely applied policy of acquiring ecclesiastical fiefs, often by the exertion of pressure, which the Hohenstaufen adopted,[48] signified a reaction against the decrease of im-

[43] No example better illustrates this fact than Frederick I's reply to the pope's enquiry in 1159 with regard to the position of the Italian bishops (MG. *Const.* I, 250): "Episcoporum Italiae ego quidem non affecto hominium, si tamen et eos de nostris regalibus nichil delectat habere."

[44] Cf. A. Pöschl, *Die Regalien der mittelalterl. Kirche* (1928), whose merit it is to have shewn the necessity for a thorough re-examination of the conception of *regalia*; cf. Degener, ZRG. *Kanon. Abt.* L, 719 sqq. For the older literature, cf. Stutz's article, "Regalie", in the *Realenzyk. f. prot. Theologie u. Kirche* XVI, 537 sqq., and Blondel, "Etude sur les droits régaliens et la constitution de Roncaglia," *Mélanges P. Fabre* (1902), 141 sqq.

[45] Cf. Gerhoh of Reichersberg, *De aedif. Dei*, c. 23 (MG. *Lib. de lite* III, 153): "regales et militares administrationes." It is to be supposed (with Pöschl, 41) that the conception of *regalia* fixed at Roncaglia in 1158 was applied analogously in the case of the German bishops.

[46] Gerhoh, *op. cit.*, 17, 21, mentions "villas regalis pertinentiae."

[47] Pöschl, 95 sq.

[48] Cf. Ficker, *Vom Heerschilde*, 16 sqq., 37 sqq., 87 sqq.; Waitz, *Verf.-gesch.* VI, 102; A. Boss, *Kirchenlehen d. staufischen Kaiser* (1886); Winkelmann, *Friedrich II.* I, 497; Hessel, "Beziehungen d. Strassburger Bischöfe z. Kaisertum u. z. Stadtgemeinde," *Arch. f. Urkundenforsch.* VI

244   H. MITTEIS

perial authority resulting from the Concordat of Worms.[49]
If it had been carried to its logical conclusion and made
an exclusive privilege of the crown, it would have provided
the monarchy with an advantage over the local powers
which could not have been revoked. But Frederick I
himself had to acquiesce in the competition of secular
" dynasts ",[50] and even Frederick II was only partially
able to make good the losses suffered during the conflict
between Philip of Swabia and Otto of Brunswick.[51]

Ecclesiastical lands were at issue also in the famous
Marseilles case of 1157 in which Frederick for the first time
enunciated the principle that all concessions of crown lands
were feudal in character and governed by the strict rules
of feudal law, even if they had passed into a second or third
set of hands.[52] If logically applied, this dictum would
necessarily have meant that all offices, counties, advocacies,
in short every exercise of sovereign jurisdiction, was to be
confined to tenants-in-chief and rear-vassals of the crown.
Even earlier than in France a situation would thus have
been created in which, as in Carolingian times, all jurisdiction terminated in the king. But the German monarchy
did not succeed in making this principle more than pro-
grammatic: it remained a mere postulate which, as the
growth of feudalism within the bounds of the territorial
principalities is sufficient to show, was frequently ignored.

As a substitute for the principle that all jurisdiction
appertained to the feudal *ressort* of the crown, there was
the much debated institution of *Bannleihe*; but this proved
inadequate. It is well known that in Germany every
person exercising high criminal justice, with the exception

(1918), 266 sqq. Characteristic of the church's resistance is a charter of
the Bishop of Speyer, dated 1157, *Württ. Urk.-buch* II, 106.
[49] Boss, 56.
[50] Riezler, *Gesch. Bayerns* I. ii, 106; Stälin, *Württ. Gesch.* II, 644;
Below, *Der deutsche Staat*, 310.
[51] Boss, 39 sqq.
[52] *Sententia de feudis imperii non alienandis* (1157), MG. *Const.* I, 235:
" quoniam ea, que ab imperio tenentur, iure feodali possidentur, nec ea
sine domini consensu ad alterius possunt transferri dominium. Intellexi-
mus autem, quod Marsilienses beneficium, quod a . ·. Arelatensi archi-
episcopo tenebant, comiti Provinciae in concambium dederint . . .". The
exchange is declared void. Cf. Scholz, *Beiträge z. Gesch. d. Hoheitsrechte*, 65.

of the margraves, was supposed to obtain judicial authority or the " ban " from the king personally and at the same time to swear an oath of office.[53] The question has, however, been raised, whether the royal ban was ever an institution of more than limited applicability.[54] And even if this question is answered in the affirmative, it is necessary to note the weakening of the ban's efficacy—a weakening which arose from the fact that the king was unable to refuse to confer the ban on anyone who had acquired a jurisdiction according to the normal rules of feudal succession.[55] What was in its nature an act of administration was thus bound by rules of private law, and permanently effective control was therefore no longer possible. When, in the end, the ban disappeared without leaving anything to take its place, the prejudice to imperial authority which resulted was nevertheless serious; for feudal methods of control, which might have replaced it, had failed to develop.

With these observations we are already in the midst of the problems of the Hohenstaufen period—the greatest of which, in spite of the work of modern historians, still remain unsolved. Whether it is really possible to speak of a " reform of the constitution " by the Hohenstaufen,[56] whether and to what degree Frederick I planned and achieved a permeation of the Empire by a novel conception of the state and of state authority,[57] how far he was in-

[53] Schröder-v. Künssberg, *Deutsche Rechtsgesch.* (7th ed.), 618 sqq.; v. Below, *Der deutsche Staat*, 236 sqq.; Keutgen, *Der deutsche Staat*, 106 sqq.; Hirsch, *Hohe Gerichtsbarkeit*, 173 sqq.—That it was an oath of office is proved by the Sachsenspiegel (*Landrecht* III. 64. § 5): " Ban liet man ane manscap ".

[54] Voltelini, " Königsbannleihe u. Blutbannleihe ", ZRG. *Germ. Abt.* XXXVI, 290 sqq. is the main opponent of the thesis of general applicability; cf. also E. Mayer, *Deutsche u. franz. Verf.-gesch.* II, 350. Heck, ZRG. *Germ. Abt.* XXXVII, 261 sqq. suggests that the ban was only used to control the criminal jurisdiction vested in religious houses. As Eike von Repgow was a vassal of Quedlinburg, it is therefore possible that he was generalizing, in those sections of his *Sachsenspiegel* where he discusses the ban, from the position which he knew personally.

[55] *Sachsenspiegel, Landrecht* III, 64. § 5 (ed. Eckhardt, 146).

[56] Cf. v. Dungern, *supra*, 203—233.

[57] The expression: " Verstaatung des Imperiums ", which defies direct translation, is due to P. Rassow, who also attributes the external form of the treaty of Constance of 1153 (MG. *Const.* I, 201) to Byzantine influence.

fluenced in his policy by French, English, and Byzantine examples—all these are questions which will only be certainly decided when the documentary evidence has been carefully edited and made available in its entirety. Yet one main conclusion is already possible: the corner-stone of Frederick Barbarossa's constitutional policy was the exploitation of the powers placed in his hands by feudalism. After the earlier administrative dominion over the national church had been taken out of the crown's hands, no other course was open except reliance on the prerogatives which the monarchy acquired from its supreme position at the head of the feudal hierarchy. In the second half of the twelfth century we find the German monarchy treading exactly the same path as the English and French kings had long taken. It was, however, precisely this difference in time which placed difficulties in the way of the German rulers: in the intervening age the local territorial powers had strengthened their position, and when the rights of the supreme feudal lord were asserted, they came face to face with consolidated rights of the vassalage of a kind which could never have been formulated in the west.

The various facts which illustrate the new situation can only be briefly sketched. Already in the first legislative act of Frederick I's reign, in the " general peace " promulgated in all probability in 1152,[58] feudal conceptions are evident: a tenement confiscated from the heirs of anyone infringing the peace is taken into royal administration, but the count can claim it from the crown as a fief.[59] The idea of execution on behalf of the state is here combined with the concession of a premium to the executive authority, and so the principle that all properties held from the crown must be granted out as fiefs has already made its way into legislation. In the same peace enactment, however,

[58] With regard to the date, cf. Küch, *Landfriedensbestrebungen Friedrichs I* (1887), 12 sqq.; Simonsfeld, *Jahrb. Friedrichs I.*, 59 with note 156.
[59] MG. *Const.* I, 195, c. 2: " Quod si heredes neglecto postmodum iuris vigore hereditatem ei dimiserint, comes eandem hereditatem regiae ditioni assignet, et a rege iure beneficii recipiat." Cap. 5: " Si autem comes eandem hereditatem regiae potestati consignet, proclamatori etiam damnum restituat et praedium a rege beneficiali iure obtineat."

questions concerning feudal possession were settled in a way which clearly indicates that the later feudal courts were not yet in existence or that they had—the very opposite to France—to yield their jurisdiction in matters of public peace to the county courts.[60]

The erection of the Austrian mark into a duchy in 1156, on the other hand, is carried out in full accord with feudal law. A constitutional act of sovereign authority, hardly surpassable in significance, is for the first time endued with the brilliant forms of an investiture *per vexilla*. This is made plain in Otto of Freising's lucid description,[61] while the charter which testifies to the act, the famous *Privilegium minus*,[62] is more concerned with the exact determination of the hotly disputed rights of the new princely vassal than with the investiture itself. The point, however, which deserves special emphasis—as contrasted with the majority of historical narratives, where the emperor is made to appear as a free agent, acting spontaneously for the furtherance of imperial interests—is the fact that the whole agreement has the unmistakeable character of a compromise. It is a sentence promulgated in a court of royal barons and pronounced by one of the most powerful tenants-in-chief, the duke of Bohemia, the execution of which was left to the emperor. And this baronial sentence extended at least to the passage in the *privilegium minus* where wide recognition was given to the hereditary rights

[60] *Ibid.*, cap. 8: " Si duo homines pro uno beneficio contendunt et unus super eodem beneficio investitorem producit, illius testimonio, cum investitor donum investiturae recognoscit, comes primo recipiat; et si idem probare poterit idoneis testibus, quod absque rapina hoc idem beneficium habuit, remota controversiae materia illud obtineat. Quod si de rapina praesente iudice convictus fuerit, rapinam dupliciter solvat, beneficio vero careat, nisi iustitia et iudicio dictante illud in posterum requirat." Thus the issue goes before the count in the county court, and not before the lord in the feudal court.

[61] *Gesta Friderici* II. 55 (ed. Waitz, 1912, p. 160); cf. Simonsfeld, *op. cit.*, 467 sq.

[62] The best edition is that of Zeumer, *Quellensammlung* (2nd ed.), 9, which follows Erben, *Das Privilegium Friedrichs I. f. d. Herzogtum Oesterreich* (1902), 137 sqq., where the older literature is reviewed. Among more recent literature, cf. Tangl, ZRG. *Germ. Abt.* XXV, 258 sqq.; Stowasser, *ibid.* XLIV, 153 sq.; Steinacker, MIÖG. *Erg.-Bd.* XI, 205 sqq.; v. Dungern, *Wie Bayern das Oesterreich verlor* (1930). Regarding the latter, however, cf. Güterbock, MIÖG. XLVI, 113, and HZ. CXLVII (1933), 509, and Holtzmann and Brunner, *Jahresberichte f. d. Gesch.* VI, 170, 448.

of women.[63]   It was directly to the princes' interest to create such a precedent for one of their fellows, and the fact that the crown surrendered on this point can only be attributed to the pressure of political circumstances.

In the feudal legislation promulgated in Italy shortly before and shortly after 1156 special mention must be made not only of the strict definition of military service, which needs special consideration,[64] but also of the extraordinarily pregnant stipulation of the law of 1169 which postulates that, in every oath of fealty, the fealty owed to the emperor shall be reserved.[65]   The formulation of this provision indicates that the idea of general fealty, strengthened by oath, such as Carolingian times had known, was still entertained.[66]   But the feudal fealty of vassals was equally at issue.   We thus find Barbarossa on the way to introducing a general reservation of fealty, such as the French monarchy later[67] introduced with more success.   For the theoretical origins of the conception of an estate of princes, this passage is of considerable significance; for if this stipulation is adopted, it is only a short step to the principle that a lay prince cannot be the man of any other layman.   As to the origins of the reservation of fealty, conjecture alone is possible.   It is perhaps conceivable that memory of a similar ruling in Carolingian times was still alive; but if external influence must be presupposed, it can have come from England alone, for such a reservation, as we have observed, only appeared in France at a later date.   The most

[63] The caesura which separates the princes' sentence (extending in Zeumer's edition, to c. 4) from the gracious acts of the monarch is very marked.   Can it be an accident that the term *regnum* is employed in the first, *imperium* in the second part ?

[64] *Lr. u. Sg.*, 613 sq.

[65] Cap. 10: " Illud quoque sanccimus, ut in omni sacramento fidelitatis nominatim imperator excipiatur."

[66] It is impossible to be certain whether the oath sworn by all subjects in Carolingian times continued in use.   None of the references brought forward in Waitz, *Verf.-gesch.* VI, 478 sqq., is conclusive; cf. v. Below, *Staat*, 233 sq., and Guilhiermoz, *Essai sur l'origine de la noblesse*, 468, who takes his stand on Wipo, c. 4, to uphold the complete disappearance of the oath.

[67] Cf. *Lr. u. Sg.*, 323.   It was still possible in thirteenth-century France for a royal vassal in his relations with the king to reserve the fealty which he owed to a feudal magnate; cf. Brussel, *Usage général* I, 160, 349.

probable source, however, is the indirect influence of ecclesiastical doctrine which was intent on refining and ennobling the conception of fealty.[68] Not only Otto of Freising but also Rainald of Dassel had studied in France:[69] it may therefore have been the teaching of the school of Chartres which now found its way into imperial legislation.

With the question of the establishment of a new estate of princes, the *Reichsfürstenstand*, we come to the culminating point in Barbarossa's reign, the struggle with Henry the Lion. The trial and fall of Henry the Lion, as I have tried elsewhere to show,[70] was a landmark in history, an event of universal significance hidden under the procedural formalities of a state-trial. In the proceedings against Henry the Lion in 1180 we see for the first time two complete trials, the one according to folk-law, the other according to feudal law. For the first time the emperor appears in his feudal court in order to direct the forces of feudal law against a rebellious vassal whom the administrative measure of prescription and outlawry could no longer curb. It was the forfeiture of all Henry's feudal holdings which was to refashion German history—though not, perhaps, in the way which the emperor intended. For the Gelnhäuser charter[71] which contains the sentence depriving Henry of his duchies includes, as is well known, the first recognition of the obstinately enforced principle of *Leihezwang*, according to which the crown was compelled to grant out all escheated fiefs within a year and a day. The effects of this principle on the position of the crown are not difficult to comprehend; but neither effects nor origin can be considered here;[72] rather we must provisionally accept the *Leihezwang* as a given fact in the framework of the general historical development of the German constitution.

[68] *Lr. u. Sg.*, 266, 312 sqq.
[69] Simonsfeld, 424.
[70] *Politische Prozesse*, 48 sqq.; cf. Güterbock, *Neues Archiv* (1932), 518 sqq.
[71] The standard edition is that of Güterbock, *Die Gelnhäuser Urkunde u. der Prozess Heinrichs des Löwen* (1920), 24; cf. Henderson, *Select Hist. Documents of the Middle Ages* (1925), 217—218.
[72] Cf. *Lr. u. Sg.*, cap. 10.

It is equally well known that the Gelnhäuser charter is at the same time the first documentary evidence for the definition of a closed estate of princes.[73] The formation of the princely estate has remained an unsolved problem for seventy years. To-day we know at least that it was really a new body and not merely a selection from a more ancient estate of princes, for it is clear that there was no such ancient estate in the legal sense of a closed corporation.[74] For this reason it is not difficult to suppose that the new *Reichsfürstenstand* was a conscious innovation with a definite political object; and this conclusion has often been drawn. But there is another question: what were the driving forces behind the innovation? And this question, although it is particularly significant, since, as we shall see, the answer is closely bound up with certain functions of feudal law, has hardly been considered. We shall therefore turn to consider this question; and in doing so, it seems to me particularly necessary to draw a sharp distinction between the years immediately following 1180 and all later developments.

We may begin with FICKER'S own view, in the lucid form in which it has been expounded by SCHÖNHERR.[75] According to him feudal considerations were predominant, although not solely operative, when admission to the *Reichsfürstenstand* was at issue. These considerations were:[76]

(i) negative—i.e. that no homage was owed to any layman save the king,

(ii) positive—i.e. the tenure of a fief direct from the king. What FICKER left obscure, and what is therefore still the subject of debate, is the problem of the further qualifications of princely tenure. Must it have any particular character in non-feudal law? Was enfeoffment *per vexilla*

---

[73] Cf. Güterbock, *op. cit.*, 69 sq.; Moeller, ZRG. *Germ. Abt.* XXXIX (1918), 1 sqq.; and particularly Keutgen, *Der deutsche Staat des Mittelalters* (1918), cap. IV.
[74] Such is Keutgen's most significant conclusion, *op. cit.*, 91 sq.
[75] F. Schönherr, *Die Lehre vom Reichsfürstenstand des Mittelalters* (1914), is a systematic analysis of Ficker's doctrine, compared with the conclusions of other scholars.
[76] For the following, cf. Schönherr, 36 sqq.

requisite, for example, and what, in this case, are we to understand by a fief conferred by *vexillum* or " banner " ? Was it a jurisdictional unit or the fief of a military commander ? And again there is the question whether the imperial princes, the tenants-in-chief, formed a closed estate in non-feudal law, like the freeborn nobility in the fourth rank of the feudal hierarchy; whether, in other words, the *Reichsfürstenstand* comprised a distinct social class. Was it, for instance, composed of all who possessed the rank of duke or its equivalent ? Were there tenants-in-chief who were not princes, counts directly enfeoffed by the king who nevertheless remained outside the princely class or could only be brought within it by an explicit act of promotion ?

Without discussing all these problems in detail, I will try to convey briefly the impression which I have formed after repeated study of the authorities. Its general implication is that the well known facts and the single elements in the situation have too frequently been treated in isolation, and that it is necessary to give greater attention to the underlying motives, which alone provide an adequate explanation of the formation of the new estate.

If we apply this method to the first of FICKER's points, the negative element, there will be no doubt that it directly furthered the interests of the crown. In this regard Barbarossa may well have pursued a conscious and systematic policy, similar to that of the French monarchy. The regulation of feudal relationships in the highest category of the feudal hierarchy in such a way that the tenants-in-chief should be bound to the crown alone, recalls the basic principles of French *ligesse*.[77] Indeed, it goes even further in so far as no allowance, so far as we can see, was made for the possibility of enfeoffments from other quarters, saving the paramount rights of the crown. The main object, without doubt, was to prevent military alliances between the princes of the empire, and we have here,

[77] This fact was already recognized by E. Mayer, *Deutsche u. franz. Verf.-gesch.* II, 133.

therefore, the beginnings of the later prohibition of leagues against emperor and realm.

This central principle, however, was undermined in two places. In the first place, the ecclesiastical princes were interposed between the king and the secular magnates. It would have been a hopeless task, at this late date, to have tried to deprive the latter of the right to receive ecclesiastical fiefs, and this practice had therefore to be tolerated in the hope that it would not occasion direct political danger for the realm. Far more serious was the fact that the systematization of the feudal hierarchy could do nothing to prevent feudal relationships between German princes and foreign powers. It is very characteristic that a writer as near to the events as Giselbert of Mons includes among the princes those who hold fiefs from neighbouring kings.[78] Here was a direct conflict of interests; but the question how the conflict of interests was to be solved, was left in each case to the terms of the specific contract entered into, and this was governed by the law of the country which entered into it. The German princes were particularly attracted by *fiefs de bourse*, and it was precisely the *fief de bourse* which—as the intervention of the French and English kings in German affairs during the contest between Philip of Swabia and Otto of Brunswick was soon to shew—was a real danger.[79]

If we turn now to FICKER's positive element, tenure from the crown direct,[80] it is clear that there is nothing in this which explicitly proves that the princes recognized as such about 1180 were the only tenants-in-chief. Modern research has nevertheless given this supposition a large

[78] Ed. Vanderkindere, p. 250: " quicumque enim in imperio principis gaudet privilegio, nemini hominium facere potest, qui consecratus non fuerit: licet eis hominia facere regibus tantummodo et episcopis et abbatibus qui regales dicuntur." Cf. Moeller, *op. cit.*, 27, and W. Meyer, *Giselbert v. Mons als verfassungsgesch. Quelle* (1888), 15 sq. The *Sachsenspiegel, Landrecht* III, 58 § 1 (ed. Eckhardt, 1933, p. 142), on the other hand, says: " Des riches vorsten ne sollen nichênen leien zu herren haben wen den coning."

[79] Cf. W. Kienast, *Die deutschen Fürsten im Dienste der Westmächte* I (1924).

[80] Cf. *Sachsenspiegel, Landrecht* III. 58 § 2, and *Lehnrecht* 71 § 21: " Svie so vanlen hevet unde vorste is, die sal nenen leien to herren hebben ane den koning."

degree of probability. The cases which were previously regarded as evidence for the existence of counts holding immediately of the crown,[81] have all been either disproved or strongly disputed. Nevertheless there is still a certain degree of uncertainty, and the discovery of new documentary evidence might force us to revise our views. It is therefore desirable to search for some positive characteristic or legal attribute by which the princes were marked out from the main body of royal vassals.

If a particular quality in the non-feudal land law was the point of differentiation, the only possible view would be that membership of the *Reichsfürstenstand* belonged to those who held the position of duke or its equivalent.[82] But such a conclusion, if true, would only be a minor gain from a legal point of view, since it is still impossible to say what constitutional powers were regarded, in the twelfth century, as essential features of the position of duke. This line of argument, therefore, rapidly leads to the legally unsatisfactory conclusion that relative power alone decided whether or not a particular magnate belonged to the *Reichsfürstenstand*. Equally unproductive in itself is the argument that princely fiefs were identical with fiefs conferred *per vexillum*,[83] for here again another unknown factor is introduced. What was the character of the " banner fiefs " ? I am inclined to adopt the view, suggested by Gerhoh of Reichersberg,[84] that they were originally fiefs of military importance. But by the end of the twelfth century the original significance was lost. The fief con-

---

[81] Thus Fehr, *Fürst u. Graf im Sachsenspiegel* (1906), 15, claimed to have evidence for Brena and Orlamünde, but later withdrew; cf. ZRG. *Germ. Abt.* XL, 350. For Anhalt (Aschersleben) cf. Schönherr, *op. cit.*, 87; Haller, *Arch. f. Urk.-Forsch.* III, 429; Rosenstock, *Königshaus u. Stämme*, 120 sq.

[82] Such, in fact, was the thesis of Rosenstock's book. A detailed criticism of Rosenstock's views is out of the question; cf. the fine judgement passed by Hampe, *Wissensch. Forschungsberichte* VII (1921), 45.

[83] Cf. Bruckauf, *Fahnlehen u. Fahnenbelehnung im älteren deutschen Reich* (1907); Heck, *Der Sachsenspiegel u. die Stände der Freien* (1905), 621 sqq.; Fehr, *Fürst u. Graf*, 7 sqq., and " Die Staatsauffassung Eikes von Repgau," ZRG. *Germ. Abt.* XXXVII, 249 sqq.

[84] MG. *Lib. de lite* III, 440: " Sicut enim hi quorum interest exercitum campo ductare, congrue investiuntur per vexillum . . . ". In subsequent writings (*c.* 1160) the idea of jurisdiction and police is already coming to the fore; cf. Rosenstock, *Herzogsgewalt u. Friedensschutz*, 144 sq.

ferred *per vexillum* acquired another purport, and the thirteenth-century law-books, which pay scant attention to military organization, place the judicial aspects to the fore. For our purpose, however, it is sufficient to note that they were compound fiefs—perhaps they might be called " honours "—to which a number of mesne-fiefs were attached. This characteristic found expression in the fact that, already in 1156 and thenceforward with striking regularity, fiefs conferred *per vexillum* were, in fact, conferred by investiture with a plurality of *vexilla*.[85] One banner at least symbolized the fief held in demesne from the crown, but the others were the symbol for the power to re-enfeoff which the holder of a " banner fief " possessed. Acceptance of this fact leads, therefore, to the conclusion that a prince was a magnate holding directly and exclusively of the king, who had also vassals of his own. But it is still necessary to examine the qualifications of these vassals, and this leads us to the question of the *Heerschild*.

It is well known that the structure of the *Heerschild* was defined in literary form by the *Sachsenspiegel*,[86] but there has been no tendency to dispute the fact that the organization itself was already actually in existence about the year 1180. The word *Heerschild* itself is older, and belongs in origin to the military sphere, where it signifies the military contingent or the right—particularly on the part of churches—to call out their rear-vassals.[87] In

[85] This fact was noted by Rosenstock, *Königshaus u. Stämme*, but he interpreted it differently.
[86] Cf. Homeyer, *Sachsenspiegel* II. ii, 289 sqq., and Ficker, *Vom Heerschilde* (1862).
[87] Cf. the copy of a charter of Conrad III (1147) in the *Cod. Laureshamensis* (ed. Glöckner) I, 432: " Tres enim curtes Oppenheim, Gingen, Wibelingen eidem ecclesie pertinentes, cum omni iure et utilitate . . . in servitium et proprietatem regni recepimus, exceptis his, que in predictis villis homines seu ministeriales Laureshamensis ecclesie iure beneficiali ex antiquo possident; que idcirco remisimus, ne forte dignitas regalis abbatie militari clipeo, qui vulgo dicitur herschilt, subhacte diminuatur."—Cf. further *Mon. Boica* XXIXa, 306 (MG. *Const.* I, 188 note): " quia ecclesia Kizzingensis regalia, quod herescilt dicitur, non haberet, nullus laicorum quicquam de iure beneficiali ab ecclesia pretaxata vel ab abbatissa obtinere posset" (1155).—Finally cf. *Cod. dipl. Saxoniae Regiae* I. ii, 222 (No. 364), where bishop Uto of Naumberg demands in 1165 an imperial sentence " de suis inbeneficiatis, qui se autumant herskilt."

precisely the same way as the idea of the " banner fief ",
however, it acquired a new significance at the end of the
twelfth century, when it came to mean capacity or qualification to have vassals—not, indeed, in the absolute sense
of the capacity to have any vassals, but in the relative
sense of the capacity to have vassals of a particular category.
What we are considering, therefore, is the concept of " relative, active feudal competence or qualification ",[88] though
I only use this expression for want of a better, since it is
easily misunderstood. It is essential not to employ the
word " qualification " in the sense which it possesses in
modern legal terminology—namely, an attribute the lack
of which renders relevant action impossible—for that is
for the most part[89] not the mediaeval meaning. The
Heerschild was a system not of compulsory rules, but of
guiding principles, of *leges imperfectae.* Anyone who disregarded them placed himself[90] under certain disadvantages
—he lost equality with his compeers, could no longer be
a witness against them or sit in judgement on them[91]—but
whatever enfeoffment he obtained was valid, and the political benefits derived in this way might well outweigh the
corresponding loss of rights. There was no direct con-
straint to obey the rules of the system. All that can be
said is that from about 1180 it was no longer regarded as
normal to enter into feudal relationships which contravened
the rules, and it is easy to understand that such a tendency
to standardisation was in itself sufficient to exert a decisive
influence over practice.

As far as the origins of the *Heerschild* are concerned, the
complicated system described in the later law-books must
be disregarded. The original hierarchy, still partly discernible, comprised three grades below the king: princes,

[88] On "relative, aktive Lehnsfähigkeit" cf. Homeyer, Ficker, Schröder,
and many others: the merit of having emphasized this fact more strongly
than before is nevertheless Rosenstock's.
[89] Only exceptionally—particularly in the case of churches—is enfeoffment by those without a feudal contingent declared void, and this
no doubt for military reasons; thus e.g. in 1155 in the case of Kitzingen
(cf. *supra,* n. 87) and MG. *Const.* II, 117 (1223).
[90] And his successors to the third generation; cf. Homeyer, *op. cit.*,
303.
[91] Homeyer, 577, 600.

nobles and freemen.[92]　That the princely class split into two—lay and clerical—thus creating a further category, was a matter of secondary importance, and probably an unavoidable consequence of the concordat of Worms. For the lay princes it signified no loss of rank: on the contrary, such a result was expressly avoided, since they remained tenants-in-chief, even if they held fiefs from ecclesiastics.　The decisive factor was rather the abrupt cleft between the third and fourth grades of the hierarchy. That the fourth class was the axis of the whole system was already perceived by FICKER.[93]　He called it the " typical grade " (*Normalschild*)—and correctly, in so far as the basis on which it was built was the most stable element of society. The free gentry, in short, " had " the fourth grade: they belonged to it irrespective of their actual feudal relationships, and even if a free baron were directly enfeoffed by the king, he did not rise above the fourth grade, unless he were simultaneously created a member of the princely class with the assent of the rest of the princes.[94]

If the view that the estate of princes was a conscious innovation, newly formed and defined, is taken seriously, it is therefore clear that what occurred in 1180 was not the rise of a new nobility of birth but the elevation of certain individuals from the ranks of the highest class known to non-feudal law, the class of noble freemen, into a special category.　The instrument through which this privileged class was created was feudal law, in both the active and the passive sense: to be both liegeman of the king and feudal lord over highborn dynasts conferred the rank of prince. Anyone who had not achieved this position by 1180 was not to be allowed to achieve it subsequently.　At the moment when the most powerful of the dukes, Henry the

---

[92] Ficker, *Heerschild*, 219.　There were, of course, regional variations: the fourth grade, for example, was later frequently subdivided in west Germany (Ficker, 131 sqq.).

[93] Cf. Schönherr, 27 sq.

[94] This is proved by the case of the count of Holland, who did not become *ipso iure* a member of the princely class, in spite of the fact that he had broken off all feudal relationships except those with the emperor (had " bettered his homage "); cf. Giselbert, cap. 179 (ed. Vanderkindere, p. 265).

Lion, was brought to nothing, an obstacle was to be created which would prevent his former vassals stepping into his more elevated place.[95] For this purpose the princes established a close corporation, with the intention of maintaining as far as possible the *status quo* of 1180, unless it were altered by co-option. But this conclusion leads directly to another: that the estate of princes, the *Reichsfürstenstand*, was a creation of the princes themselves. And this view can be accepted without supposing that the princes formulated their decision in a sentence of the imperial court, which has been lost to posterity; for it was an adequate method of dealing with the new situation for the chancellor to order his staff to employ the word *princeps* in its new meaning alone in all future writs and charters.

The estate of princes was thus defined in essence by feudal law. Its strictly juridical formulation is based on the hierarchy of the *Heerschild*. Nor is this incompatible with the further historical consideration that it was the *de facto* successors of the dukes, rather than their successors *de iure*, in whom the legal qualifications for the new class were found united. That leads us one stage further: proof might, in effect, be required for the statement that all those recognized as princes of the empire after 1180 really had counts and freeborn dynasts as vassals. Nevertheless I can claim to be relieved of this proof, in the first place because it is the basic object of the third section of FICKER's second volume on the *Reichsfürstenstand* to show that feudal lordship over counties was the substance of the ducal position and subsequently of the princely estate.[96] Only the circumstance that his conclusions only recently became available[97] has prevented this becoming a commonplace of historical knowledge. FICKER proved his point, as far as the available material permitted. Where gaps still

---

[95] In particular, no doubt, the Saxon counts were to be prevented from obtaining once again the ducal rank which (according to Ficker, *Heerschild*, 154) had been theirs in the days of the Billunger.

[96] Ficker-Puntschart, *Vom Reichsfürstenstande* II. iii, 13, 84, 164, 209, 281, 391, etc.; cf. also Mayer, *Deutsche u. franz. Verf.-gesch.* II, 356.

[97] The second volume of Ficker's *Vom Reichsfürstenstande*, of which Vol. I appeared in 1861, was rediscovered and published by P. Puntschart in three parts between 1911 and 1923.

remain, we have, in the second place, the evidence of contemporary writers. The best informed of all, Giselbert of Mons, tells us that it is the essential characteristic of a duchy to consist of counties which can be re-enfeoffed, and that, on the other hand, no one can be a prince of the empire within whose territory another prince is exercising overlordship over counties.[98]　An " active feudal capacity " was, in short, the juridical bridge across which even the dukes had to pass, in order to become imperial princes.

For the counts, who in non-feudal law belonged to the highest class of the freeborn nobility, attachment to the fourth grade of the feudal hierarchy meant nothing less than the beginning of " mediatization ".　This transformation was not, indeed, carried out so rigorously as it was in all probability conceived: a few counts were subsequently successful in entering the ranks of the princes, others remained immediate vassals of the crown,[99] and still others kept free from all feudal connexions.　But in all essential points the fate of the county dynasties was sealed in 1180. Between them and the monarchy an estate of princes was interposed, which was already on the way to sovereign powers.　Henceforward it was normal for the count to receive his fief not directly from the crown but at second hand, and with the acceptance of this rule the " horizontal " stratification of the feudal pyramid became an irrevocable fact.　" Vertical " pillars and connecting links, which might have enabled the crown to maintain direct relations with its rear-vassals, could not be constructed.　The systematic

[98] He is discussing the elevation of the count of Hainault to the estate of princes at the meeting of the imperial court in Schwäbisch-Hall in 1190. The count of Flanders, with the assent of the rest of the princes, pronounces " quod comes Hanoniensis super terris illis iuste posset fieri et marchio et princeps, cum dux tenorem ducatus in terris illis se vel suos antecessores habuisse non posset monstrare.　A marchione de Minse [Meissen] ibidem iudicatum fuit, et inde pares habuit principes sequaces, quod dux Lovaniensis ducatum non habebat, nisi in comitatibus quos tenebat vel qui in eo tenebantur, cum ipse in aliis comitatibus vicinorum suorum tenuram suam monstrare non poterat " (Vanderkindere, 252).—On the relations between the county of Chiavenna and the duchy of Swabia, cf. Scheffer-Boichorst, *Zur Gesch. d. 12. u. 13. Jahrhunderts*, 105 sqq.; Simonsfeld, *Jahrb.*, 175, 508; Ficker, *Reichsfürstenstand* II. iii, 159; Rosenstock, *Königshaus*, 167; *St.* 3667.
[99] On the Swabian counts, cf. A. Mock, *Entstehung d. Landeshoheit d. Grafen v. Wirtemberg* (1927), 42 sq.

regulation of feudal relationships by means of the *Heerschild* thus worked, in the last analysis, against the crown. When the legal position was definitely formulated in the *Sachsenspiegel*, conceptions were incorporated which represented the interests of the princes themselves and therefore formed an insuperable obstacle in the way of a " monistic " or centralized solution of the constitutional problem.

With these considerations before us, there is no difficulty in understanding how inevitable was the inclusion in German feudal law of the *Leihezwang*[100]—the principle that all fiefs which escheated to the crown must be redistributed within a year and a day.[101] It is characteristic that this principle made its first practical appearance in the proceedings against Henry the Lion. His fall involved a gap in the feudal hierarchy between the crown and the fourth feudal category of counts and free barons, which it seemed reasonable to fill by the formation of one or more new princely honours. But it was only too easy to impose the filling of the empty place on the king as a permanent constitutional duty. The rear-vassals—namely the counts —could not complain, as they might reasonably do, if the feudal chain were extended by the " intercalation " of another link; for the filling of an empty place could not result in a lowering of the tenant's rank. Thus we arrive at the simplest of all conceivable explanations of the *Leihezwang*: namely, derivation from the internal development of the feudal system itself. Whether other additional factors were at play is a question which we can no more consider now[102] than we can enter on a discussion of the

[100] Cf. *supra*, 249.

[101] The authoritative passages in the Sachsenspiegel are *Landrecht*, § 147 (III. 53. § 3), ed. Eckhardt, p. 138; *ibid.*, § 153 (III. 60. § 1), p. 143; and *Lehnrecht*, 71 § 3.—Eike, in accordance with his general outlook, explains the principle of *Leihezwang* as enunciated in the interests not of feudal organization but of a sound judicial administration—in order, in other words, that the courts should function with regularity. But the argument is unconvincing, in so far as administrative appointment would have been more consonant with the needs of judicial organization than enfeoffment. And the Schwabenspiegel (*Landrecht*, 121 c.) lets the cat out of the bag when it grants the princes the right, if the king withholds a fief, to bring an action before the count-palatine. This passage is a clear indication that feudal, not judicial, interests were at stake.

[102] Cf. *Lr. u. Sg.*, cap. X, § 3.

resistance which the monarchy opposed to this potent check on its freedom of action.

In the three major constitutional events connected with the year 1180, the formation of a closed estate of princes, the definition of the *Heerschild*, and the formulation of the *Leihezwang*, we can, in my view, perceive compromises forced on Frederick I by the political situation. The princes demanded the payment of a big price, if they were to condemn Henry the Lion and so bring one of their fellows to nought.[103] The fall of the mightiest among them was certainly to their advantage, as well as that of the crown— but only on condition that they succeeded in saving for themselves the powers which he had won. And in this they were successful. Thus it came about that the development of feudalism in Germany was centrifugal in effect, and opened the way for the growth of the sovereign principalities. With the increasing emphasis on the real-property side of feudalism, as opposed to its personal aspect, this tendency became even more marked. Soon not only the man but also the property came to have a fixed place in the feudal hierarchy;[104] and so the princely fief became a permanent element in the constitution, immutable and indivisible, and the principle of *Leihezwang* developed into a guarantee of territorial stability at the same time as it assured the maintenance of the princely office, in the sense that the number of princedoms could no longer be reduced, or could only be reduced with the consent of the whole princely estate. Once this point was attained, development during the thirteenth century could only proceed as in fact it did proceed. For if it is true that Frederick II's legislation, above all the *Statutum in favorem principum*, was promulgated in favour of many varied interests,[105] it remains a fact that the three most important privileges were only guaranteed to the princes as such: the right to grant safe-conduct (§ 14), the right to issue coin (§ 17), and

---

[103] Lerche, *Eheverbindungen des welfischen Hauses*, 80, pertinently remarks that all the princes who passed judgement must have been related to or allied by marriage with Henry.
[104] Cf. Ficker, *Heerschild*, 209 sqq.
[105] Keutgen, 124.

particularly the recognition of customary law within the principalities (§ 6), which implied that the imperial government concurred in the view that the princes, unlike the emperor, were free from the feudal obligation to confer escheated fiefs.[106] But it would be a fatal mistake to judge all this simply as an expression of brutal dynastic egotism or of that individualism or particularism which was later termed " liberty ". The princes no doubt regarded themselves as the spiritual heirs of the ideas of Henry the Lion, particularly in the sphere of internal settlement and colonization; and it is easy to see that fidelity to those eminently statesmanlike conceptions may well have involved violent struggles with the conflicting claims of fidelity to the not always clearly recognizable aims of Hohenstaufen imperial policy. In the last analysis, therefore, it is the peculiar character of the feudal conception of fealty and of loyalty in a more general sense, with which we time and again find ourselves face to face, when we seek a juridical foundation for the political events of this critical period.

We have arrived at the point when we must ask the question whether the far-reaching constitutional changes which we have considered may be regarded as having transformed Germany into a " feudal state ". The answer we shall give depends on the view we adopt of the meaning of this far from clearly defined term.

If the term is intended to imply that all or at least the most important constitutional relationships within the German state were transformed into purely feudal relationships, so that new constitutional relationships could only be constructed on the basis of feudal law,[107] the answer can only be in the negative. Even at the time when

---

[106] Cf. *Stat. in fav. princ.* § 6: " Item unusquisque principum libertatibus, iurisdictionibus, comitatibus, centis sibi liberis vel infeodatis utetur quiete secundum terre sue consuetudinem approbatam." This clause has been preceded by Otto IV's charter of 16 June 1209 (*Reg. imperii* V, No. 284) and by the statute of 1216 (MG. *Const.* II, 90); cf. Blondel, *Politique de l'empereur Frédéric II en Allemagne*, 137 sqq.

[107] This sentence closely follows v. Below's formulation, *Territorium u. Stadt* (2nd ed., 1923), 162; cf. also *Der deutsche Staat* I, 319 sqq.

feudal law had reached the height of its development, there was a whole series of genuinely public, non-feudal institutions. Non-feudal, for example, was the procedure of royal election; for the college of electoral princes arose without any contribution from feudal law. Jurisdiction, also, was to a very considerable degree non-feudal. The king remained the head of the common law and of the courts which applied the common law; and even if this notion could never be completely applied, there were always royal courts directly dependent on the crown,[108] which successfully withstood all attempts to incorporate them within the organization of the princely territories. The relations of the cities with the imperial government, even if influenced by feudal conceptions, were not conditioned by feudal law.[109] And the position with regard to military organization, *regalia* and financial administration was exactly parallel. In all these connexions feudal law was only one juridical influence, not the only possible but one among many ways of approach to constitutional problems.

Among the instruments of truly royal, non-feudal administration the imperial *ministeriales* rank high. Without doubt an increasing use of this class of the population, bound by birth to their lord as no freeman was bound, was an essential feature of Hohenstaufen policy. And this for a very good reason. The legal principles which governed ministerial tenure enabled the lord to make full use of his seignorial rights—simply because the *ministerialis* was servile in origin and therefore unable to leave his lord—in a way which was impossible in feudal law, where the rights possessed by the vassalage as a whole against their lord were firmly entrenched. For this reason the imperial government made every endeavour to prevent any amalgamation of ministerial and feudal law, wherever it seemed to be taking root and notably in ecclesiastical lordships.[110]

[108] Schröder-v. Künssberg, *Rechtsgesch.*, 623 sq.
[109] Gierke, *Genossenschaftsrecht* II, 731 sqq.; Below, *Staat,* 321 sqq.
[110] Cf. Henry V's charter of 1107 for Corvey (Wilmanns, *Kaiserurkun-den d. Provinz Westfalen* II, 279): " officium quod quidam Escelinus sibi pro hereditario beneficio vendicabat, iudicio contubernalium suorum ei

The state had a strong interest in maintaining the servile bond, in which the idea of unqualified obedience (*obsequium*) was still powerful, for the very reason that, by comparison with the western powers, the idea of obedience was weak in the feudal relationship between lord and vassal in Germany. In the west, the growth of the idea of liege homage and of the *homo ligius* had brought about a reaction to a stricter interpretation of feudal obligations.[111] In Germany the process was the very opposite. There the loose conception of fealty common among the vassalage made its way into ministerial relationships, and finally robbed them of their absolute, unqualified character. It is the merit of a work which KEUTGEN published some years ago,[112] to have placed this development in the right perspective, and more recent investigations have been dominated by this aspect of the question.[113] The *ministerialis* can— indeed, in certain circumstances he must—receive a fief from his lord; but the law-books do not hold it to be a genuine fief, since it is held without homage.[114] This theoretical distinction, however, was doctrinaire and hardly of practical importance, for the obedience which

ablatum congregationi remisimus, et, nisi predictus abbas cum fratribus suis intercessisset, digna ipsum ultione pre iniusticia ei illata punissemus." —In DL. (MG. *Dipl.* VIII), 108, Lothar's *curia regis* gives sentence on a plea prosecuted by the bishop of Cambrai against a *ministerialis* who claims to have received a household office " in pheudo." The judgement is issued in generally binding form: " Eadem sane sententia de omnibus officiis non feodatis in presentia nostra a prefatis principibus data et confirmata est."—Finally a charter of 1194, issued by Henry VI for Minden (Erhard, *Reg. Westf.* II, 238) pronounces that anyone claiming enfeoffment of an office in the city or in the country must prove his claim by ordeal of hot iron—a pronouncement which clearly indicates a strong presumption against feudal tenure.

[111] Cf. *Lr. u. Sg.*, cap. 7, § 4.

[112] " Die Entstehung der deutschen Ministerialität," *Vierteljahrschr. f. Sozial- u. Wirtschaftsgesch.* VIII (1910), 1 sqq., 169 sqq., 481 sqq. and in particular 492 sqq. The idea was already to be found in Ficker, *Heerschild*, 176 sqq.

[113] Cf. among the abundant literature, Molitor, *Der Stand des Ministerialen vornehmlich auf Grund sächsischer, thüringischer u. niederrhein. Quellen* (1912), cap. 5; Winter, *Ministerialität in Brandenburg* (1922); Weimann, *Ministerialität im späteren Mittelalter* (1924); Ganshof, *Etude sur la ministerialité en Flandre et Lotharingie* (1925); Klewitz, *Ministerialität in Elsass* (1929); Ganahl, *Studien z. Verf.- Gesch. d. Klosterherrschaft St. Gallen* (1931), 113 sqq.

[114] Cf. *Sachsenspiegel, Lehnrecht*, 63 § 1; *Deutschenspiegel*, 175; *Schwabenspiegel, Lehnrecht*, 111.

was owed as a consequence of servile birth, and which
was an essential element of the ministerial relationship,
obviously did not need to be renewed when a ministerial
fief was granted.[115] It is certain, on the other hand, that
only the acceptance of a ministerial fief qualified the
ministerialis for and obliged him to the performance of a
number of particularly important services, not only of a
military character.[116] Indeed, we may go further and say
that only a *ministerialis* who had been granted a ministerial
fief was raised out of the social category of servile bondman
into the knightly class, which gradually cast off the marks
of servile origin as its capacity to accept non-ministerial
fiefs, from the immediate lord or even from others,[117]
won increasing recognition. It is easy to understand that,
in the end, vassals and *ministeriales* intermingled to such
a degree that in many cases differentiation was impossible.[118]

This process can be more readily observed in the territorial principalities than in the imperial lands, and for this

[115] So, very pertinently, Keutgen, *Ministerialität*, 509.

[116] I agree with Stengel, *Papsttum u. Kaisertum* (*Festschrift f. Kehr*),
168, that the controversy whether the origin and function of the *ministeriales* was predominantly military or non-military, has led nowhere. The
situation was exactly parallel to that of the vassals in the Carolingian
epoch: peaceful occupations during the intervals between warfare no
doubt took up the larger share of their time, but military employment
was equally certainly more characteristic of the class. Cf. further Stowasser
" Das Tal der Wachau u. seine Herren," *Mitteil. d. Vereins f. Gesch.
Wiens* VII (1927), 17 sqq., and Lechner, " Ein Ineditum Heinrichs IV ",
MIÖG. *Erg.-Bd.* XI, 155.

[117] An excellent example is found in c. 4–5 of the *Constitutio de
expeditione Romana* (MG. *Const.* I, 662)—a document written in Reichenau
some time before 1160, which, although dated back to Charles the Great,
must be accepted as authentic in itself (Scheffer-Boichorst, *Zeitschr. f.
Gesch. d. Oberrheins, Neue Folge* III, 173 sqq.), and which contains valid
law (Brandi, *Quellen u. Forsch. z. Gesch. d. Abtei Reichenau* I, 88 sq.).
In this document we even read of *ministeriales* who have accepted fiefs
from a number of lords in return for homage. Keutgen (p. 512 n. 1) very
acutely notes that in these circumstances the *constitutio* puts the state in
a privileged position; the *ministerialis*, it is stated, who is serving the
crown, and cannot therefore perform his stipulated service for another
lord, shall not lose his fief through default of service. Because of this
Keutgen concludes that the *constitutio* is to be regarded not as a code of
Reichenauer ministerial law, but as imperial law—" a stroke by which
Frederick I sought to bring the vassals of the imperial churches once again
into direct relations with the crown, and so a counterpart to his policy
of getting himself invested with ecclesiastical fiefs."—Cf. further *Urkundenbuch d. Hochstiftes Hildesheim* I, 504 (1196) and 509 (1197).

[118] Winter, *op. cit.*, 104 sqq.; Pfitzner, *Besiedlungs-, Verfassungs-
u. Verwaltungsgesch. d. Breslauer Bistumslandes* (1927), 332 sq.

reason the advice to seek a solution of the ministerial problem by regional investigation has been taken almost too
literally: the imperial *ministeriales* have, as a consequence,
fallen somewhat into the background. But there are striking examples to prove that developments within the imperial demesne were exactly the same as elsewhere.[119]
For this reason, without doubt, the *ministeriales* do not
in the end play the great part in imperial government
which we should expect after their brilliant start in the
eleventh and twelfth centuries. A real imperial bureaucracy
could not be built up out of their ranks. The mere circumstance that, in the organization of the *Heerschild*, they were
placed on the last rung of the feudal ladder necessarily
meant that their inclusion in the feudal hierarchy involved
a loss of direct contact with the throne. The territorial
princes, on the other hand, were fully capable of reducing
the feudalized ministerial offices once again into real
administrative posts—a process which the lack of a *Leihezwang* in the principalities immeasurably furthered.

We have considered one use of the term " feudal state ".
If, on the other hand, it is meant to indicate that the central government made full use of feudal relationships and
of feudal measures to replace the directly exercised sovereign
powers which it had lost,[120] then the Germany of Frederick I
and Frederick II can well be called a feudal state. The
centralizing policy of the Ottonian house and of the earlier
Salians was no longer practicable after the events of Henry
IV's reign. By the second third of the twelfth century at
latest a new situation had arisen. The Hohenstaufen had
no difficulty in realizing the fact, but they were unable to
master the problems which had come to the fore in the
intervening age. The twelfth century was an age of in-

[119] Niese, *Verwaltung d. Reichsguts*, 151 sqq.
[120] This second definition corresponds in some, if not in all points
with v. Below's conception of the " feudal state "; cf. *Der Deutsche Staat*
I, 322 sqq., and *Territorium u. Stadt* (2nd ed.), 162. But it is impossible
to speak, as v. Below does, of a breach in the connexion between subject
and ruler, of a " loss of subjects " by the state. The idea of " subjects "
only came to the fore in the territorial principalities. The number of
" subjects of the empire ", on the other hand, had always been severely
limited, for only the free element in the population was in direct contact
with government.

tensification in every sphere of life, and not least in the
sphere of law. The material with which rulers had to deal
became increasingly obdurate, ever more difficult to mould.
The legal outlook of the vassals—and particularly of the
immediate vassals of the crown—had hardened and become
so rigid that it was impossible for the king to take full
advantage of his position as paramount feudal suzerain.
Compared with England or with France, Germany was
not sufficiently a feudal state. The constitutional guarantees which feudalism placed in the hands of the vassalage
were by now too exclusively the preponderant factor in
the situation: the apt combination or balance of rights
and authority which might have led to feudal centralization,
was lacking. Central government in Germany suffered a
constant loss of specific instruments and weapons of public
authority—of *regalia* in the widest sense—which passed
into the hands of the later territorial princes. To regard
this process as simply a question of " usurpation " or
" appropriation " would, however, be totally wrong:
what occurred was a large-scale transference of competence
in the sphere of government, in which feudalism helped
on the movement and guaranteed its results.

We maintain, therefore, that there was nothing essentially centrifugal in feudalism itself, but only in the specific
form which it assumed in the Empire under the influence
of specific political factors. This is proved by the very
fact that its effects, in the territorial principalities, resulted
for the most part in consolidation and in a strengthening
of the central power. From this point of view, therefore,
we can only confirm an observation which others have
made,[121] but which is still far from being a generally accepted fact: that it was the German principalities, and not
the German Empire, which in constitutional development
ran parallel to the western powers. The process of creating
a non-feudal state in the German principalities was absolutely analogous to constitutional development in the west,
though it was, of course, smaller in scale. In administrative

[121] Cf. v. Below, *Territorium u. Stadt*, 167, and Hintze, " Zur Typologie
der ständischen Verfassungen ", HZ. CXLI, 242.

technique the principalities were ahead of the imperial government; and the consequence was that, by about 1250, it was clear that the rise of the modern state in Germany would take place, not in the Empire as a whole, but within the confines of the separate princely territories. Centuries of effort were needed before the diverse currents of German constitutional life could again be reduced to unity.

We turn, therefore, to the German principalities; but we must begin by emphasizing the fact that their origins and the process of their formation form too big a subject to be discussed in detail. There has been much controversy about the foundations of territorial sovereignty; and it still remains an acute problem how far manorial lordship and the possession of land provided the essential basis; how far, on the other hand, it lay in the possession of judicial powers, whether ordinary jurisdiction or the jurisdiction in life and limb which was the essence of *haute justice*; whether the exercise of count's functions was decisive, or whether advocacy or *regalia* supplied the constitutive element.[122] Where all these possibilities have been widely canvassed, it is, however, essential not to overlook the fact that none of these rights or institutions was more than raw material, and that the raw materials needed to be combined together—no doubt in a wide variety of compounds—before a new structure could be produced. The question: what was the driving force, what was the dynamic factor, to which the coalescence of all these elements was due, is the really important question, but it is a question which is very rarely asked. And yet it is precisely this question above all others which interests us here, for it can be shown that the leading part in the process by which the principalities were constructed, must be assigned to the powers inherent in feudalism. This statement will be proved in the following pages as far as is possible with the help of a few recent works and without too great a burden of facts.

---

[122] The controversy is summed up by v. Below, "Entstehung d. Landeshoheit," *Territorium u. Stadt*, 1 sqq.

The best examples are provided by the lands of ecclesiastical princes. In the territory of Mainz, for example, we
can observe, from the twelfth century onwards, an unbroken
series of transfers of feudal property to the archbishopric,
and as these transactions often involved fortified places
and other strategically important points, their acquisition
is to be attributed to a conscious and consistent archiepiscopal policy.[123] If some of these connexions were
subsequently broken, positive and permanent gains are
demonstrable, above all in the Rheingau. Even more
successful in the utilisation of their feudal position were
the bishops of Halberstadt.[124] In Bremen, according to
the account given by the chronicler, Adam of Bremen,[125]
archbishop Adalbert had made it his programme to acquire
all the counties within his diocese; and the execution of
this programme can be followed in the obstinate struggles
for feudal lordship over the county of Stade.[126] For
Utrecht OPPERMANN'S investigations[127] have provided full
confirmation of the view which FICKER formed of the major
rôle played by feudalism.[128] Particularly instructive,
however, is the course of events in Cologne.[129] Here it is

[123] M. Stimming, " Entstehung d. weltlichen Territoriums d. Erzbistums Mainz," Quellen u. Forsch. z. hessischen Gesch. III (1915), 39 sqq.;
cf. Schmidt-Ewald, Vierteljahrschr. f. Sozial- u. Wirtschaftsgesch. (1918), 400.
    [124] Cf. Schmidt-Ewald, Entstehung d. weltl. Territoriums d. Bistums
Halberstadt (1916), 52 sqq., 62 sqq.
    [125] Ed. Schmeidler, 188: " Solus erat Wirceburgensis episcopus, qui
dicitur in episcopatu suo neminem habere consortem, ipse cum teneat
ómnes comitatus suae parochiae, ducatum etiam provinciae gubernat
episcopus. Cuius aemulatione permotus noster praesul statuit omnes
comitatus, qui in sua dyocesi aliquam iurisdictionem habere videbantur,
in potestatem ecclesiae redigere." Cf. Hauck, " Entstehung d. geistlichen
Territorien," Abh. d. sächs. Akademie XXVII (1909), 654 sqq.
    [126] Ficker, Reichsfürstenstand II. iii, 402 sqq.; Dehio, Hartwig v.
Bremen (1872); Orig. Guelf. III, 126, 622, 626; Sudendorf, Urkundenbuch d. Herzöge v. Braunschweig u. Lüneburg, Einl., xiii sqq.; Dehio,
Gesch. d. Erzbistums Hamburg-Bremen II, 104 sqq.; Hüttebräuker, Das
Erbe Heinrichs d. Löwen, 39 sqq.
    [127] Westdeutsche Zeitschr. f. Gesch. u. Kunst XXVII (1908), 185 sqq.
    [128] Reichsfürstenstand II. iii, 220. Utrecht (according to Oppermann)
was the legal successor of a Frisian " stem duchy ". As long as the king
maintained his right of Bannleihe (cf. supra, 244) there was no growth of
territorial sovereignty. With its disappearance the church of Utrecht
was able to bind the local baronage to itself by feudal ties. Cf. further
Muller, Inleiding tot de middeleeuwsche rechtsbronnen der stad Utrecht
(1885), 9 sqq.
    [129] Ficker, op. cit., 230 sqq., 255 sq.; Aubin, Entstehung d. Landes-

possible to see the movement proceeding wave by wave. Already in the eleventh century there was a well-developed system of feudal tenure; but the strengthening of the rights of the rear-vassals, sponsored by the imperial government, brought to nothing this early phase of centralization. The same forces which the princes were later to mobilize against the central government, were directed at this stage against themselves.[130] Then followed the attempt at government through archiepiscopal *ministeriales*,[131] which must, however, be considered a failure, since by the end of the thirteenth century at latest the ministerial class had become thoroughly feudalized. A new situation only arose with the growth of a real bureaucracy after 1300. In the meantime, however—and particularly under archbishop Philip of Heinsberg—the network of feudal relationships had been constantly extended, and particular care had been taken to see that connexions with the rear-vassals were kept alive: they were given guarantees which prevented their medial lords from refusing, except on cogent grounds, to enfeoff them or from depriving them of their fiefs.[132]

Information about the Franconian dioceses of Bamberg

hoheit nach niederrhein. Quellen (1920), 397 sqq.; Jansen, *Herzogsgewalt d. Erzbischöfe v. Köln* (1895).—For Trier cf. Rörig, *Entstehung d. Landeshoheit d. Trierer Erzbischofs* (1906).—In Osnabrück the bishop obtained feudal supremacy over the church's advocacies, partly through renunciation by the tenants-in-chief, partly through outlawry of the count of Tecklenburg for participation in the murder of Engelbert of Cologne; cf. Ficker, *Engelbert d. Heilige*, 145 sq.; Sopp, *Entwicklung d. Landeshoheit im Fürstentum Osnabrück* (1902), 37 sqq.

[130] Aubin, 407 sqq.; for interesting parallels, cf. Baldes, *Die Salier u. ihre Untergrafen in d. Gauen d. Mittelrheins* (1913).

[131] Cf. the analogy of bishop Meinwerk of Paderborn, who got permission from Henry II to administer his counties through *ministeriales*; *Vita Meinwerci (ad ann.* 1021), MG. *Script.* XIII, 145, and Aubin, *Verwaltungsorganisation d. Fürstentums Paderborn* (1911).—For Hildesheim, cf. O. Müller, *Entst. d. Landeshoheit d. Bischöfe v. Hildesheim* (1908), 11 sqq. and particularly p. 37, on the bishop's use of feudal measures to obtain the forfeiture of the county of Winzenburg. For the episcopal policy of castle-building, cf. H. W. Klewitz, *Studien z. territorialen Entwicklung d. Bistums Hildesheim* (1932), 32 sqq.—On Verden, cf. A. Siedel, *Untersuch. ü. d. Entwickl. d. Landeshoheit d. ehem. Fürsterzbistums Verden*, 11 sqq.: here again consolidation was achieved by feudal methods.—In Breslau the policy of rounding off the episcopal territory was furthered by the exchange of fiefs and by the acquisition by agreement of rights over escheats; cf. Pfitzner, *op. cit.*, 338 sq.

[132] Aubin, 419.

and Würzburg is especially abundant.[133] It can now be considered certain that neither the direct conferment of sovereign rights by the crown nor the guardianship of public peace throughout the region was the ultimate source of the bishop of Würzburg's ducal position, but rather the acquisition of paramount feudal lordship over counties and hundreds.[134] The course of events in Würzburg can be compared with that in Trent and Münster, where there was a parallel attempt to secure a ducal position for the bishop.[135] The feudal policy of Bamberg, on the other hand, was not so successful: it failed to secure count's rights in the Bavarian Nordgau, acquired those in the Radenzgau too late,[136] and so had to give up its attempts to compete with Würzburg on an equal footing.

In following the history of the ecclesiastical principalities, it is occasionally possible to observe how the clerical lawyers manipulated the burden of proof in such a way as to create a presumption that any land at issue—unless direct proof to the contrary were produced—was held of the territorial lord.[137] They sought, in other words, after the same results as were realized in France by the principle

---

[133] On Würzburg cf. particularly G. Schmidt, *Das Würzburgische Herzogtum u. d. Grafen u. Herren v. Ostfranken*, and W. Miessner, *Der literarische Streit um die Herzogsgewalt in Franken* (typewritten dissertation, Würzburg 1923), where the older literature (Henner, Zallinger, Rosenstock, E. Mayer, etc.) is surveyed.—For Bamberg cf. the outstanding work by E. Freiherr v. Guttenberg, *Die Territorienbildung am Obermain* (Bamberg, 1927)—as E. Mayer wrote (ZRG. *Germ. Abt.* XLVIII, 589), a model for all future studies in legal history.

[134] Guttenberg, 234. Cf. the quotation from Adam of Bremen, *supra*, n. 125, which contains much if not all of the truth, and is a particularly weighty statement, if, as Schmeidler maintains (*Hist. Vierteljahrschr.*, 1921, 141), Adam was really a Franconian by birth.—The bishop of Würzburg's complaints about the usurpation of feudal jurisdiction by the imperial cities are noteworthy; MG. *Const.* II, 434 (1234).

[135] The comparison has been made by Miessner, 96 sqq. For Trent cf. Ficker, *Reichsfürstenstand* II. iii, 133 sqq.—here the survival of the *Codex Wangianus* enables us to follow the bishop's feudal policy in detail.— Brixen pursued similar objects, but (like Bamberg) was unable to overcome the resistance of the neighbouring baronage (particularly the counts of Meran and Tirol); Ficker, *op. cit.*, 143 sq.

[136] Guttenberg, 203 sqq., 223 sq.

[137] Cf. for example *Mon. hist. ducatus Carinthiae* I, 170, where the bishop of Gurk in 1160 demands evidence from a vassal of possession for a period of thirty years. Thirty years was also the term set by imperial law for the proof of prescriptive rights; cf. Frederick I's charter of 1156 for Hilwartshausen, *St.* 3740; Simonsfeld, *op. cit.*, 422 n. 20.

nulle terre sans seigneur.[138] The consequence was that
anyone claiming to hold from the crown had to undertake
the burden of proof;[139] and since feudal relationships were
still only rarely attested by charter, the result might well
be the elimination of royal rights by a deft employment of
legal procedure. Thus the state may have suffered many
a loss which can no longer be traced to-day, for the simple
reason that ancient feudal ties had sunk into oblivion;
and it has been argued that the " allodial county ", which
was unknown to early constitutional law, came into existence in this way.[140] Thus the aversion, so evident in German legal procedure, to the rational conception of written
proof made itself grievously felt in the constitutional
sphere, and the situation was made worse by the lack of
well-organized imperial archives, through which knowledge
of the state's rights might have been kept alive.

This, however, is a side issue, and with it we must leave
the history of the ecclesiastical principalities. The formation of the lay principalities, on the other hand, was a
process which went on for many centuries, and it is not our
business to describe the effects of feudalism in the later
phases of their history. Our task is rather to attempt, on
the basis of a few selected examples, a sketch of the beginnings of the process, and thus to discover the principles on
which the development of the principalities was based.
And the first point to note is the existence of marked
regional differences. In south-west Germany, for example,
it is impossible to trace any uniform line of development.
It was perhaps a direct consequence of geo-political circumstances that the region inhabited by the Swabian race
was the classical home of an untold variety of constitutional
forms, each reflecting its own particular environment, each
a law unto itself, and all in consequence resisting inclusion
in any system. If conscious feudal policy was ever pursued in this land, it took place within such petty limits

[138] Cf. *Lr. u. Sg.*, 318 sqq.
[139] Cf. Guttenberg, 294: the count of Orlamünde was forced in 1260
to prove that he had been enfeoffed by the crown with the hundred of
Steinach.
[140] Cf. Ficker, *Heerschild*, 162; similarly *Reichsfürstenstand* II. iii, 272.

that no decisive results were left, and often, indeed, no traces on which we can seize. FICKER attempted to prove that all the Swabian counties were feudally dependent on the Swabian duchy; but in this case his arguments cannot be regarded as successful.[141] We are, therefore, thrown back for the most part on conjecture and analogy, if we set out to discover how far a skilful utilisation of feudal relationships contributed, in this district as in others, to the subsequent rise of the territorial princes.[142]

If we turn to the region inhabited by the Frankish folk, the most outstanding of the new territorial states within the district is without doubt the Rhenish Palatinate. There is, in FICKER's judgement, no other principality in which we have such complete evidence of the control of the counties by the feudal lord as in the later Palatinate, though it must be admitted that his masterly knowledge of the authorities and his powers of inference were alone able to sift out the original position from the scattered and often relatively recent evidence.[143] In Hessen during the last quarter of the thirteenth century the conscious and systematic policy of the landgrave, Henry the Child—the son of Henry II of Brabant and of the landgravine Sophia of Thüringen—strengthened the loose feudal ties by which the barons and *ministeriales* of the land were bound to their lord, and by creating new bonds averted the alienation of territories which was threatened by Mainz.[144] Along the lower Rhine, on the other hand, the situation was incredibly complicated, for the disintegration of the Lotharingian duchies and the scattered character of the properties held by imperial bishoprics and abbeys resulted in such a variety of political groups that systematic investigation is practically impossible. The tendency during the thir-

---

[141] *Reichsfürstenstand* II. iii, 150 sqq.: against his views, among others, A. Mock, *Entstehung d. Landeshoheit d. Grafen v. Wirtemberg* (1927), 42 sq.

[142] Cf. for example Fehr, *Entst. d. Landeshoheit im Breisgau*, 30 sq., 178 sq. On the policy of the Zähringer regarding the advocacy at St. Gallen, cf. Ganahl, *op. cit.*, 81 sq.

[143] Ficker, *Reichsfürstenstand* II. iii, 198; Mayer, *Deutsche u. franz. Verf.-gesch.* II, 330.

[144] Hattemer, *Territoriale Gesch. d. Landgrafschaft Hessen* (1911), 32 sqq.

teenth century, at all events, was towards the removal of intermediate authorities and the creation of a number of consolidated territories, at loggerheads among themselves, but all equally held by direct tenure from the crown.[145] Here consolidation was achieved gradually from below; and in the process of consolidation feudal policy was repeatedly effective. The count of Guelders, for example, was able to concentrate sovereign jurisdiction within his own hands, by forcing the baronage to hold their jurisdictional rights and districts as fiefs from himself, and his political motive is very clearly apparent in the limitation of this policy to those parts of the baronial fiefs which lay within his own county.[146] In Cleves, also, very similar developments have been observed: there the growth of a feudally dependent but socially superior class of urban freemen was encouraged—a class which competed with the *ministeriales* of the county in the development of the estates and of a representative constitution, and so strengthened the hand of the duke against his feudatories.[147]

In the Saxon region, also, uniform development was lacking. As we have already remarked,[148] the social conditions of early Saxony made a complete penetration of feudalism unlikely. And with this factor we must take account, also, of the limited authority of the Saxon duke, who was unable to raise himself to supremacy over the old Saxon nobility.[149] The Billunger were only dukes in, and not dukes of Saxony; and the evidence indicates that they had few vassals.[150] Not even Henry the Lion realized

[145] Ficker, *op. cit.*, 282.
[146] G. Müller, *Entstehung d. Landeshoheit in Geldern* (1889), 13 sqq., 20 (with n. 1)—though without a clear perception of the legal situation.
[147] Ilgen, *Das Herzogtum Cleve* I (1921), 528.
[148] *Supra*, 238.
[149] Already in Widukind (II. 6) we find the statement that the Saxon magnates were unwilling to suffer "mediatisation": "Nam Saxones imperio regio gloriosi facti dedignabantur aliis servire nationibus, quaesturasque quas habuerunt ullius alii, nisi solius regis gratia, habere contemptserunt." Cf. Dümmler, *Otto d. Gr.*, 62, 78, 92; Ficker, *op. cit.* II. iii, 298 sqq.
[150] Weiland, *Sächs. Herzogtum*, 11. The exceptional independence of the Saxon county families—which had, however, mostly died out by about 1180—led Ficker to the hypothesis that the idea of the *Reichsfürstenstand* originated in Saxony; cf. Schönherr, 39.

what was presumably his object[151]—feudal control of the whole network of Saxon counties.[152] Where feudal rights were in existence, however, they were transferred by the sentence of 1180 to Henry's successors in the duchy and in the ducal rights.[153] The Gelnhäuser charter makes express mention of the *comitatus* in the clauses which enumerate the appurtenances of the duchy. The Ascanian house may therefore be presumed to have acquired *de iure* rights over the Saxon counties, but there is no reason to conclude from this that they were therefore recognized *de facto* by all the former Guelf vassals.[154] On the contrary, recent investigations have shewn that the Guelfs not only kept their rich allodial possessions, which they used as a basis for creating new feudal connexions, but that they also kept alive some of their old feudal relationships. It may therefore be said that feudalism was of prime importance in the rise of the duchy of Brunswick-Lüneburg, and that the privilege of 1235, by which the new duchy was created, was in the main simply the formal recognition of a situation which already existed in fact.[155]

Still another picture is presented by Bavaria, about which we have on the whole the fullest information. Here feudalism had made its way into the land as early as Carolingian times, and the way was paved for a course of constitutional development remarkably similar to that in the West Frankish realm.[156] The secularization of church lands carried out by duke Arnulf (907—937) furthered this development, and led of necessity to the creation out of church lands both of innumerable fiefs which were held from the duke and of a corresponding number of mesne tenements.[157]

[151] Weiland, *op. cit.*, 88 sq.; Toeche, *Heinrich VI*, 13 sq.; Hampe, *Herrschergestalten*, 245: the authority is Helmold's *Chronica Slavorum* II. 6.
[152] Hüttebräuker, 59.
[153] Weiland, 169 sqq. Evidence is provided by Otto IV's charter of 1201 (*Orig. Guelf.* III, 762) in which his brothers definitely renounce all claims to *feoda* and *comitatus*.
[154] For cases where this occurred, cf. Grauert, *Herzogsgewalt in Westfalen seit dem Sturze Heinrichs d. Löwen* (1877), 56 sq., 68 sq.
[155] Hüttebräuker, 61.
[156] Waitz, *Verf.-gesch.* IV, 286.
[157] Schulte, *Die Adel u. d. deutsche Kirche*, 204; Doeberl, *Entwicklungsgesch. Bayerns* (3rd ed.), 109 sqq. A charter of Frederick I (*Mon.*

In this way feudalism, by concentrating power and ultimate feudal control in the duke, strengthened and confirmed the tendency to separate local development which was already apparent in a strong sense of racial unity and a tenacious adherence to native law. Nor even the frequent changes in the person of the duke during the tenth and eleventh centuries could undermine this sense of Bavarian unity. As early as the beginning of the twelfth century the Guelf dukes appear to have succeeded in binding a large part of the Bavarian nobility to themselves by feudal ties, though it is not certain whether the Bavarian counties as such were held as ducal fiefs.[158]   After 1180, however, doubts are no longer possible.   Otto of Wittelsbach demanded and—after initial resistance—received the homage of all Bavarian counts and noblemen,[159] though naturally with the exception of those, such as the dukes of Styria and Istria, whose lands had been expressly separated from the Bavarian duchy.   With this fact in mind, it is easy to understand why the extinction of the majority of Bavarian county families brought the first Wittelsbachs so remarkable an accretion of power.[160]   The decisive factor was their ability to make the utmost use of the principles of feudal

Boica XXIX A, 369) says that many properties " per beneficium transierunt in usum laicorum." Hermann of Altaich states, no doubt on documentary authority, that " per ipsos potentes (qui ipsa praedia in feoda receperant) ad minores personas fuerant hinc et inde feudaliter derivata." Cf. Doeberl, 110 n. 2.—Pöschl, *Arch. f. kath. Kirchenrecht* CVI, 427, points out that feudalisation within the Bavarian church proceeded on the same lines as in France.

[158] Cf. Heigel and Riezler, *Das bayr. Herzogtum*, 155 sqq., 199, and Otto of Freising II. 43 (ed Waitz, p. 151) for the year 1155: " Igitur . . . Heinricus dux possessionem suam patrumque suorum recepit sedem. Nam et proceres Baioariae hominio et sacramento sibi obligantur "—the citizens of Regensburg, on the other hand, have to swear and to give hostages. The one is, of course, a feudal, the other a non-feudal procedure. —As regards the counties, Riezler is more cautious in his *Gesch. Bayerns* I. ii (2nd ed.), 407, than in the work cited above, probably because Doeberl (*op. cit.*, 171) considered the counties as such to have been held from the crown. But it is unlikely, according to Ficker, *Reichsfürstenstand* II. iii, 55 sqq., that there was ever a considerable number of counties held immediately of the crown. On the other hand, there were certainly completely independent franchises like that of Welf VI; cf. Adler, *Welf VI,* 34 sq.

[159] Boehmer, *Wittelsbacher Regesten*, No. 1; Riezler, *Gesch. Bayerns* I, ii, 361.

[160] Doeberl, 259, gives a list of counties which escheated between 1182 and 1268, cf. Riezler, *Herzogtum*, 200.

succession, and to insist, in particular, on strict application of the rule of exclusive male inheritance;[161] and we can see how profitable this feudal policy was, if we compare their success in this direction with the difficulties they encountered in their attempts to secure the reversion of allodial heritages.[162] Escheated church fiefs, obtained in the main by agreements in which the reversion to the fief was secured in exchange for rights of comparable value, also played a major part in the building up of the Wittelsbach demesnes.

In the counties which passed in this way into the duke's hands, centralized courts and a centralized administration were immediately set up.[163] It has been suggested[164] that this change was hardly lawful, and that the Wittelsbach dynasty was under a legal obligation to hand out the counties again as fiefs;[165] but such a suggestion can only be due to a misunderstanding of the historical situation at the time. It is based, without doubt, on the belief that the *Leihezwang* was a general rule of law, binding throughout the Empire. But the fact is that there were no general rules of law which were applicable throughout the Empire, and there could be no question of " abrogating " the *Leihezwang* within each single territorial state, since it had never been enforced in the principalities. It is a mistake to regard the law of the principalities simply as an exception to the law

[161] Ficker, *op. cit.*, II, iii, 87; Huschberg, *Gesch. d. herzoglichen u. gräfl. Hauses Ortenberg*, 64, 70.

[162] Cf. Ficker, *op. cit.* II. iii, 88 sqq.

[163] Doeberl, *op. cit.*, 260; Wohlhaupter, *Hoch- u. Niedergericht in d. mittelalterl. Gerichtsverf. Bayerns*, 169, 193; Rosenthal, *Gesch. d. Gerichtswesens u. d. Verwaltungsorganisation Bayerns* I, 51 sqq.

[164] Ficker, II. iii, 90.

[165] If it is true that the *Schwabenspiegel* was composed in Augsburg (Brunner-v. Schwerin, *Grundzüge*, 8th ed., 113) and, on the other hand, that Augsburg belonged to Bavaria after 1272 (Eckhardt, *Rechtsbücherstudien* I, 139), it is reasonable to suppose, as Ficker has already suggested, that the *Schwabenspiegel* was written with an eye to the legal situation in Bavaria. In these circumstances it is noteworthy that the *Schwabenspiegel*, *Lehnrecht*, c. 133, makes considerable changes in the text of its prototype, the *Sachsenspiegel*, *Lehnrecht*, 71 § 3. There is no longer a direct statement that the duke must hand out escheated counties again as fiefs: instead, those who have a claim to any fief are given the right of recourse to the king, as supreme feudal lord, if their claims to succeed are denied. The *Schwabenspiegel*, therefore, only considers the case where there are legitimate feudal heirs: nothing is said of fiefs for which there is no heir or of forfeitures, which the duke may therefore be presumed to have been entitled to retain.

of the Empire—an exception created by " overcoming "
the strict rules of imperial law. On the contrary, both
legal systems grew up side by side, and the princes never
needed to " overcome " the binding feudal principles which
dominated the legal system of the Empire, for the simple
reason that these principles had no force within the internal
organization of the principalities. All that was necessary
within the principalities, therefore, was a deft utilization of
the forces inherent in feudalism itself. Where such a
policy could be adopted, feudal law underwent rapid
evolution, and the feudal constitution was successfully
guided through a period of transition to an age of new
constitutional forms. This was the normal course of
development; but it took place not in the Empire itself,
but in the principalities which grew up within the Empire.
In the principalities a healthy development was still possible; but in the Empire itself, which was affected to a much
greater degree by external political influences, the healthy
development which had begun in the earlier centuries of the
middle ages was succeeded by a long period of weakness
and decline, which ultimately resulted—it is hardly too
much to say—in morbid degeneration.

We have reached the end of our survey of the history of
feudalism, and if we cast our eye not only over Germany
but also over the other major states of mediaeval Europe
we can safely say that, in the period between the tenth and
the thirteenth centuries, there was no land in which
feudalism failed to prove its potentialities as a decisive
factor in constitutional life. In every country there
existed side by side a feudal hierarchy and a series of
non-feudal institutions, organized on truly monarchical
principles. But in each country the influence of feudalism
varied in degree. France alone passed through an era of
complete feudalisation; and for a period feudalism was
there the one and only substitute for the earlier bureaucratic
organisation which had decayed and passed away. The
king, in other words, was forced to make his position at the
head of the feudal hierarchy the sole basis of his government.

But France also saw the fullest and most unswerving application of those defensive forces which sprang from the heart of feudalism itself and yet led to the destruction of the feudal system: it saw an attack on feudalism which was fought with the very weapons which feudalism itself had forged. In Germany, England and Italy, on the other hand, the influence of feudalism was more limited in extent, though still of immeasurable service in building up the authority of government. But the constructive powers inherent in feudalism were used in Germany—and in Italy as well—to build up the authority not of the central government itself, but of the rulers in the smaller territorial units, and the result was therefore an arbitrary and ultimately unsatisfactory political system. In Germany, in short, feudalism never arrived at that stage of consistent, balanced and systematic development which was characteristic of the west.

But there is still one further point. Whatever the land and whatever the circumstances, the main constructive force in feudalism found expression in the development of a sovereign key-stone to the feudal arch, a culminating point in the feudal hierarchy; and success or failure in this regard was the crucial test. And yet there was no country, not even France, where what we may call the " seignorial element" was strong enough to win complete ascendancy. Everywhere we find, side by side with the rights exercised by the overlord, the formulation of complementary rights which accrued to the vassalage. And these rights were not merely the uncoordinated rights of single vassals, but were rather the corporate rights of the vassalage as a whole—the rights of the estate of vassals. When in the thirteenth century new waves of political development began to rise— waves which brought about the rise of the modern state— the new constitutional structure was consequently neither solely seignorial nor solely corporative in character. Each element was forced to concede a place for the other within the new political structure. The state which succeeded the feudal state, therefore, necessarily emerged as a dualistic organism—in other words, as a body politic with representative institutions and representative estates.[166] This is a development which we cannot follow further in this place: it is sufficient if we have shown that its germs can already be discerned in the feudal organization of mediaeval Europe, and that the constitutional forms of later centuries thus spring directly from the conceptions of law and the constitution which were evolved during the feudal period.

[166] This is naturally not all that can be said about this problem; cf. for example Spangenberg, *Vom Lehnsstaat zum Ständestaat* (1912), 39 sqq., Wolzendorff, *Staatsrecht u. Naturrecht in der Lehre vom Widerstandsrecht* (1915), 46 sqq., 171 sq.

IX

THE BEGINNINGS OF THE NATIONAL STATE IN MEDIAEVAL GERMANY AND THE NORMAN MONARCHIES[1]

By ALBERT BRACKMANN

LET us set back the clock some eleven hundred years. The political map of Europe about the year 800 was far and away less complicated than the political system of to-day.[2] The imperial coronation of Charles the Great had created a universal empire which included practically the whole of the Christian west, and the independent regions on its frontiers, with the exception of the Byzantine empire and a few outposts of the great Mohammedan world-power, had little political significance. The empire which arose in the year 800 was superficially a continuation of the

[1] " Der mittelalterliche Ursprung der Nationalstaaten," *Sitzungsberichte der preussischen Akademie der Wissenschaften, Phil.-hist. Klasse,* 1936, No. XIII (pp. 128—139). An Address delivered in the Prussian Academy on 11 March 1936, and translated with the Academy's permission. —The paper is printed in the form in which it was delivered, and this has necessitated certain limitations. In the first place, all that could be included was the early mediaeval phase in the political developments which led to the splitting up of Europe into a series of national states. In the second place, I have necessarily based my narrative on the conclusions arrived at in a number of more specialized essays which I have published in recent years: these essays are referred to at the appropriate place in the text, and provide an amplification of my arguments. There could, in any case, be no question of supporting my arguments by detailed proofs in a paper of this size and character. But it was necessary also at certain points to ignore incidental complications, if the essential factors were to be properly emphasized; and for this reason the picture which I have drawn is sometimes simpler and bolder than the reality. This is the third unavoidable limitation; but I hope later to supply the gaps and fill in the detail in a more comprehensive work on the structure of the Norman states and their significance in the general historical development of mediaeval Europe.

[2] Cf. my essays, " Die Erneuerung der Kaiserwürde im Jahre 800," *Geschichtliche Studien für Albert Hauck* (1916), 121—134; " Die Anfänge der Slavenmission und die Renovatio imperii des Jahres 800," *Sitzungsberichte d. preussischen Akademie, phil.-hist. Kl.,* 1931, No. IX; " Der römische Erneuerungsgedanke u. seine Bedeutung für die Reichspolitik der deutschen Kaiserzeit," *ibid.,* 1932, No. XVII; " Reichspolitik u. Ostpolitik im frühen Mittelalter," *ibid.,* 1935, No. XXXII.

Frankish state; but as a result of the imperial coronation
it was imbued with the new conception of an *imperium
christianum*, a universal Christian empire. Neither the
pope nor his Roman clergy had expressed any decided
views about either the extent or the boundaries of the new
empire. If its sphere had been limited, forty years earlier,
in the forged Donation of Constantine, which was fabricated
in the papal court about 760, to " Italy and the provinces
of the west," it seems that the Roman clergy who did homage
to the new emperor in St. Peter's on Christmas Day 800,
had already cast their eye on the whole of the ancient
Roman empire; for there is no reason to doubt the correct-
ness of the account given by the Byzantine chronicler,
Theophanes, of a plan to unite the empires of east and west
by a marriage between Charles the Great and the empress
Irene. After Rome it would, they hoped, be possible to
incorporate Byzantium into the universal Christian commonwealth. And this aspiration, fragmentary though our
knowledge of it is, serves to reveal the magnitude of early
mediaeval political conceptions: the ideal was a Europe
united in one single empire, and even if this conception was
never substantiated, it remained strong enough to dominate
the whole political outlook of the early middle ages.

But the ideal was vitiated from the very beginning by
a flaw which was to be of immense consequence. Even in
the so-called " Theory of the Two Swords ", which was
originally formulated by pope Gelasius I at the end of the
fifth century, it has been maintained that of the two powers,
spiritual and secular, which should rule the Roman empire,
the authority of the ecclesiastical power—that is, of the
bishops—" weighs heavier " than that of the king.[3] Such
was the phrase used by Gelasius in the letter he wrote
to the emperor Anastasius I in 494. This conception was
subsequently taken over by the author of the forged
Donation of Constantine in the slightly altered form of the
superiority of the clerical over the secular power,[4] and its

[3] Cf. the new and authoritative interpretation in E. Caspar, *Gesch.
d. Papsttums* II (1933), 64.
[4] Cf. E. Caspar, " Das Papsttum unter fränkischer Herrschaft,"
Zeitschr. f. Kirchengesch. LIV (1935), 139 sqq.

effects were seen in actual practice in the coronation of 800
when pope Leo III handed over the crown to the Frankish
king. In this act the pope was the donor, Charles the Great
the recipient: the pope appeared as the superior, the new
emperor as the inferior power. The scene in St. Peter's on
Christmas Day 800 thus contained the germ of the whole
conflict of church and state, which reached its dramatic
culmination at Canossa.

But development was at first slow. During the two and
a half centuries which followed the coronation of Charles
the Great, the factors which bound church and state together were normally stronger than those which drove them
asunder. The idea of one united Christian commonwealth
comprising the whole of the west and represented by
empire and papacy, prevailed throughout Western Europe;
for the boundary states—Poland, Bohemia and Hungary
in the east, the Scandinavian peoples in the north, and in
spite of some resistance the Anglo-Norman and Romanized
peoples of the south and west—soon surrendered to the
idea of one emperor. The whole conception was so generally accepted a fact that not a single chronicler of the
Carolingian, Ottonian or early Salian period ever thought
of discussing the significance of the *Weltanschauung* of his
day. The first time we find it placed in the forefront of
discussion is in the " World Chronicle " written about 1145
by bishop Otto of Freising, the historian of Frederick
Barbarossa, by which time it was already in danger of
perishing. Otto of Freising not only placed the universal
empire in the very centre of his narrative but also, following
the example of St. Augustine in his " City of God ", reduced
the political ideal of the early middle ages to a coherent
system by treating of the " two cities ", temporal and
eternal, human and divine. We see here a process which
can often be observed in the course of history: not until
the peak of a development is past do men begin to realize
what its significance was. The contemporaries of Frederick
Barbarossa lived one and all in the shadow of the unparalleled might of the emperor, and it is readily comprehensible
that they never for one moment conceived that the future

belonged not to the emperor and the conception of a world commonwealth for which he stood, but to the kings and their territorial states. But already at the end of the eleventh century, fifty or sixty years before Frederick Barbarossa succeeded to the throne, the forces which were to lead to a complete transformation of the European political system were beginning to stir into activity. So we are brought face to face with the question to which we are seeking an answer: how was it that the conception of a united western empire, which had dominated Christian thought for so many generations, suddenly gave way before the growth of separate and distinct national states ?[5]

The first stimulus was provided by the struggle of church and state. In the closing years of the eleventh century, it is well known, the ideas which had been propagated by the Burgundian monastery of Cluny for a century and more began to exert an influence in the domain of high politics. The political significance of the Cluniac movement has been denied, its effectiveness has been limited to the influence which the strict Cluniac rule exerted over western monasticism.[6] But this view is wrong.[7] The great abbots of Cluny were politicians and strove to realize a concrete political objective. Even the first abbot, Odo (910—942), revealed the goal which he had set himself, when he said that he aimed at imbuing the whole of mankind with the spirit of the church. At first sight his words seem anything but political. But what did these abbots, who were as much at home in the courts of France, Spain and Germany as at the court of their own Burgundian ruler, understand by the phrase " the spirit of the church " ? Once again it is the first abbot, Odo, who reveals their meaning when

---

[5] In using the expression "national state" in this connexion, I am following the usual convenient practice; but there is, of course, a vast difference between the term "national state" as applied to the middle ages, and the modern connotation of the term. The first great national state in the modern sense was the France which was created by the revolution of 1789.

[6] Cf. for example L. M. Smith, " Cluny and Gregory VII," *Engl. Hist. Review* XXVI (1911), 20—33.

[7] Cf. my essay, " Die politische Wirkung der kluniazensischen Bewegung," *HZ.* CXXXIX (1929), 34—47.

he declaims in the acid phrases of his sermons against the secular princes and sets the authority of the priesthood over secular authority. In this way Cluniac conceptions gradually merged with the Gelasian theory of the two swords and with the doctrine of the superiority of clerical over secular authority; but it was not long before they outstripped the older theories. If, for a century and a half, the abbots of Cluny had confined their energies to counselling and advising kings and princes, by the middle of the eleventh century they had attained the position of uncrowned kings of western Christendom. It was no accident that abbot Hugh of Cluny stood between Gregory VII and Henry IV during the fateful days of 1077 in the castle of Canossa. In estimating the part which the abbot played in the scene at Canossa, historians have been led astray by the fact that, as Henry IV's godfather, he was seeking a compromise. But it was after Canossa that his real aim became evident, when he sent Cluniac monks to Germany with the task of establishing what we can only call a German " ecclesiastical state " with its centre in Hirsau. If Hugh's pupil, the French pope Urban II, who was Henry IV's bitterest opponent, subsequently placed Cluny and Hirsau in the background and directed the struggle from Rome itself, the new phase of policy amounted to no more than a change of tactics. In their ultimate objects the popes and the abbots of Cluny were united: in both cases the goal was to bring the secular power under the leadership of a church which was fully conscious of its ultimate aims. Already in 1075 these aims had reached their highest point and received classical expression in the famous maxims of the *Dictatus papae*, the summary statement of guiding principles from which papal policy took its direction. It is sufficient for our purpose to recall the most outstanding of these pronouncements: all princes must kiss the pope's feet (c. 9), there is but one name in the world, the pope's (c. 11), the pope may lawfully depose emperors (c. 12). These rigorous pronouncements transformed the theory of the two swords into the doctrine of the supremacy of papacy over empire. The universal empire had become under Cluniac and Hildebrandine influence an out-and-out theocracy.

But immediately and everywhere, in the realm of politics and in the domain of thought, men rebelled against this claim to subject the world to theocratic rule. The first thinker, so far as we know, to turn away from the political philosophy of the early middle ages was an English churchman in York, whose name remains unknown. In a series of treatises written about the year 1100 he relentlessly attacked the theories of the papal party, and set up in their place a totally new conception of the world order.[8] He contrasted Gregory VII's theocracy with the divine will as seen in nature; he placed the king above the priesthood; state and church, he maintained, were one and both in his view should be subject to the monarch who was appointed by God. In this way his treatises proclaimed the state's independence from the church. We are accustomed to separate church and state, and so his words no longer sound so revolutionary as they rang in the ears of his contemporaries. But at the beginning of the twelfth century they must have had all the appearance of an incitement to mutiny; and such without doubt would have been their effect, if they had not been silenced by opponents and hidden in the depths of the library at York, until they were discovered three centuries later by Wycliffe and put by him to political use. In spite of their ineffectiveness, however, the York treatises remain invaluable to the historian as first-rate evidence for the existence of a new *Weltanschauung*, born from opposition to the theocratic system of Gregory VII.[9]

No other thinker of the day was as radical as this English theologian. But he was not the only man of his age who developed novel ideas. His contemporaries in England were Lanfranc and Anselm, both monks in the Norman monastery of Bec and subsequently archbishops of Canterbury. Of the two, it was Anselm, known as " the father

---

[8] Cf. my essay, " Die Ursachen der geistigen und politischen Wandlung Europas im 11. u. 12. Jahrhundert," HZ. CXLIX (1934), 229—239.

[9] In regard both to these points and to those which follow, it is sufficient to refer to my arguments in the essay cited in the previous note.

of scholasticism ", who won the more lasting importance in the intellectual development of Europe. In formulating the principle: *credo ut intelligam*, he inaugurated a new age of philosophical thought in which reason " guided by faith " sought to obtain a more profound insight into the fundamental problems of life. But Anselm, like the Anonymous of York, was writing and working at the time of the English investiture contest, and in both cases it is easy to perceive the inner connexion between the events of their day and the development of their personality: the contest between church and state, in other words, awoke in these men both the impulse to independent thought and an unquenchable need for a new philosophical outlook.

But the age of Anselm and of the anonymous writer of York was also the period of the foundation of the Anglo-Norman state in England, and with this further point we come to the second factor which led to a transformation of the early mediaeval political system. Henry I, who began the investiture contest in England, was at the same time the real founder of the Anglo-Norman state, which introduced a new type of political organisation into mediaeval Europe. I have already pointed out the general significance of this new Norman or Nordic form of state in a recent essay.[10] I drew attention there to the fact that the new type of political organisation is first found in the small duchy of Normandy, founded by Rollo in 911; that its characteristic features were a strong royal authority and a systematic centralisation of the administration; that the duke and his successors took not only criminal jurisdiction in life and limb but also supreme military authority and the nomination of bishops firmly into their own hands, and thus eliminated the most typical feature of continental feudalism, the control of administrative functions by the feudatories, lay and ecclesiastical. In this way they prepared the way for the later bureaucratic state. If in addition we recall the fact that it was here in Normandy and in Norman England at the end of the eleventh century

[10] " Die Wandlung der Staatsanschauungen im Zeitalter Kaiser Friedrichs I," HZ. CXLV (1932), 1—18.

that the theologians of whom I have spoken formulated
their novel ideas, interrelated developments are disclosed
which were of decisive importance not only in the intellectual and political development of Europe generally
but more particularly in the transition from the concept
of universal empire to the era of national states. It was,
in short, the Normans who reshaped the life of Europe,
both politically and intellectually, and who set the development of European civilisation on a new course.

Such a judgement would, of course, be unjustified, if it
were merely based on what took place in Normandy itself.
But the petty duchy of Normandy was not the only state
in which a transformation occurred at the period with which
we are dealing. Wherever they went, the Normans transformed political life, exactly as they had changed it in
their Norman duchy. They were the Ruriks who organized
the Russian state between the ninth and the eleventh
centuries, and they helped also in the foundation of the
new Polish state, which made its first appearance in 963
and, as Polish scholars have admitted, was moulded in its
early stages by Norman influences.[11] But it was above
all in England and southern Italy that the new conceptions
of the state exerted the greatest influence during the eleventh
and twelfth centuries: England which was transformed by
the Norman conquerors after 1066 and brought into line
with the Norman duchy, and Southern Italy which at the
same period was consolidated into one united kingdom
by Robert Guiscard and his successors in the Norman
ruling dynasty, Roger I and Roger II. The significance of
the Norman achievements in the constitutional sphere can
only be fully appreciated if the institutions of the continental feudal state of the earlier middle ages are compared
with those of the Norman monarchies. The continental
feudal state was characterized by a perambulating court,
wandering ceaselessly from royal manor to royal manor:
the Norman states in England and Sicily had fixed royal

[11] Cf. my essays, " Die Anfänge des polnischen Staates," *Sitz.-ber. d.
preuss. Akademie, phil.-hist. Kl.*, 1934, No. XXIX, and " Reichspolitik u.
Ostpolitik im frühen Mittelalter," *ibid.*, 1935, No. XXXII.

residences. In the continental state of the old type administration was the hereditary possession of the feudatories and was consequently loose and decentralized: in the Norman states there was a dependent bureaucracy, appointed by the crown. The army, in the older system, could only be summoned with the consent of the magnates in the great council of the realm: in the Norman states there was, if not a professional standing army, at least an attempt to create one.[12] Instead of badly organized revenues, dependent on the irregular income derived from the crown lands and the *regalia*, the Norman monarchies had a systematic economic and financial policy, directed by the central government and based for the most part on money economy and state monopolies—a foretaste of the mercantilism which was later to be the characteristic of absolutism. Instead of a combination or juxtaposition of independent and even incompatible legal systems, one uniform law and a uniform legal procedure was the rule in Norman constitutional organisation. The dangerous slackening of the bonds between ruler and subject by "immunities" and franchises, particularly by the immunity or exemption of ecclesiastical lands, was replaced in the Norman states by the endeavour to incorporate the church into the governmental organisation of the state by royal investiture of bishops.[13] And finally, where art and learning were otherwise in the control of the church, the Norman monarchies introduced not only a conscious policy of state encouragement for all cultural activities, but also —what other states lacked—a cult of the monarch and of the royal dynasty. There is no better way of obtaining a true notion of the profound transformation in the forms of government and public life than to go in spirit to the residence of the Norman kings in Palermo and picture in

[12] Cf. among others P. Schmittbenner, "Lehnskriegswesen u. Söldnertum im abendländischen Imperium des Mittelalters," HZ. CL (1934), 229—267.
[13] It is only necessary to mention as an example the "Monarchia Sicula" of Roger II, a sort of concordat between the Curia and the Norman monarchy, which recognized the Sicilian king as apostolic legate in his lands, so that the papacy could not intervene except through the ruler himself, and defined the spheres of church and state.

one's mind the city's harbours, warehouses and public buildings. Even to-day the Palazzo Reale with the Capella Palatina and its mosaics, and the cathedral with the porphyry tombs of the Norman royal dynasty and its Hohenstaufen successors, are a living witness to the conscious fostering of artistic life by Roger II and his successors.

And yet contemporary literature—exactly as in an earlier generation—shows hardly a sign of the impression which must have been created by the new type of political organization. In Normandy alone we see something of its effects, when Orderic Vitalis, a monk in the Norman abbey of St. Évroult who died in 1142, relates with enthusiasm the deeds of Robert Guiscard and his successors and of the Norman kings of England and only makes incidental mention of the emperors, or when the philosopher, John of Salisbury, writing in 1159 in his " Polycraticus " denies the supreme authority of the empire and places the *princeps* instead of the *imperator* in the forefront of discussion. In spite of its ecclesiastical wrapping, John of Salisbury's " Polycraticus " contains the first political theory which breaks with the conceptions of the early middle ages and leads onwards to an era in which discussion of the rights and duties of " princes " takes the place of the old theory of the two swords.[14]

The most important question, however, is how the new Norman conception of the state affected the rest of Europe, both intellectually and politically; and this is without doubt a question of particular difficulty, especially where Germany is concerned. At the very moment when Roger II's Norman monarchy in Sicily and southern Italy reached the peak of development, and when the investiture contest in England was at its height, Germany saw the empire raised under Frederick Barbarossa to glory and splendour, and it is well known that Barbarossa entered into direct relations with the Norman monarchy in Sicily through the

[14] On Orderic Vitalis and John of Salisbury cf. further the recent work of J. Spörl, *Grundformen frühmittelalterlicher Geschichtsanschauung* (1935).

betrothal of his son, Henry VI, to Constance in 1184. But the power wielded by the Hohenstaufen emperor is for the most part regarded less as a result of the new Norman conceptions of the state than as due, on the one hand, to a more rigorous enforcement of ancient royal rights, and, on the other hand, to a revival of the traditions of Roman antiquity, which reached the emperor as a consequence of his close relations with the learned representatives of the reawakened school of Roman law in Bologna.

In one sense it is impossible to quarrel with this interpretation; for it cannot be denied that the orthodox point of view fully corresponds with the conception of the emperor's personality which has been handed down to us by his biographer, Otto of Freising. For Otto, Frederick Barbarossa was an emperor in the ancient style, a " rex iustus " in the sense of St. Augustine, a Roman *imperator* and the legitimate heir of the ancient Caesars. But this conception, created by Otto of Freising and accepted as authentic from his time onwards, is far from being an exhaustive analysis of the character of Hohenstaufen rule. Earlier writers have pointed out that the principles on which the Hohenstaufen crown and family demesnes were administered in Alsace and Swabia, reveal a new tendency at work : the administration of the whole district by dependent officials or *ministeriales* and the centralization of administration in a series of castles or royal palaces, which were spread in a dense network over the land.[15] If little has been made of this observation, the failure is to be attributed to the fact that our information about the new administrative machinery is very inadequate, and a further reason, without doubt, lies in the fact that our vision is obscured because Hohenstaufen government still contained many elements taken over from the early mediaeval state. But when we see how Frederick Barbarossa, and still more his grandson, Frederick II, created a well-disciplined and trustworthy bureaucracy from the ranks of the royal *ministeriales*, how they erected magnificent palaces and residences

[15] Cf. among others H. W. Klewitz, *Geschichte der Ministerialität im Elsass bis zum Ende des Interregnums* (1929), 52—64.

on their demesne lands, how they sought by codification
to create a uniform law for the whole realm and endeavoured
to build up a standing army, how Barbarossa himself
already began the attempt to incorporate the Norman
kingdom of southern Italy into his empire, and how Frederick II was bent on introducing the administrative organisation of his Sicilian kingdom throughout his realm, it is so
clear that all these new elements in Hohenstaufen government are closely similar to the institutions developed in
the Norman monarchies that we cannot doubt that Norman
political conceptions were effective both in Germany itself
and in the empire as a whole.   And there is still one other
characteristic feature of the new state, which is very marked
in the case of Frederick Barbarossa and which is found in
a similar form in the case of all Norman rulers: the conscious endeavour, which is intimately bound up with all
that is essential in Norman government, to enhance the
king's sovereign authority.   No ruler before Barbarossa
had so exalted a conception as he of his royal position.
When he received the legates of republican Rome in 1155,
he answered their boasts about the magnificence of ancient
Rome and the legacy it had handed down to the city which
they represented, with the words: " You speak of the
former glory of Rome, of the dignity of the senatorial
office . . . ?   Look upon our state; everything of which
you boast is in our hands . . . Your consuls, your senate,
your nobility are in our power . . . We are the lawful possessor of all you have.   Let anyone who can, wrest the
club from the hands of Hercules."[16]   And when Barbarossa,
in the same oration, dismissed all memories of ancient Rome
as empty words, and evoked instead the names of his
predecessors, Charlemagne and Otto the Great, who had
won Rome and Italy not as a gift of pope or Roman senate
but as a result of valiant fighting, he expressed for the first
time the idea of the independent, unqualified sovereign
rights of the monarch, which was even more clearly
formulated two years later in the well-known encounter
with the papal legates at Besançon in 1157: " We hold

[16] *Gesta Friderici* II. 30.

our kingdom and our empire not as a fief of the pope, but by election of the princes from God alone."[17] With these words, however, Barbarossa entered into the very realm of thought which had been opened up at the beginning of the twelfth century by the unknown English church-man in York, who had set the divinely appointed king above the priesthood. And in the years which followed, this new conception of the monarch's independent rights was refined and intensified until it produced the idea of the sacred and inviolable majesty of the ruler, and led in 1165 to an incident which was almost unique, the canoniza-tion of Charles the Great. There can be no doubt that this act was undertaken with the express political object of setting up the imperial idea in opposition to the theocratic doctrines of the Curia, of bringing the great emperor of the past into play against the papal claim to world dominion; and it is very noteworthy that the canonization of Charles the Great by Barbarossa's nominee for the papal throne, Paschal III, was preceded in England by the canonization of Edward the Confessor in 1161 by Henry II—by the very king, in other words, who, a year before the canonization of Charles the Great, established his authority over the English church in the Constitutions of Clarendon. It is impossible to explain this striking growth in the respect claimed for the person of the monarch except as a corollary of the conscious intensification of monarchical authority which was practised in the Norman lands. Many super-ficial features—the conception, for example, of the in-violability of imperial majesty—may have been copied from precedents in Roman law; but the driving force was clearly provided by Norman example in the south, west and north-east of Europe, and by the specifically Norman conception of the state and of monarchy. A distinct re-flection of the new emphasis on the person of the emperor is found in the historical literature and the poetry of the Hohenstaufen period. We know that the emperor himself

[17] *Ibid.* III. 11: "Cumque per electionem principum a solo Deo regnum et imperium nostrum sit . . . quicumque nos imperialem coronam pro beneficio a domno papa suscepisse dixerit, divinae institutioni et doctrinae Petri contrarius est et mendacii reus erit."

provided bishop Otto of Freising with the material for his history, and that the imperial chancellor, Rainald of Dassel, encouraged the " Archipoeta " to sing the emperor's praises. When the latter in his magnificent verse acclaimed the emperor as " lord of the world " and as *princeps terrae principum*, or when the poet who wrote the " Ludus de Antichristo " put into the French king's mouth the words —naturally fictitious and untrue—" we are proud to serve the emperor ", their conception of imperial omnipotence corresponds exactly with the whole political outlook of the imperial court as revealed in the words of the chancellor, Rainald of Dassel, at the synod of Dôle in 1162, when he forbade *reguli* or " petty kings " to meddle in the filling of the Holy See, since this was the prerogative of the emperor alone.   But it corresponds equally with Norman practice, in which the authority of the ruler was made the sole and absolute criterion in public life.   At the end of Barbarossa's reign there flourished in Germany the poet Henry of Veldeke, whose " Eneis " forged a link between the Hohenstaufen empire, supported by the flower of European chivalry, and ancient civilization—a mediaeval Virgil who ascribed to the Hohenstaufen the same exalted lineage as the Roman poet had attributed to the dynasty of Augustus.   The church, in short, had passed into the background and " mother earth " ruled mankind.

Against this picture which I have painted, the objection might be raised that ancient or Byzantine traditions and parallels were a stronger incentive to the Hohenstaufen than Norman example.   To meet such a charge, however, it is only necessary to point out that twelfth-century Germany provides still another example of the new type of state, and this example can never be explained by reference to classical antiquity.   I am refering to the " state " which Henry the Lion built up in north Germany.[18]   There are few more controversial subjects to-day than the personality and policy of Henry the Lion.   Once again, as in the nineteenth-century controversy between *Grossdeutschen* and *Klein-*

[18] For the literature on this subject cf. my references, HZ. CXLV (1932), 8—10.

deutschen, the Welf duke with his east colonial policy is depicted as the opponent of the Italian policy of the Hohenstaufen. But this forced antithesis was disproved in the nineteenth century, and it must be resisted with equal spirit to-day. In order to realise that history which pictures Henry the Lion as a determined and consistent opponent of Italian policy and a champion of the idea of eastern expansion is measuring the past by the standards of the present, it is sufficient to remember that Henry the Lion's participation was the decisive factor in Barbarossa's first Italian expedition—he rescued the emperor from a very threatening situation in Rome in 1155—and that Henry's son, Otto IV, undertook as emperor a more thorough-going Italian policy than Barbarossa ever pursued. Henry the Lion's significance in German history lies rather in the new form with which he invested his rule in northern Germany. It is precisely his new principles of government which make it necessary for us to class him not with the old " tribal " dukes of earlier generations— whose successor he is still widely considered to have been— but with the monarchs who ruled the Norman states in his own day. His biographer, Helmold, in his " Chronicle of the Slavs " said of Henry the Lion: " In the various military expeditions which the duke led into the Slav lands, the question was never Christianity but always money." In those words Helmold reproduces the impression which the calculating, materialistic policy of the duke made on his contemporaries: Henry, in other words, only went to war for economic reasons. And that, reduced to a short formula, is exactly the same practice as we find in Norman Sicily, and is a general characteristic of all Norman military undertakings. Just as the commercial and trading classes of Palermo followed Roger II's fleet when it attacked the coasts of Greece or Africa, so Henry the Lion's army was accompanied by merchants from Lower Saxony, who profited from the duke's protection to carry their trade as far as Gotland, Sweden or Novgorod. But this far-seeing commercial policy, which extended over the whole of northern and eastern Europe, was only one part of Henry the Lion's general economic activity; and if we want evidence of his economic interests, we need only select from the mass of information which has come down to us, the carefully planned refounding of Lübeck in the north and the foundation of Munich in the south. Such a policy was hitherto unknown in Germany and could only be paralleled in the Norman state of southern Italy. But the parallelism extends to other spheres as well. Apart from the Hohenstaufen and the Zähringer,[19] Henry the Lion was the only territorial prince in Germany who administered his lands through a dependent ministerial bureaucracy and organized the administration in fixed centres. To avoid unnecessary complication, I must deliberately ignore the methods which the Hohenstaufen, the Zähringer and the Welf duke employed in order to get rid of the various feudatories and ecclesiastical establishments within their lands, to break down their franchises and bring them under the control of superior authority;[20] for what matters to us is not so much the process by which the new states were gradually built up by consolidation from below, as the essential form and character of the new administration. From this point of view there are two further factors important enough to be mentioned. On the one hand, Henry the Lion obtained from Barbarossa in 1154 the right to invest the bishops within his east colonial lands, and thus embarked, like Roger II in Sicily and Henry II in England, on an attempt to incorporate the church into his growing " state ". On the other hand, he built himself a princely residence in Brunswick, which could compete in size and splendour with the majority of Norman royal palaces; it is not necessary to describe in detail the castle of Dankwarderode, the cathedral of St. Blasius or the numerous objects of art in the so-called " Welf treasure-house "; and I need only refer incidentally to the fact that it was through Henry's encouragement that the " Lucid-arius "—the first scholarly work in the German language—

[19] For the Zähringer, cf. Th. Mayer, *supra*, 175—202.
[20] Theodor Mayer's essay emphasizes the important part which the occupation of the land by colonization played in the construction of the Zähringer " state ".

was written, just as it was one of the duke's *ministeriales*, Eilhart of Oberg, who sang the tale of Tristan and Isolde in his native tongue. The general picture which we can form in this way of Henry the Lion's rule in his north-German " state " proves beyond doubt that he closely followed the model provided by the Norman monarchies, and one way in which Norman influence was readily effective is apparent enough: betrothed in 1165 and married in 1168 to Matilda, the daughter of Henry II of England, Henry the Lion maintained the closest relations with the English royal court and finally went to Normandy after his fall and exile in 1180.

With this review of the administrative organisation introduced into north Germany by Henry the Lion, we must halt and survey once again the development which led from the theory of universal empire to the theory of the national state. The early mediaeval conception of a united Christian commonwealth, imposing though it was in appearance, was vitiated from the beginning by the curial doctrine of the two swords and by the ever-widening breach between empire and papacy. The decisive blow to the old order was delivered when the pretensions of the church, formulated in the first place by the Cluniac leaders and perfected by Gregory VII, culminated in the claim of the Curia to bring the direction of secular politics into the pope's hands. Against this pretension radical opposition was aroused, though not so much in the empire itself as in the border-states of Normandy and Norman England. At the very moment when the reaction against Gregorianism and the consequent revolution in thought took place, a new form of political organisation was growing up within the Norman states. The concentration of public life in the state itself and in the royal government drove the clerical element into the background and stimulated the growth of new forces in every sphere of political, economic and cultural life. The Europe of the dying eleventh and the twelfth centuries experienced for the first time in the whole of the Christian era a spiritual revolution of immeasurable importance, which amounted in essence to a secularization of the whole of human life. Intimately connected with it was the revolution in the political sphere, which replaced the loosely-knit feudalism of the early middle ages by a centralized, authoritarian bureaucratic state. It is impossible to emphasize too strongly the fact that the age of the Hohenstaufen, the most brilliant period in the whole of German history, can never be explained as a mere continuation of the early mediaeval empire. Its source was rather a violent revolution in men's souls, which made its influence felt in every sphere of human life. On this foundation the Hohenstaufen built anew, using the new forces, born of the reaction to clerical pretensions, to mould a state suited to the circumstances of their day. But the complexities of political life cut short the early prospect that the first great revolutionary movement in European history would lead directly to the results which the early development of the Norman monarchies had seemed at first to promise. The conservative elements were still too strong to surrender without a struggle. Among the causes which checked the systematic development of the new principles of government, not the least were the decline of the Sicilian state in the struggles of the Hohenstaufen with the Roman Curia and later with the house of Anjou, and the Anglo-French wars which lasted from the thirteenth to the fifteenth centuries. These wars led everywhere to a weakening of the central authority and the rise of an overmighty aristocracy: in England after the concession of Magna Carta in 1215, in Italy after the extinction of the Hohenstaufen in 1268, in Germany after the Interregnum which established the territorial principalities firmly in the saddle and placed the destinies of the monarchy in the hands of the electoral college. In this way the development of the authoritarian principles introduced by the Norman monarchies was checked, and Europe passed instead into the age of representative estates. But the great revolution of the eleventh and twelfth centuries was not without durable effects. The secularization both of intellectual and of political life which it inaugurated was a permanent gain, and even in the sphere of government and administration what could not be enforced on a large scale, was maintained in part at least within narrower limits. If the Hohenstaufen failed to rebuild the empire in accordance with the new conceptions of their age, much that they created and adapted from their Norman contemporaries was taken over by the German princes and proved to be a pillar of strength in the construction of the German principalities. In this way the reaction which set in, changed the course of development; but the endeavours of twelfth-century statesmen and the ferment of twelfth-century thought were not wasted. The gains were more indirect, progress was less rapid, than at first seemed probable; but the revolution which undermined both the political structure and the spiritual and intellectual life of early mediaeval Europe, permanently altered the course of European development. When the twelfth century ended the state had effectively ousted the church from its predominance, and the future lay with the princes and the national states.

INDEX

Adalbert, archbp. of Bremen, 108—
109, 268.
Adalbert, count of Chalw, 133—
134, 139.
Adalbert of Kärnten (Carinthia),
102, 240.
Adolf of Nassau, 201.
Advocate (*Advocatus, Vogt*), 17,
100, 143, 145—147, 150, 155,
157—167, 169, 171—172, 185,
186, 193, 217, 222, 226.
Agilolfinger, dukes of Bavaria, 7.
Agnes, empress, 107, 111, 118.
Albrecht I, 201.
Alexander II, 109.
Alexander III, 69, 168.
Alpirsbach, mon. of, 134, 140, 142,
147, 157—159, 182—183.
Alsace, 77, 111, 182, 200, 211, 291.
Altenburg, 91.
Anno, archbp. of Cologne, 108.
Arnulf, duke of Bavaria, 80, 83,
236—237, 274.
Augsburg, 6, 75, 122, 276.
Augustinian canons, 161.
Austria (Ostmark), 79, 84, 85, 91,
194, 228, 247;
Austria, dukes of; cf. Babenberger,
Habsburger.

Babenberger, dukes of Franconia
and Austria, 79, 84, 172.
Bamberg, 83, 85, 132, 134;
Bamberg, dioc. of, 86, 89, 93, 164,
186, 270.
Bamberg, bishops of; cf. Suidger.
Bann (*Bannleihe*), 28, 158—159,
229, 244, 268.
Bannbezirke, 20.
Basel, bishop of, 104.
Basel, dioc. of, 6, 179—180.
Bavaria, 6, 14, 21, 75—78, 83, 84,
88, 106—107, 152, 237, 274—
276;
Bavaria, dukes of: cf. Agilolfinger,
Arnulf, Henry, Henry the Lion,
Henry the Proud, Otto of Nord-
heim, Otto of Wittelsbach,
Tassilo.
Bernard of Marseilles, 154, 183.
Berthold I of Zähringen, duke of
Carinthia, 107, 154, 181.

Berthold II of Zähringen, 147, 181,
185.
Berthold III of Zähringen, 186.
Billunger, dukes of Saxony, 273.
Black Forest, 179—181, 183, 184.
Bohemia, 18, 78, 82, 84, 86;
Bohemia, duke of, 247.
Boleslav Chrobry (King of Poland),
86.
Breisach, 182, 190.
Breisgau, 154, 180—181, 188.
Bremen, archbps. of: cf. Adalbert.
Breslau, bishopric of, 18.
Bruno, bishop of Strassburg, 188.
Brunswick, 296;
Brunswick, duchy of, 274.
Burckhard, count of Nellenburg,
154.
Burgundy, 77, 78;
Burgundy, rectors of, 165, 181, 197.
Burkhard, duke of Swabia, 237.

Canossa, 88, 95, 114, 122—123, 283,
285.
Carinthia (Kärnten), 107;
Carinthia, dukes of: cf. Adalbert,
Berthold.
Carloman, 47.
Castles, construction of, 20, 153,
209, 241, 269.
Chalon-sur-Saône, synod of, 45.
Chalw, counts of, 156; cf. Adalbert.
Charles the Great (Charlemagne), 3,
63, 73, 74, 96, 98, 104, 216, 217,
223, 235, 281—283, 292, 293.
Charles Martel, 46.
Chiavenna, 78.
Chur, bishopric of, 46.
Cistercian order, 160.
Cleves, duchy of, 273.
Cluny, 106, 132, 134, 143, 144, 180,
284;
Cluny, abbots of; cf. Hugh, Odo.
Cologne, archbishopric of, 268;
Cologne, archbishops of: cf. Anno.
Colonisation, 17—24, 31, 74, 79,
111, 180, 182—183, 191, 192,
195—196, 207, 209, 261.
Concordat of Worms, 10, 68, 95,
127, 171, 242—244, 256.
Conrad I, 12, 30, 79, 96.

301